L.P.

Metropolitan Transportation Politics
and the New York Region

NUMBER SIX: METROPOLITAN POLITICS SERIES

Metropolitan Transportation Politics and the New York Region

By JAMESON W. DOIG

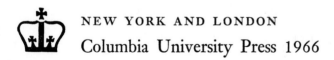

NEW YORK AND LONDON
Columbia University Press 1966

Jameson W. Doig is Assistant Professor of Politics and Public Affairs at Princeton University.

Preface

This study of metropolitan politics has benefited from the advice and assistance of a number of friends and colleagues. I am especially indebted to Michael N. Danielson, a member of the Princeton University faculty and the author of a companion volume in this series, for his many thoughtful and constructive suggestions. Wallace S. Sayre of Columbia University, Herbert Kaufman of Yale University, and Duane Lockard of Princeton University also provided valuable advice during the course of the study. In addition, the counsel and encouragement of Marver H. Bernstein of Princeton University, Richard T. Frost of Reed College, William N. Cassella of the National Municipal League, and David B. Truman of Columbia University are very much appreciated.

The research on which this volume is based could not have been carried out without the active cooperation of many persons who participated in the events described in the study. Most cannot be cited by name, but their important assistance is gratefully acknowledged. One exception to the rule of anonymity is warranted. The late John F. Sly, a member of the Port of New York Authority and the Metropolitan Rapid Transit Commission, and Professor of Politics at Princeton, offered encouragement throughout the study. Our interpretations of events and institutions sometimes differed, but he was always a kind and perceptive critic.

The study was made possible by grants from the Metropolitan Region Program of Columbia University and the Princeton University Research Fund. The Brookings Institution also gave assistance during my two years as a member of the Institution's research staff.

In preparing the manuscript, I was fortunate to have the services of several excellent typists, Evelyn Datz, Doris Lake, and Priscilla Benoit, and a fine editor, Katherine M. Purcell of the Columbia University Press. Glenn Shafer, my research assistant, provided valuable assistance in preparing the book for publication.

To my wife, Joan, who offered constant encouragement and assistance during the study, this volume is dedicated.

Jameson W. Doig

Princeton, New Jersey
September, 1965

Contents

Metropolitan Politics Series

This is the sixth in the series of books resulting from the metropolitan study program begun at Columbia University in 1957 and supported by a grant from the Ford Foundation.

The faculty committee supervising this program and serving as editors of the series are Wallace S. Sayre, Chairman, Richard E. Neustadt and David B. Truman of the Department of Public Law and Government of Columbia University, and William N. Cassella, Jr., of the National Municipal League.

Abbreviations

H&M	Hudson and Manhattan Railroad
ICC	Interstate Commerce Commission
IMGBRS	Inter-Municipal Group for Better Rail Service
LIRR	Long Island Rail Road
MCTA	Metropolitan Commuter Transportation Authority
MRC	Metropolitan Regional Council
MRTC	Metropolitan Rapid Transit Commission
MRTS	Metropolitan Rapid Transit Survey
NJMRTC	New Jersey Metropolitan Rapid Transit Commission
NJRPC	New Jersey Regional Planning Commission
NYMRTC	New York Metropolitan Rapid Transit Commission
PATH	Port Authority Trans-Hudson Corporation
PNYA	Port of New York Authority
RPA	Regional Plan Association
TBTA	Triborough Bridge and Tunnel Authority

Metropolitan Transportation Politics
and the New York Region

CHAPTER I

Introduction

This study is concerned with the nature of political power in the metropolis. The focus of the study is intensive rather than extensive: it explores one major regional issue, transportation, in the largest of our urban complexes, the New York area (Figure 1). Our concern is with the patterns of cooperation and conflict involved in the making of the region's postwar transport policies and especially in the efforts to obtain coordinated or balanced development of rail and road facilities.

Because efforts to devise and carry out transportation policies entail a large measure of interaction among private and public groups in the region, this arena is especially useful for the student of metropolitan politics. Here the perspectives, motivations, and actions of a wide variety of participants—local public officials and private interests, regional authorities and study groups, governors, state legislators, and state and federal agencies—are revealed. Therefore, while the research focus is limited, the study has several broader purposes. It explores the nature of political fragmentation of the metropolis, as shown in the views and actions of the region's many spokesmen. It examines the development of relatively well-integrated political subsystems along functional lines, as a way of overcoming the general fragmentation of power and responsibility. Finally, it is concerned with the conditions that facilitate or retard policy innovation in the metropolis. Politics in metropolitan areas is, as one observer recently noted, "still a frontier"; this study explores that frontier.[1]

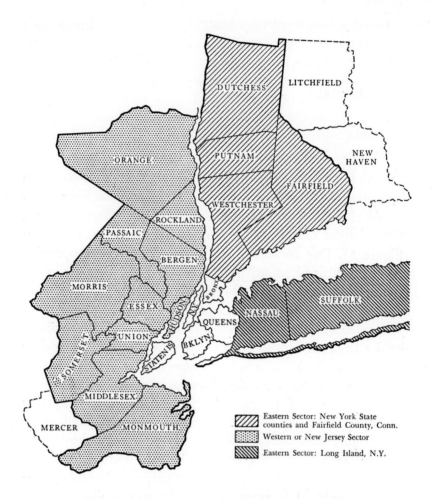

FIGURE 1. THE TRISTATE METROPOLITAN REGION
Source: Institute of Public Administration

In the remainder of this chapter, the general pattern of political behavior in the metropolis, as derived from this and other studies, is outlined. Chapter II describes the development of the New York region's transportation system and of the region's postwar problems of rail-service deterioration and highway congestion. It also examines the structure of political power that supported and was sustained by the highway-oriented policies of the early postwar years. In Chapters III to VIII, the efforts during the 1950s to devise new transportation policies within a regional framework are analyzed. A bistate Metropolitan Rapid Transit Commission (MRTC) was created and, in reluctant collaboration with the Port of New York Authority (PNYA), the Commission conducted an extensive study, culminating in proposals for the creation of a regional transit district, the granting of large public subsidies to existing rail lines, and construction of new transit facilities. These recommendations were widely debated in the region and were supported in part by the governors of New York and New Jersey and by the New York legislature, but were ultimately defeated in New Jersey. The processes through which the MRTC was formed and its proposals developed, and the two years of debate stimulated by its report, illustrate the narrow perspectives and limited concerns that shape regional development and the difficulties in this environment of generating new policies.

Chapter IX considers the most recent attempts to cope with the transportation problems of the New York region. In some ways these efforts differ from those of the 1950s. A few state officials play dominant roles, relegating local public officials, private organizations, and study groups to secondary positions. Policy is developed primarily in confidential negotiations, rather than through widespread public debate. The main concern is with limited steps which can be carried out quickly, rather than with expensive rail improvements and major institutional changes. Some shifts in policy have emerged, but the behavior patterns of the 1960s have much in common with those of the previous decade. The region lacks a central institution to take responsibility for transportation policy-making, the participants in the region's political system approach metropolitan transportation problems in terms of their narrow responsibilities and therefore disagree on goals and priorities, and the policies that emerge from this system generally fail to advance the region significantly toward permanent solutions.

In a final chapter, some concluding observations are offered concerning the capabilities and limitations of major participants in the metropolitan political system and the conditions under which changes in regional organization and policies may occur.

POLITICAL BEHAVIOR IN THE METROPOLIS

The dominant characteristic of metropolitan areas is fragmentation of political power and responsibility. In each urban region one finds divided and overlapping governmental responsibility, wariness of closer cooperation among units, and hesitant, piecemeal action on such major regional problems as transportation, water supply, and recreation.[2]

The Local Scene. Divided authority is especially evident as one surveys the many cities, towns, and other municipal units that inhabit the metropolis. In the larger regions, dozens of these governments exist side by side, each with responsibility for serving only its limited segment of the metropolitan population. The municipal official—and in regions with several counties, his colleague at the county level too—perceives problems not in a regional frame of reference but primarily in terms of his own narrow institutional base. Narrowness of perspective is especially prominent in the suburbs, owing to territorial limitations and to the desire of the suburban electorate to avoid the problems of the larger metropolis. The suburban mayor or county official is usually willing to act only when his own local-

ity is directly threatened—as by loss of commuter rail service—
and even if willing, he is unable to act effectively on such major
problems as regional transportation and water pollution.[3]

Because of the dominant role of the central city in the region,
its public officials are likely to take a broader view of their responsibilities than their suburban counterparts. Also, the central
city has the geographical scope and financial resources to exercise significant influence in the development of regional policies.
At times, as one commentary suggests, the mayors of the core
cities and their associates may be able to "play the part of regional statesmen," sacrificing when necessary the "short-run
special interests of the central city to its less immediate, but no
less real, interest in the welfare of the area as a whole." [4] This
study is consistent with a less optimistic view: the central-city
mayor will often find his inclination and his ability to act severely circumscribed because of opposition from private groups
in the city, or from specialized agencies of his own government
which would be affected by changes in regional policies.[5]

The perspectives of most private groups in the region are as
narrow as those of local public officials. Most newspapers, business organizations, and civic groups in each city, town, and
county represent primarily the immediate interests of their
own sectors of the metropolis. Some—the central-city dailies,
downtown business organizations, and suburban interests with
close ties to the core city—often speak in terms of the broader
region. Usually, however, such views are fully compatible with
the aim of maintaining the economic strength of their own
sector of the region.[6]

The relationship of the central city to outlying areas of a metropolis is frequently referred to in terms of "city versus suburbs." [7] The pattern is often more complex. Some suburban
interests and areas will at times join with central-city groups
to defend a certain policy for the region, while other suburban
and city interests will be allied in opposition. If the outlying

areas include not only small bedroom communities but larger and older centers as well, such as Oakland in the San Francisco area or Newark in the New York region, the patterns of economic interdependence and political cooperation and rivalry will be further complicated.

Given the fragmented responsibilities and perspectives of local participants, it is not surprising that the net effect of their actions is often unsatisfactory. Traffic congestion becomes worse, railroad passenger service deteriorates, each town adds its share to pollution of water resources, and coordinated action to meet these problems is avoided. At times more positive, though limited, efforts occur: two or three towns may agree on cooperative measures to meet their joint needs for traffic control or refuse disposal or a county may contract to perform public health services for the cities within its borders. Such steps, however, constitute a "decidedly piecemeal approach" to the problems of larger regions.[8]

Another approach to the problem of fragmentation has been the development of regional councils of local public officials, created to encourage discussion of mutual problems and to devise coordinated policies. Such councils have been established in Detroit, New York, Washington, D.C., San Francisco, and other areas. These councils are voluntary in nature, however, and their members carry with them the limitations of their one-city or one-county base. They have achieved some positive results but their achievements have been decidedly limited.[9] Yet efforts to go further, granting effective central power over major services to a regionwide government, have invariably faced determined opposition from local groups and have almost always failed.[10]

Independent Regional Authorities. The difficulties of attaining coordinated policy-making through the efforts of local officials or through creation of a metropolitan government have led to widespread use of independent authorities, each authority handling one or more specific functions (for example, bridges, highways, water supply) on a regional or subregional basis. Most authorities are supervised by appointive boards, and financed largely from service charges, rents, and tolls. This approach has gained wide acceptance because it does not threaten the existence or independence of local governments and because of the attraction of the "businesslike" procedures which characterize the public authority.[11]

Opinion is probably more sharply divided on the impact of the authority than on the role of any other government institution in the metropolis. In view of the broad geographical scope and visible achievements of many authorities, some observers conclude that it is an "effective instrumentality for the unified planning . . . and development" of a region. The success of the authority, it has also been argued, is rooted in its freedom from normal political restraints. The initiative and efficiency of this independent agency are contrasted with the parochialism and hesitancy, the "bureaucracy and . . . waste," of other government institutions.[12] Fundamentally, this view of the authority is closely related to an argument made long ago by Woodrow Wilson—that politics can be excluded from administration and must be, if efficient administration is to be achieved.[13]

Another view, which this study supports, questions both the interpretation of process and the assessment of results held by those favorable to the authority. It is true that a regional authority has a relatively large degree of formal independence in financial and administrative terms. This autonomy is usually reinforced by a number of related factors: narrow functional responsibilities which limit the range of potential opposition to authority policies, widespread public acceptance of the position that the authority should be kept "out of politics," a reputation for success, close relationships with state governors and other public officials who can alter the authority's freedom of action, and a high level of skill in areas of functional responsibility and in political strategy. Politics is not excluded. Rather, the channels of political influence are altered and the effective access of various groups modified, producing a pattern of politics distinctive to the public authority. Whereas elected officials must be attuned to the wide variety of groups of potential value in the next election, the authority looks to the governmental leaders and investment circles primarily able to affect its discretion, and calculates policy and tactical maneuvers accordingly.[14]

Insulation from normal political pressures is frequently defended in terms of results—"efficiency, . . . enterprise and long-range planning." If assessment of the authority is limited to its restricted functional domain, this conclusion is often valid. But many authorities are concerned with pieces of the region's transportation system or other functions that may require broader coordination for effective development. Here, particularly if the agency tries to maintain maximum independence of action, the results may be piecemeal and unsatisfactory.[15]

State and Federal Action. The limitations of local governments and independent authorities often give state institutions significant responsibilities in coping with major regional problems. The governor's role is especially important, at least potentially. With his constituency increasingly metropolitan, the governor is likely to be responsive to metropolitan needs. As Wood has argued,

The chief executive office faces every major functional decision through the filter of metropolitan life. Most of the problems are likely to be urban, or at least attached with a definite urban opinion. The Governor knows that the crucial vote lies within the city and its suburbs.[16]

Yet the governor must look beyond the metropolis. Because his responsibilities are statewide, his immediate concern will often be with different problems from those which agitate the residents of any one region. And when he does respond to metropolitan demands, his actions will be tempered by the anticipated reactions of other state interests and—frequently—by the relatively low degree of concern among wide segments of his metropolitan constituency.[17]

The state legislature is less likely than the governor's office to respond effectively to regional problems. Obstacles to legislative action are more complex, however, than a rural-urban dichotomy would suggest.[18] Representatives from the region reflect the fragmentation that exists within the metropolis. Delegates from other areas of the state are reluctant to spend state funds without expectation of direct benefit of their own areas; but if this is not a significant factor, they may be willing to aid colleagues in their party from the region in deciding issues in which they have no direct stake. Thus, legislative alliances may join some city and suburban interests from the region with their nonregional allies on one side of an issue and find an equally diverse group, geographically, on the other. The result is likely to be inaction or stopgap activities in the face of crisis. Whether the outcome will represent the views of a majority of the region's legislators will depend on the representative structure of the legislative body and the alliances formed on the specific issue.[19]

The past two decades have seen an increasing concern with regional problems on the part of the national government. However, the difficulties of obtaining adequate federal action resemble the obstacles encountered at the state capital. Diverse constituencies and the pressures of other demands limit the ability of national as well as state political leaders to respond effectively to metropolitan problems.[20]

Special Interests and the Making of Policy. The limited capability of elected officials to meet regional problems leaves a vacuum which more specialized interests try to fill. Impelled by their desire to control policy and aided by their functional expertise, private interests and government agencies primarily concerned with transportation, housing, and other regional problems build alliances across local, state, and federal levels and exercise major influence at all stages of policy-making and execution. In so far as action is taken at all in the fragmented metropolis, these interests are likely to provide the essential leadership, narrow in conception and execution though it may be.[21]

The traditional model of special-interest action emphasizes the efforts of private interest groups, which press their demands upon government agencies.[22] In some fields, including transportation and urban renewal, an alternative conception is often more accurate. Here narrow-purpose governmental units frequently provide the initiative in policy development and marshal political support for the alliance's preferred plans.

Special-interest alliances in various policy areas differ considerably in structure and behavior. In urban transportation, we can distinguish two coalitions—road and rail—which often pursue separate lines of development and engage in sporadic cooperation and conflict.[23] The highway coalition includes as central participants the state highway departments, the federal Bureau of Public Roads, and such regional bodies as the Port of New York Authority and the Golden Gate Bridge and Highway District. Closely associated with these are the bus companies, the truckers, the automobile associations, and other user groups; the shopping centers and other commercial interests which benefit from expansion of the road network; oil, automotive, road construction, and other related industries; and the political spokesmen for these interests. The main goal of the road coalition is expansion of the network of highways, bridges, and tunnels; maximum freedom of planning and financing are deemed essential to this end. Supported by public preferences and a ready supply of funds from tolls and excise taxes, the regional authorities and state agencies take the initiative in recommending dramatic new facilities, obtain support from other public and private interests, and carry out their activities with speed and efficiency. Conflict among coalition members concerning routes, jurisdiction, and distribution of user costs is not unknown, but cooperation is the dominant theme.

The other coalition includes those who support the railroad and transit systems which once held sway in freight and passenger transport and which have been battling, especially since the close of World War II, to retain traffic in the face of the highway challenge. The railroads themselves are central participants on the freight side; in the passenger field, however, their position is often that of a reluctant partner who would gladly retire from the fray. Here the pressure to retain and expand service is more likely to come from rail commuters and from the realtors and others in suburbia who benefit economically from their convenient commuting access to the central city. Merchants and other businesses with an important economic stake in the downtown areas may also join this alliance. In addition, support often comes from regional planners and civic organizations whose primary focus is on the development of a coordinated transportation system. Finding an overemphasis on highway transport, they join with the rail coalition in the hope of redressing the balance.

In the relationships between rail and road groups, conflict has been the dominant theme. Rail interests criticize highway expansion for siphoning off rail traffic; they demand closer control over road planning, and financial coordination of highway and rail efforts. Members of the highway coalition attack these views and prophesy further decline in the importance of rail travel in the metropolis. At times, though, cooperative efforts take place. Faced with vocal public criticism, elements of both groups may coordinate their plans in certain specific areas or agree to the need for financial assistance to rail lines —usually at the expense of the general taxpayer, not the highway agencies. In any event, the road coalition, widely supported by the public, is likely to maintain its essential financial strength and a large measure of autonomy. The rail system, suffering from a decline in ridership and division within the ranks of its supporters, limps along in most regions with the assistance of temporary palliatives.[24]

CHAPTER II

Transportation in the Metropolis:
Problems, Policy, and Political Power

Soon after the close of World War II, New York and other urban regions found their transportation systems under severe strain. Rapid increases in population and income levels resulted in major expansion of passenger and freight traffic. These changes were coupled with a shift of traffic from rail and bus to truck and automobile, causing heavy congestion during commuting hours and on weekends. In regions traditionally dependent on rail service for a significant share of transportation, falling revenues and rising costs brought economic difficulties for the mass transit systems and railroad companies, leading to fare increases and reductions in service.

The primary response of government agencies to these problems was to expand the network of highways serving urban regions. While curtailment of intercity rail service was slowed by regulatory agencies, almost no public funds were allocated to aid the private railroad companies. These approaches were consistent with policies developed before the war, and public preferences reinforced historical trends. Yet in the New York area—as in other regions with highly concentrated employment centers and residential developments built up in the rail era —continued and perhaps expanded rail service seemed to be required if the region were to prosper. Although the strength of the highway coalition, public apathy, and the fragmentation of regional leadership were impressive obstacles, in the New York region a small band of railroad men, commuters, and business groups argued that reassessment of current highway-oriented policies was essential.

In this chapter, the historical development of the rail system and the impact of the motor age are first outlined. The political structure which supported the postwar transportation policy of the New York region is then analyzed, providing a backdrop for the efforts of the rail coalition to alter that policy during the 1950s.[1]

DEVELOPMENT OF THE RAIL SYSTEM

The century prior to World War I saw the construction of the rail networks which lace the New York area. The first railroad was the Camden and Amboy, later part of the Pennsylvania system, which opened a line across New Jersey in 1831. During the next four decades it was followed by the Central of New Jersey, the Lackawanna, the Lehigh Valley, the Erie, and finally, in 1870, the Susquehanna. These lines crisscrossed New Jersey and terminated at the western bank of the Hudson River. There they were halted by the wide expanse of water which cuts the metropolitan region in two, and passengers and freight bound for Manhattan and points east relied on ferries for this part of the journey.[2]

The Hudson River remained a major obstacle throughout the nineteenth century as several efforts to tunnel under the river failed.[3] In 1908–09, however, the Hudson and Manhattan (H&M) Railroad completed two trans-Hudson tunnels, connecting Newark, Hoboken, and Jersey City with Manhattan; and in 1910 the Pennsylvania Railroad completed its tunnel between New Jersey and midtown Manhattan.[4]

East of the Hudson, rail lines were constructed between New York City and outlying areas, and by 1850 both the New York Central and the New Haven railroads brought passengers directly into Manhattan. Long Island commuters were served by several lines of track laid down by the Long Island Rail Road.[5]

Within New York City, a number of elevated rail lines were constructed during the late nineteenth century, and during the first years of the twentieth century the city government embarked on a major program of subway construction. The first section of the Manhattan subway system was placed in operation in 1904, and in the next few years the system was extended into Brooklyn, Queens, and the Bronx.[6]

By the beginning of World War I the major rail facilities of the New York region had been constructed. (See Figure 2.) The eastern sector had a combination of privately and publicly owned facilities, including three important railroad networks and a growing complex of subway and elevated lines in New York City. In contrast to New York City's important rail contribution east of the Hudson, the New Jersey sector, with no dominant city and hundreds of separate municipalities, left the development of a regional transport network entirely to private enterprise. Six major rail systems crossed that state, and all but one terminated at the Hudson River. There, Jersey Central and West Shore passengers were required to take the ferry in order to reach Manhattan, and travelers on three other lines could either use ferry service or transfer to the H&M tubes. Of the major rail systems, only the Pennsylvania ran its trains directly into a Manhattan terminal. The inconvenience of travel from New Jersey to Manhattan, the center of the region, was clearly the main weakness in the urban transportation network.

The next two decades (1920–40) produced a number of studies aimed at improving the rail network. Among the major surveys were several by a state-sponsored North Jersey Transit Commission in the 1920s and by a joint board of private and public bodies during the years 1928–31.[7] The Port of New York Authority (PNYA) and the Regional Plan Association (RPA) also outlined plans for possible improvements. Most of these studies were primarily concerned with the problem of replac-

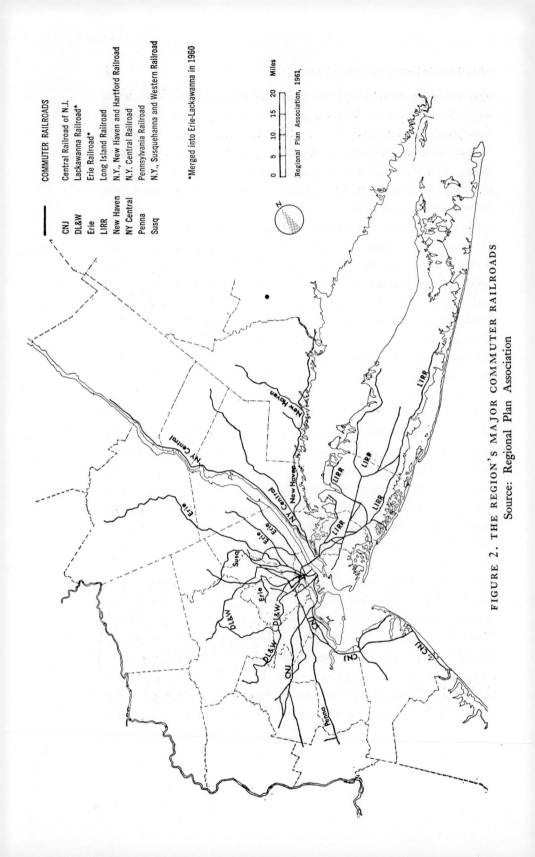

FIGURE 2. THE REGION'S MAJOR COMMUTER RAILROADS
Source: Regional Plan Association

ing trans-Hudson ferries with rail facilities, but proposals for adding rail lines in Westchester, Long Island, and Staten Island were also included.[8]

Although plans were prepared, citizens' committees formed, and resolutions adopted calling for action, no action was forthcoming. It seemed highly unlikely that major improvements in the passenger systems would be self-supporting, and the railroads showed no interest in underwriting such projects. Yet action by public agencies faced major obstacles. The region-wide extent and the deficit nature of the problem, further complicated by the interstate character of the region, made it difficult to find a governmental agency to take responsibility; the states, the local governments, and the PNYA all were reluctant to act. Even these obstaces might have been overcome, however, had not growing efforts toward action been twice blunted, first by the depression, then by World War II.[9]

IMPACT OF THE MOTOR AGE

Even as the New York region sought ways of improving its rail facilities, this system was being challenged by the automobile, the bus, and the truck. Part of a nationwide development and linked to the general trends of population increase and suburban growth, the expansion of motor transportation began well before World War II and accelerated rapidly in the postwar era.[10]

In 1930 about 24 million people entered New York City from New Jersey by automobile. Twenty years later this number had risen 390 percent, to 94 million; over half of this increase took place between 1945 and 1950. Similar trends, though less pronounced, occurred in automobile travel from the Westchester and Long Island sectors of the region. Bus and truck travel also increased sharply.[11]

As traffic increased, new vehicular facilities were constructed; and each additional artery seemed to stimulate still more traffic.

Billions of dollars of state and federal funds were poured into highways,[12] and the activities and importance of the agencies concerned with motor traffic expanded greatly. The chief beneficiaries in the New York region were two semi-independent agencies, the Port of New York Authority and the Triborough Bridge and Tunnel Authority. By 1931 the bi-state PNYA had constructed the George Washington Bridge and three bridges linking Staten Island and New Jersey and was operating these as well as the Holland Tunnel (first opened in 1927 under another agency). All were operated as toll facilities, and the Holland Tunnel and George Washington Bridge were immediate financial successes. As a result the PNYA was soon able to undertake construction of the Lincoln Tunnel, the first tube of which was opened in 1937, the second in 1945. By the early 1950s consideration was being given to constructing additional trans-Hudson crossings.

In the eastern half of the region, authorities were established during the 1930s to construct and operate the Triborough Bridge, the Bronx-Whitestone Bridge, and other major New York facilities. Through mergers of several agencies, the Triborough Bridge and Tunnel Authority (TBTA) was formed in 1946 and given responsibility for constructing and operating toll bridges and tunnels within the five boroughs of New York City. In the postwar traffic boom, the Triborough Authority joined the Port Authority as a financially successful regional body.[13]

While vehicular traffic in the New York region was expanding, the rail lines found their traffic decreasing. The decline was most severe on the New Jersey railroads, which had carried 171 million riders across the Hudson in 1930. After a sharp drop during the depression, these railroads regained part of their traffic loss during the war and in 1945 carried about 140 million. But by 1950 traffic had fallen to a new low—slightly under

100 million a year. Among those severely affected were the West Shore and the Erie, which lost two-thirds of their traffic between 1930 and 1950. The decline in Westchester and Long Island traffic was less severe, but still substantial: between 1945 and 1950 Westchester traffic dropped from 65 to 50 million, Long Island traffic from 110 to 85 million.[14]

The causes for this postwar decline were several. The dispersion of suburban growth, abetted by highway expansion, reduced the percentage of the population which could conveniently use rail service for home-to-work and home-to-store trips. The shift in Manhattan destinations from downtown to midtown reduced the usefulness of the ferry system. The direct cost of auto and bus travel was often less than that of rail travel. Reduction from a six- to a five-day workweek cut rail usage significantly. Finally, the increased ownership of automobiles and the popularity of television reduced evening and weekend rail travel.[15]

But while rail travel diminished, expenses were not reduced proportionately. The rail companies retained most of their rush hour passengers while non-rush hour traffic declined sharply. Thus, the companies were required to keep manpower and equipment available to meet peak-hour loads, although most of the personnel and equipment were idle much of the day. In addition, wages and material costs continued to rise, and railroad taxes remained at high levels, with New Jersey and New York having the highest tax rates per rail mile in the country.[16]

Faced with declining passenger traffic and more rigid costs, the railroads sought to raise fares and curtail service. In 1946 and 1947 the New Jersey roads obtained their first postwar fare increases from state and federal regulatory commissions, and a second increase followed in 1949. The Lackawanna Railroad was given permission to abandon the 23rd Street ferry in 1946, and several lines eliminated little-used trains. Each fare rise or

service reduction was followed by further declines in passenger
traffic, however, leading the railroads to seek still further
fare increases and train curtailments.[17]

Massive highway construction and a relatively passive public
attitude toward rail deterioration characterized these first postwar years, but it was doubtful that present policies would adequately meet the region's future transportation needs. Although
vast sums of public funds were poured into building roads,
bridges, and tunnels to accommodate expanding motor transport, congestion continued to be a major problem, especially
in the downtown business areas into which most of the additional traffic poured. And in spite of the declining use of rail
transport, the rail network was still of great importance during
rush hours. During peak hours each day in 1950, 240,000 commuters entered New York City by rail, most of these bound for
midtown and downtown Manhattan. Only 103,000 commuted
by automobile and bus. Even the highway enthusiast could
foresee difficulties in absorbing increasing numbers of rail
travelers on the highway system if rail service continued to
deteriorate.[18]

What should be done to meet these problems? Ideally (at
least from a planner's point of view), an immediate evaluation
of current highway-oriented policies should be carried out and
recommendations adopted to provide coordinated planning and
balanced financing of the rail and road systems. As the Regional Plan Association argued in 1951, "The issue here is the
paramount public need for a well balanced regional transportation system of highway, parkway *and* railroad development." [19]

But planning standards often conflict with political realities.
So it was in this case. Efforts to provide a more "balanced"
transportation policy would challenge the freedom enjoyed by
the opulent and politically powerful road coalition, and the
forces supporting the challenge were relatively weak and divided. Such efforts would also require guidance and leadership

from political institutions with regionwide perspectives, and in the fragmented metropolis such leadership was difficult to locate.

TRANSPORT POLICY: THE POLITICAL SUBSTRUCTURE

"Certain characteristics of groups," writes Eckstein, "are likely to determine decisively their effectiveness" in the political arena. Among the most important are the cohesiveness and prestige of the group and its size, wealth, and leadership. In addition, the pattern of existing policies and the structure of relevant government institutions will aid some interests and retard the efforts of others.[20]

These are the characteristics that concern us in analyzing the political forces involved in transportation policy-making in the New York region. We first consider the alliance pressing for innovation during the first postwar decade, the rail coalition, and then examine the elements supporting the *status quo*.

The Rail Coalition. As one surveys the interests actively concerned with obtaining changes in regional transport policy, their relatively low potential for politically effective action emerges clearly. Compared with the highway coalition, this alliance of railroads, central-city groups, and suburban interests rated poorly in organizational unity, general prestige and wealth, breadth of membership, and leadership skills. Its difficulties were reinforced by the nature of existing policy and of governmental structure. Even so, these active elements provided continued pressure against highway-oriented policies during the first postwar years and the nucleus for a broader and perhaps successful campaign if the crisis were to worsen.

The suburban railroads in the region were important participants in the coalition. Their most immediate concern, however, was the reduction of financial losses from passenger service, and much of their energy went into efforts to persuade regulatory commissions to permit fare increases and train service reductions.[21] These efforts inevitably brought the rail carriers into conflict with other members of the coalition, particularly suburban commuter interests and their allies in the state regulatory commissions.

Yet some rail officials were concerned with more basic causes and more positive solutions as well. Spokesmen for the rail lines criticized the pouring of "billions of dollars into new highways, tunnels, and bridges," while the mass transit problem was "ignored." Several, including officials of the H&M, the Lackawanna, and the Susquehanna, advocated the construction of new river crossings and additional Manhattan stations in order to eliminate reliance on ferries for trans-Hudson commutation. And a few, led by H&M president William Reid, called upon the states, the Port Authority, and the Triborough Authority to undertake such construction and other improvements, in order to provide a more stable and efficient transportation system for the region. Here the views of the rail companies and those of the other members of the coalition tended to coincide, although for somewhat different reasons: the rail officials were primarily interested in shifting their financial burdens to public agencies, the suburban and central-city spokesmen in improving the economic vitality of various parts of the region.[22]

Although suburbanites were basically allies of the railroads, their organized efforts were built mainly upon conflict with the rail lines. Suburban interests during these first postwar years were most actively represented by municipal-commuter groups, organized in response to railroad attempts to reduce service to their communities. As a consequence, their approach tended to be anti-railroad and geographically narrow. Each of the half-dozen or more commuter groups was organized along a specific rail line and focused its attention primarily upon pressing state and federal regulatory bodies to deny railroad requests to increase rates and cut service.

The most active of these groups in the region, and the organization with the longest history, was the Inter-Municipal Group for Better Rail Service (IMGBRS). Formed in 1945 in response to efforts of the Central Railroad of New Jersey to cut back on service, the IMGBRS was composed of local public officials and appointed private citizens in sixteen towns along the Central's route. As each railroad proposal was submitted to the regulatory commissions, IMGBRS representatives appeared with evidence which purported to show that losses were not as large as stated by the railroad, that improvements in service rather than reductions might increase net passenger income, and that "inefficient management and the use of obsolete equipment"—not the provision of passenger services—caused the Jersey Central's financial difficulties. The IMGBRS also emphasized the adverse impact on suburban economic development that might result from continued service deterioration. The trend of fare increases and service reductions was never halted, but the Inter-Municipal Group could claim that its efforts often helped to persuade the regulatory commissions to grant less than the railroad had requested and that the delays in final commission action caused by IMGBRS' objections saved "hundreds of thousands of dollars to the commuters of northern New Jersey." [23]

Similar organizations sprang up in various parts of the region during the late 1940s and early 1950s: the Westchester Commuters Group, the Transit Committee of Bergen County, the Jersey Shore Protective Committee, the Boonton Line Transportation Association, and several others. Some of these groups were composed primarily of municipal officials, while others were run by commuters; each was limited to a narrow geographic slice of the region, and each fought a rearguard battle against unrelenting railroad pressure.[24] Usually, these local groups could expect sympathetic treatment from the state commissions, which were sensitive to local economic and political pressures. But when service across state lines was involved, the Interstate Commerce Commission was normally allied with the railroads in placing primary emphasis on railroad financial needs, not on "the uneconomic costs of fare increases to the public." [25]

Suburbia agreed with the railroads, however, on the need for more positive approaches to the rail problem, and a number of possible steps were suggested. The IMGBRS and the Transit Committee of Bergen County pressed for construction of trans-Hudson tunnels in order to attract more passengers to the rails, and the Westchester County Planning Commission foresaw possible advantages from building new rail lines to serve Westchester and Connecticut commuters entering New York City. These and other groups called for immediate studies of the transit problem, leading to effective long-range improvements. Several major newspapers in the region urged that the PNYA consider taking action, and a few spokesmen suggested the possibility of regional tax support to maintain and improve rail services in the region.[26]

In terms of political effectiveness, however, the suburban interests had significant weaknesses. Potentially, the commuter element was important. There were more than 200,000 railroad commuters to Manhattan and thousands more with destinations in Newark, Jersey City, and other cities, and the economic significance to their local areas of these rail passengers was substantial. But few suburbanites were actively involved in the commuter associations, or in more positive efforts to improve transportation services. Most commuters limited their activities to following the controversies in local papers and in flyers passed out during recurrent crises. The pressure of other concerns and the nature of commuting itself raised obstacles of time and communication that few managed to overcome.[27]

The third major group in the rail coalition was composed of central-city business and civic interests. Most active here were such organizations as the New York Chamber of Commerce, the Citizens Budget Commission, and the Regional Plan Association, together with New York City newspapers, especially the New York *Times* and the New York *Herald Tribune*.[28] For some of these participants, the primary motivation was protection of Manhattan's economic dominance in the region. The Avenue of the Americas Association, for example, argued that traffic congestion was "causing large organizations and taxpayers to move from Manhattan into the surrounding areas" and advocated improvement of the rail system in order to relieve this congestion and thus reverse the "loss in taxable and other vital economic values" in the central city. But others, particularly the RPA (which had members throughout the area), emphasized the importance of an efficient rail system to the prosperity of the entire region.[29]

In contrast with the suburbanites, the central-city interests were sympathetic toward the railroads' financial difficulties and saw little long-run advantage to be gained from contesting fare increases and service reductions.[30] Instead, they emphasized the need for more positive action: studies, short-range improvements, and construction of expensive new facilities were advocated by various groups. Because of their concern for the economic health of both the region and the railroads and their familiarity with local subsidies for the city subway system, some of these groups were willing to support the use of public funds in order to improve the rail system. Action by the regional authorities was also suggested; Goodhue Livingston of the City Planning Commission, for example, criticized the "sprawling operations" of the Port and Triborough Authorities and argued for creation of a new transport authority to supervise both rail and road operations in the region.[31]

Conflicts of perspective and interest thus characterized the rail coalition. Much of the energy of the railroad and suburban groups, together with their regulatory commission allies, was focused on skirmishes over particular fare and service schedules. And while all three segments of the coalition agreed that more positive action was needed, they differed as to what kinds of action. Some were especially concerned about the impact of highway developments on rail service, and emphasized the need for coordinated planning and perhaps financing of the entire transport system; others, viewing such coordination as unnecessary or unfeasible, favored rail aid from general public funds. Some felt that the immediate effort must be regionwide; others would give first priority to a particular sector of the region. Finally, the coalition was divided as to whether short-range action or major improvements should be emphasized.[32] These differences did not represent definite cleavages within the coalition, but they suggested the need for establishing priorities before action could be taken.

Even if agreement on these issues were obtained, the coalition faced several difficulties in reversing existing policy. Although the central-city interests and the suburban groups included some members with prestige and political influence, it was doubtful that a unified and vigorous campaign for action could be based upon such a diversity of voluntary associations. The railroads themselves, though not without influence at the state capitals and in the region, lacked the political support to lead an effective campaign. Also, the strength of the highway coalition and the fragmentation of governmental power were major obstacles. What the coalition needed most, perhaps, was the threat of an immediate and major loss of rail service. Such an emergency could have expanded the small group of activists into a politically significant share of the region's voters and could have forced the political leaders at regional and state levels to take action. Ironically, the commuter organizations, in their stopgap efforts before the regulatory commissions, helped to avert such a dramatic crisis. The wearing away of rail service proceeded slowly during this first postwar decade, and most of the region's populace were unaware of any major transport crisis, present or potential.

The Road Coalition. In contrast to the rail group, the alliance marshaled behind postwar highway policy was highly effective politically. In the New York region, it was organized primarily around two regional agencies, the Port Authority and the Triborough Bridge and Tunnel Authority. Closely linked with them, especially as highway construction and the need for coordination increased, was a network of county and state highway agencies and the federal Bureau of Public Roads. Supporting these agencies, although not usually central participants in policy-making in the New York region, were the bus companies, automobile associations, and other beneficiaries of highway expansion.

The members of the road alliance were not necessarily opposed to maintaining rail services. Although they were inclined to doubt the need for major improvements, the Port Authority and other road interests favored public action to stabilize railroad commutation. Without such efforts, large numbers might transfer from rail to highways during the next few years, overtaxing the facilities available even with a massive road-building program. The road coalition objected, however, whenever it was suggested that highway expansion should be coordinated with rail planning or that highway funds should be used to aid the railroads. Modest efforts to aid the rail system, paid for by the general taxpayer, might be acceptable, but funds required to expand the highway network could not be diverted in order to save the railroads.

Because of their highly visible role in the region's highway program, the Port and Triborough Authorities were major objects of attack as criticism of the New York area's transport policy grew. The PNYA, owing to its interstate jurisdiction, financial strength, and original mandate to aid the railroads, was the primary target. Its efforts to retain its independence of action form a central part of the story that follows; the actions of the TBTA are also involved, though more peripherally. The background and behavior patterns of these two agencies are outlined here.[33]

The Port of New York Authority. Established in 1921 by interstate compact, the PNYA was charged with responsibility for developing the "terminal, transportation and other facilities of commerce" in the New York–New Jersey region. The compact gave the PNYA broad responsibility in the Port District, a bistate area extending about 20 miles in radius from the Statue of Liberty; its capacity to carry out these duties was limited, however, by its inability to levy taxes or assessments or to issue orders binding upon private or other public agencies.[34]

The Port Authority was at first expected to devote its main energies to the problem of freight distribution in the region. However, it found the railroads unwilling to cooperate in the establishment of joint yards, joint rights of way, or other plans to rationalize the harbor and rail system; and little progress was made toward carrying out the original program. In the late 1920s, the PNYA turned to vehicular facilities. Its network of toll bridges and tunnels was highly successful financially, and it was able to branch out. In 1932 a freight terminal was opened in Manhattan, in 1944 a grain terminal was acquired, in 1947 the PNYA leased Newark Airport and La Guardia and Idlewild Airports, and between 1948 and 1951 it took over administration of Port Newark and of Teterboro Airport and began operating two truck terminals and a bus terminal.[35]

Passenger rail operations were not entirely neglected during these three decades. Between 1928 and 1931, the Port Authority joined with other groups in the region in a study of the passenger problem, an effort abandoned because of traffic decline during the depression.[36] In 1937 the PNYA submitted a report recommending that a trans-Hudson rail tunnel be constructed;

and in 1949, at the request of New Jersey Governor Alfred E. Driscoll, the PNYA submitted a report concerning a proposed rail line between Newark Airport and the waterfront.

Although the PNYA was willing to study the problem, it showed no interest in expanding its own responsibilities to include rail passenger service. In its 1937 report, the Authority estimated that the proposed project might run a yearly deficit as high as $5.3 million. The report concluded that the Authority itself could not undertake the project, since lack of taxing power limited it to "self-liquidating projects." The 1949 plan carried an estimated annual deficit of $1.2 million, and again the Authority declared its inability to take on such a deficit operation.[37]

As the vehicular projects, wealth, and diversity of operations of the PNYA increased, criticism of its "neglect" of rail transit also grew. Commuter associations and the railroads were joined by the RPA, the Newark *News,* and other regional spokesmen in urging the PNYA to reconsider its opposition to undertaking a direct role in rail transit. By 1950, as the need for some public action to stem the rail decline seemed more apparent, the governors of New York and New Jersey also began to show some interest in the Port Authority's changing its position.[38]

In response to these criticisms and queries, the PNYA took a firm stand, a position which it was able to maintain until 1959–60. The PNYA argued, first, that it was "completely unable to purchase or otherwise assume deficit financing of rail transit operations." Any passenger rail facilities, the PNYA asserted, would operate at substantial deficits, and an integrated transit system in the New York–New Jersey area would probably involve annual losses of $35 to $40 million. Since the Authority was required to support its program entirely on the basis of its own income, such a deficit operation would make it impossible for the PNYA to sell revenue bonds for new facilities and would force contraction of its entire program. In fact, "any implication that the Port Authority was even considering the financing of rail transit," its officials maintained, would "seriously impair" its credit structure. The Authority also opposed any plan that would provide tax resources to meet PNYA deficits, for such a step would subject it to "political influence," thus destroying the "sound business" principles on which it was operated.

"The only long range solution" to the transit problem, the PNYA argued, was the creation of an interstate public corporation, with power to "make up deficits out of taxes apportioned equitably among the communities which depend upon rail service." [39]

The position taken by the PNYA was in part unassailable. It could not expand and perhaps not even survive if required to assume a continuing rail deficit so large that other income could not offset it. But some of its arguments were open to debate. Might it not be able to assume limited responsibilities in the rail field, either directly or via allocation of some of its surplus bridge and tunnel revenues to a separate organization? Also, was it in fact preferable as a matter of regional policy to create a separate and perhaps competing agency for rail, rather than integrating both rail and road under one authority, supported by its own revenues and taxes?

In maintaining its position, the Port Authority was not limited, however, to the logic of its arguments. As it entered into a long and intensive campaign to ward off responsibility for rail passenger service, the PNYA possessed a number of politically significant advantages—widespread public support, a relatively large degree of formal independence in policy-making, and well-developed political skills. The nature of each of these advantages deserves further comment.

The Port Authority's achievements and current plans have generally been supported enthusiastically by business groups, newspapers, public officials, and other regional spokesmen, and the admiration of state legislators and the two governors has usually been evident as well. Acclaimed during the postwar period for its "far-reaching program," for "imagination and resourcefulness, . . . vigor and initiative," and for its "great service to business and industry" while avoiding the "evils of governmental bureaucracy and governmental waste," the PNYA has been able to count upon widespread backing for its desire to maintain its financial autonomy and its preferred range of activities.[40]

The ability of the PNYA to determine its own policy preferences and to avoid transit projects has been greatly aided by several structural characteristics and related traditions. Whereas most state agencies are under the supervision of a single official, appointed by the governor and removable at will, the PNYA is guided by twelve commissioners, six appointed by each governor, for overlapping six-year terms. The chairman of the board of commissioners is chosen by the members themselves, and no commissioner may be removed by the governors except for cause, after a hearing. These legal factors have substantially modified the influence that either governor can wield over PNYA policy-making.

Still, the appointive power itself provides the governors with the means to select persons to represent their own views or a range of views which they believe should have influence upon an agency. In some public authorities the appointive power has been used in this way; the Chicago Housing Authority, for example, included in 1949 "a Jew, a Catholic, a Negro, a small businessman, a big businessman, a labor leader, and a social worker–intellectual." [41] Traditionally, commissioners of the Port Authority have been drawn from a far narrower stratum; banking and business predominate, and members of the board are frequently wealthy. In 1952, for example, two commissioners were presidents of banks in the region, six were board chairmen, presidents, or vice-presidents of business firms, and one was the publisher of a large newspaper, the Bergen *Evening*

Record; the other three included a member of a major law firm, a consulting engineer, and a university professor. That year, commissioners of the PNYA sat on the boards of directors of more than sixty corporations, including such major companies as Prudential Insurance, American Can, Remington Rand, and New Jersey Bell Telephone.[42]

This is not to imply that business experience should disqualify one for service on the Port Authority. On the contrary, given the importance of financial criteria in its work and the complexity of management involved, it is perhaps desirable and inevitable that business competence would be sought for the PNYA. Nor should one infer that the commissioners are concerned only with business criteria and values. Some have had careers outside the business community, some of the businessmen have held other public posts, appointive or elective (and party service has at times been a criterion in appointment), and a few commissioners have identified themselves as much with their governors and broader regional concerns as they have with the immediate goals of the PNYA. On balance, however, the previous experience of the board has been consistent with the conservative approach taken by the PNYA—in opposition to taking action on a problem as financially uncertain as rail transit or to any actions which might reduce the financial and administrative autonomy of the Authority.

The relationship between the commissioners and the PNYA staff has further reinforced these policies and the general ability of the agency to determine its own priorities. The twelve commissioners are unpaid, each has a full-time job elsewhere, and the PNYA's complex activities have traditionally been carried out with great skill and success. As a result, many commissioners have lacked the time and inclination to master the Authority's methods and problems; the hurdle has been especially great for those who might consider pressing for a rethinking of traditional PNYA goals. Inevitably, the full-time staff has exerted substantial influence in the development of overall and instrumental policies.

Staff influence has been heightened by the high quality and long tenure of most top-level officials at the Authority. The executive director, Austin J. Tobin—"stocky, . . . vigorous and pugnacious-looking"—is one of the nation's outstanding administrators.[43] Although less well known than some of his counterparts, Tobin fits admirably the characterization used to describe J. Edgar Hoover and General Curtis E. LeMay:

Both presided over major expansions of the organization while refusing to take on functions not closely related to its fundamental purpose. Both cultivated reputations for themselves as tough, nononsense, hard-driving administrators, and for their agencies as efficient, technically expert, hard-working organizations, employing the most up-to-date devices of technology in the singleminded pursuit of their mission.[44]

Closely allied with Tobin have been a number of highly qualified officials in such fields as aviation, port development, and public relations. The PNYA has been able to obtain officials of high competence in part because of the agency's high reputation and in part because it offers salaries unmatched in most public agencies. Tobin receives $60,000 a year, a government salary exceeded only by that of the President of the United States; seven top officials are paid $40,000 annually, and thirteen others receive between $27,000 and $33,000.[45]

Many of the Port Authority's senior career officials combine ability with long service in the agency. Tobin joined the PNYA in 1927 as a law clerk and worked his way up through the ranks during the next fifteen years. Several of his top aides in the early 1950s also counted their service from the 1920s. With extended service, staff members accept and indeed absorb the goals of the organization. When appointment to top positions comes after many years in an agency, officials are therefore less inclined to reassess past policy or in any way to "shake up" the

organization. So it is with the PNYA, and the ability and commitment to the agency of its senior officials operates to reinforce
its independent position.

Autonomy in policy-making is also a product of the Authority's independent financial resources (from tolls, rents, and
other charges) and its independence in personnel and other
administrative matters. Budgetary autonomy is especially important. As Sayre and Kaufman have pointed out in their analysis of authorities operating in New York City, there are several
advantages here:

First, the authorities do not have to undergo the public budget
hearings before the Board of Estimate, at which so many of the
pressures on ordinary line agencies are brought to bear. Second, the
authorities do not have to defend their plans and projected expenditures to budget and fiscal officers of the city or any other government. . . . Third, they are not exposed to deprivations of income
through appropriations delays or slashes, a common means of sub-
duing line agencies. Fourth, they are not limited by the detailed
appropriation items of the regular expense budget of the city. In
sum, their operating policy decisions, as these are reflected in their
budgets, are made internally rather than in dealings with outside
agencies and officials, in private rather than in public, and the
authorities are the undisputed masters of their own operating
resources.[46]

The broad impact of these structural characteristics is to
give the PNYA a degree of independence more often associated
with a private corporation than with a public agency. Such a
conclusion has been accepted and indeed favored by PNYA officials. As Tobin asserted in 1953,

An authority is designed to put revenue producing public facilities
on their own feet and on their own responsibility; to free them
from political interference, bureaucracy and red tape. . . . This test
of management, the administrative standards of a well-managed
private corporation, is the test that should be applied to the [Au-
thority's] responsibilities and duties.

"The Commissioners of the Port Authority function as a Board of Directors," Tobin concluded. "My own executive office has the same normal responsibilities as those of the president of a private corporation." [47]

One can carry the emphasis on PNYA independence too far, however. There are several ways in which outside interests can affect its policies directly and effectively. The governor of either state may veto any action taken by the PNYA, or the state legislatures may refuse to enact laws needed for new projects. Certain municipal and other controls can also be cited.[48] The PNYA has found it necessary to develop strategies to neutralize potential opposition from these sources, and it has executed these strategies with great political skill during the postwar period.

The Authority's basic strategy has been to carry out a vigorous program along the lines of its preferred goals. Vehicular, airport, and other facilities are constantly being built and improved. This policy provides a basis for obtaining widespread public approbation; it has also insured that large reserves are not built up—reserves that the Authority might be asked to apply to rail transit.

Closely joined with its expansion policy has been a skillful public relations program, aimed at persuading the general public and political leaders of the region of the importance of current PNYA activities. The director of public relations participates in policy meetings, issues a constant stream of press releases (more than 600 from 1946 to 1951), and has made available to newspapers "reliable background information for use in determining editorial policies." [49] These publicity efforts have emphasized the achievements and "nonpolitical" nature of the PNYA and the intimate relationships between these two factors.[50]

The PNYA has not relied only on these indirect methods in warding off political pressures. The agency's views have been presented informally to the governors of both states and to influential members of the two legislatures. These efforts have been continuous and have been carried out by commissioners and top staff officers closely acquainted with the officials concerned. State legislators have also been given special tours of Port Authority facilities, and new projects have been presented to the legislatures and to the general public with a substantial publicity build-up.[51] These strategies have been largely effective in securing political support for PNYA goals and independence at the state capitals; the governors' veto power has been used infrequently, and the legislatures have rarely failed to authorize new projects.[52] The comments of New York Governor Thomas E. Dewey in 1952 typify the general view taken of the PNYA during the first postwar decade and suggest the success which the agency has had in maintaining public acceptance of its goals and methods:

In its thirty-one years of service to the two States the Port Authority, without burden to the general taxpayer, has provided almost half a billion dollars' worth of terminal and transportation facilities. Through its great public works, it has set an example for the administration of public business on a sound and efficient basis.[53]

Because of these several factors, the PNYA was able to maintain a substantial degree of independence in policy-making during the early postwar period and was largely able to decide when and where to expand its facilities. Pressure from the rail coalition for action on rail transit posed no immediate threat to the politically powerful Authority. Still, the PNYA found it necessary to remain alert. Further rail-service deterioration could increase the size and importance of the rail coalition, and the rail group might expect to find allies in any concerted attack upon the PNYA from among those who criticized the agency for other reasons. There were the residents of the areas around PNYA airports, who were critical of the noise and danger involved in airport operation, and those from towns which lost land to PNYA projects. There were groups which attacked it concerning toll rates and other policies—positions especially prominent in Hudson County—and scholars and planners who criticized the public authorities for increasing the fragmentation of metropolitan areas. Although these critics were usually isolated minorities, their political strength could increase dramatically upon occasion (as it did temporarily following a series of plane crashes near Newark Airport in 1951–52).[54] Since pressure from the rail coalition could be augmented greatly by such groups, the PNYA could be expected to exert its considerable resources to divert the region from itself as a "solution," and if possible to help locate an alternative approach that would leave it unfettered by rail transit.

The Triborough Bridge and Tunnel Authority. The region's other major road agency—the Triborough Bridge and Tunnel Authority—is in some ways similar to the PNYA. But there is a basic difference: the PNYA is an organization headed by a skilled leadership group; the TBTA might more accurately be viewed as one man—Robert Moses—with an agency appended. The role of the TBTA, though secondary in this study, warrants a brief review of Moses and his works.

Robert Moses has long been an important and controversial figure in New York. Since working with Governor Alfred E. Smith in the 1920s, he has accumulated a series of titles and a reputation for success rarely matched in the field of public administration. In 1922 Moses prepared a plan for a state system of parks, and he began carrying it out in 1924 as president of the Long Island State Park Commission and chairman of the State Council of Parks. Subsequently, he was made chairman of the Jones Beach State Parkway Authority and the Bethpage Park Authority, both on Long Island. In 1934, he was appointed by Mayor Fiorello H. LaGuardia to be Park Commissioner for New York City and chairman of both the Triborough Bridge Authority and the Henry Hudson Bridge Authority. Other city positions followed, including membership on the City Planning

Commission (1942), chairmanship of the Triborough Bridge and Tunnel Authority (formed in 1946, consolidating several previous authorities), and appointment to the newly created position of City Construction Coordinator (1946) and to the chairmanship of the Committee on Slum Clearance (1948). Moses continued to hold all these positions throughout the 1950s.

During these years, he became well known as a man who "gets results"—impressive, easy-to-see results—among the most prominent of which are the Triborough Bridge, the Queens-Manhattan tunnel, the Brooklyn-Battery tunnel, and the Whitestone Bridge. As one commentator has said, Moses has built himself a "city–state park–parkway–highway–bridge–tunnel empire." [55] And to that must be added power dams, for on becoming chairman of the New York State Power Authority in 1954 Moses directed his considerable energies toward the Niagara–St. Lawrence power projects (not the least important of which is the Robert Moses Dam).

The nature of his work—combined with his proclivity for invective—has led Moses into conflicts with political leaders, administrative agencies, residents in the paths of his projects, and many others. He has been criticized for "arrogance" and accused of wanting to "do away with the democratic process." Yet the dominant view within the New York region and in Albany is highly favorable. Endowed with intelligence, imagination, and tremendous amounts of aggressive energy, Moses has demonstrated a unique capacity to overcome bureaucratic complexity and inertia and to produce major achievements. As one legislator concluded during a debate in Albany several years ago, "There have been times when he has been somewhat vitriolic, to state it mildly, but Mr. Moses has rendered a greater service to the State than any of his contemporaries." [56]

The Triborough Bridge and Tunnel Authority has been one of Robert Moses' major enterprises. At the time of its formation in 1946, the Triborough Authority controlled five toll bridges and one tunnel connecting New York City boroughs. As the postwar travel boom developed, the agency grew financially stronger year by year, and in 1950 a second tunnel connecting Brooklyn and Manhattan and a Manhattan garage were completed. By 1952, with an annual net income exceeding $20 million, the Triborough had developed a $90-million construction program and was looking forward during the next few years to the building of a coliseum at Columbus Circle and a gigantic bridge across the Narrows, connecting Brooklyn and Staten Island.[57]

Financial affluence and expansionist tendencies have brought attacks upon the Triborough Authority, just as they have upon the Port Authority. Critics argued that some of the agency's income should be devoted to meeting New York City's subway deficits and that the plans of the Triborough should be closely coordinated with rail service planning in the city and the region. A few, the most tenacious being New York City Planning Commissioner Goodhue Livingston, have gone further. In public statements beginning in 1951, Livingston argued that the Triborough should be merged into a new Regional Transport Authority, which would control the subway system, the H&M Railroad, the Long Island Rail Road, and some Port Authority bridges, as well as all bridges and tunnels between the city boroughs. Such an authority, he asserted, would provide a means for more effective coordination of transportation development, and for more balanced financing.[58]

Moses has taken a different view. The railroads might properly be aided by tax reduction and by the states' assuming the cost of most grade-crossing eliminations, but he has seen little need for an expansion of railroad commuter facilities and no advantage in an "official, all-powerful regional agency" to coordinate and improve rail service. As to the suggestion that the Triborough Authority aid in solving rail problems, Moses was more critical. Triborough's "first rate reputation," he asserted, was based upon the "definite, limited and financially sound" nature of its program. To combine with it all of the "dubious projects" that could be called transportation would "wreck" the Authority:

Putting all of the problems into a big new shiny basket is just a way of hastening their trip to the dump heap or the incinerator. . . . We no doubt need some smarter, more forceful and more independent people in the existing agencies, here and there less pride of authorship and more sacrifice for the common good, but we don't need powerful, new expensive bureaucratic regional administrations staffed by ambitious second rate planners, railroads eager to rid themselves of their less profitable business, and public officials anxious to dump their tougher problems on someone else.[59]

But the Triborough Authority has seemed in little danger of becoming involved in rail operations. In maintaining its independence, this Authority has been able to depend upon the political strength of chairman Moses and upon legal restrictions. In contrast to the PNYA, Triborough's jurisdiction is limited to New York City, and its contracts with current bondholders appear to prohibit it from using its borrowing authority to undertake rail transit responsibilities.[60]

The Port Authority and the Triborough Authority were major participants in the road coalition. Closely allied with them were a number of other public institutions and private groups. Several of these were coordinated through the person of Moses himself; his multiple positions provided the basis for insuring close cooperation among the Triborough Authority, the office of the City Construction Coordinator, the City Department of Parks, the Long Island State Park Commission, the Jones Beach State Parkway Authority, and the Bethpage Park Authority on Long Island. Other agencies directly involved in planning and constructing the region's arterial highway system included the New York State Department of Public Works, New York State Thruway Authority, New Jersey State Highway Department, New Jersey Turnpike Authority, New Jersey Highway Authority, the federal Bureau of Public Roads, and state and county park commissions. Bus companies and associations, automobile clubs, truckers, and other beneficiaries supported and applauded their efforts. Although conflict arose occasionally within the coalition—especially between Moses and the Port Authority—"close contact" and cooperation were the rule.[61] The alliance was reinforced by the service of other officials (in addition to Moses) in more than one of the agencies. Charles H. Sells, for example, had been Superintendent of Public Works for New York State and Westchester Commissioner of Public Works before becoming a Port Authority commissioner in 1949.

When any serious threat to the independence of the road coalition arose, auto groups and other members might be expected to voice strong objections. Usually, however, they left the battle to those most directly threatened and most capable of effective defense and counterattack—the Port Authority and Robert Moses.

A Multitude of Governments. In pressing for changes in regional transport policy, the rail coalition not only found itself divided on goals and priorities while facing a politically powerful alliance of road interests. In addition, the structure of general governmental institutions in the region provided significant obstacles to action. Barring a sudden conversion of highway interests to the transit cause, the rail coalition would need assistance from local and state governmental leaders if its goals were to be achieved. This support would be essential if general tax funds were to be tapped to aid the rail system or if sufficient leverage were to be applied to the highway coalition to yield funds from that source. Yet the characteristic

fragmentation of government in the metropolis made it difficult to focus responsibility on any local or state leader, and thus
favored the *status quo*.

The problem of divided authority was unusually great in the
New York region. Here twenty-two counties and more than
500 cities and towns compete and cooperate in the making of
governmental decisions affecting the metropolis. The interstate
nature of the region adds officials at three state capitals as well
as the federal government to this diversity.

The typically narrow perspective of local governments in a
metropolis is found throughout the New York region. Each local
unit is "preoccupied with its own problems," and conflicts over
zoning, roads, and other issues are frequent. Cooperative agreements on some services have been made by small groups of
adjoining municipalities, but most cities and towns lack the territorial breadth or inclination to exercise leadership on transportation development or other major regional issues.[62]

In some regions other factors have served to offset this
fragmentation. In Miami and in a number of other areas most
of the metropolitan growth is contained within one county; the
county government can serve in such cases as a source of regional leadership. And in such large regions as Detroit and Pittsburgh, a central economic and social focus exists, facilitating
private as well as public leadership on a regionwide basis.[63] But
the New York region is favored with neither of these advantages. In addition to New York City, there are seventeen counties in the region; and twenty-one cities (as of 1960) with
50,000 or more inhabitants—cities that in other locations would
themselves be nuclei for separate metropolitan areas. One of
these, Newark, had a population of 405,000 in 1960, while
Jersey City counted 276,000 residents.[64] Business and political
leaders in the larger cities of the region have long felt a strong
sense of competition with New York City. Intraregional rivalry,
especially on an interstate basis between New Jersey cities and

New York, has been a significant limiting factor in attempts to develop coordinated policies. The nature and extent of this problem were clearly outlined during the efforts (described below) to develop regional transport policies during the 1950s and early 1960s.[65]

In spite of these limitations, New York City provided an important potential base for coordinated regional action. In terms of geography and economic factors, the city holds a central role in the region. Its business and civic leaders and its public officials—especially the mayor—are more likely to view problems in a regional perspective than spokesmen from any other sector of the metropolis.[66] On the transportation issue, two specific factors reinforced the positive potential of the city. New York had a long tradition of providing public support for local transit services and thus might look favorably upon extending such aid to the suburban railroads. Also, by the early 1950s several influential private groups in the city had already declared their support for regionwide public action to improve rail service.[67]

Yet it was not certain that the city would be able to exert vigorous leadership on regional transportation. New York seemed unable to coordinate the planning and financing of its own transportation facilities. The Triborough Authority, the Department of Traffic, the city's transit agency, and several other city units worked semi-independently and often at cross purposes. Also, important as a new regional transport policy might be to New York City, the mayor and his aides found their energies occupied during the early 1950s with the problems of subway fares and deficits. Creation of a Transit Authority in 1954 reduced city-state conflict on the issue, but the complexities and political difficulties involved did little to encourage the mayor to venture into the broader intercity problem.[68] Finally—and related to these other difficulties—the mayor's office has not traditionally been a strong center of leadership, in part, because of weaknesses in the mayor's formal powers. As Sayre and Kaufman conclude,

His fiscal powers are few; his managerial reach is curtailed by insufficient staff inadequately organized for his own needs; his powers to supervise are reduced by the numerous islands of autonomy among the administrative agencies; his inclinations toward initiative and innovation are resisted by the inertial weight of the bureaucracies and their constituencies.

And in part it has been a matter of personality; many of the incumbents have lacked the capacity to use the strength of the office to its full potential.[69]

Fragmentation at the local level has left a leadership vacuum which state officials might fill. The governors of New York and New Jersey have had important incentives to respond to regional needs. In New York State, about 60 percent of the votes for governor during postwar elections have been cast by residents of the New York metropolitan region; the New Jersey proportion has exceeded 70 percent.[70] Also, the public has tended to look to the governor for leadership because of the state's important role in local affairs, the visibility of the gubernatorial chair, and the lack of an alternative source of action.[71]

On the rail transit issue, however, several obstacles stood in the way of gubernatorial action during the first postwar decade. First, there was no established pattern of active state leadership on rail transportation problems—of the sort that characterized education and highways, for example. Although in the early 1950s New York took more positive steps to meet the special problems of the Long Island Rail Road, traditional state policy had been concerned almost entirely with regulation of passenger service. Second, it was not clear what actions would be useful. The technical and financial complexities were considerable, especially when the question of constructing new rail lines was involved and when interstate coordination might be required. Vigorous gubernatorial action would be difficult under these circumstances. Third, no major crisis developed during the first postwar decade. Pressures upon the governor to overcome past tradition and cut through the complexities to a prompt solution were not strong.

Finally, the governors faced many other demands upon their limited resources. State programs in education, welfare, and other areas demanded the executives' attention and tended to take precedence—since the traditional role of the states was larger in these areas, the political costs of inaction were perceived to be greater, or at least more immediate, and the possible lines of productive action seemed clearer. Little time or political energy remained for the rail transit issue.[72]

During the early postwar years, gubernatorial action was tentative and exploratory, except under conditions of crisis. Between 1951 and 1954, after bankruptcy and a series of major accidents had beset the Long Island Rail Road, New York State did act to stabilize and improve that line's financial condition.[73] In the late 1940s, New Jersey's Governor Driscoll investigated several plans for improving rail service in northern New Jersey, but no action was taken because of the projected deficits involved. And sporadically during the early 1950s, Governors Dewey and Driscoll explored the possibility of Port Authority action to build a New Jersey–Manhattan rail system.[74] These were the limits of gubernatorial action on the region's rail problem during the early postwar period.

Important obstacles also stood in the way of effective legislative action on the region's transportation problems. Although representatives from the region held a majority in three of the four legislative houses of New York and New Jersey (all but the New Jersey Senate), they did not form a self-conscious, organized bloc. On the contrary, they were divided by political party and, on some problems, further subdivided by geography. Since in this period the Republicans usually controlled all four houses, Republican legislators from the region—from suburban

Bergen and Westchester, for example—were especially influential in the making of policy affecting the metropolis. To some extent this Republican bias improved the outlook for legislative action on an issue as important to the suburbs as commuter rail service, but nonregional delegates were not dependable allies if the use of substantial state funds to assist one area was involved. In addition, the limited influence of the Democratic leaders of the region's major cities in the state legislatures might make it difficult to develop policies which would obtain the cities' positive cooperation.

The pattern of political forces in the New York region thus provided a firm base for continuing the highway-oriented policies of the first postwar decade and little reason for optimism on the part of those who wanted more "balanced" development of road and rail facilities. The road coalition was opposed to contributing its funds to aid rail services or to restricting its independence through a cooperative planning effort, and the fragmentation of governmental leadership mitigated against a reassessment of transport policy by local or state officials. Even so, continued deterioration of rail service could unify and extend the rail coalition and increase the possibility of direct action in the future, especially from two sources: the governors, who—though reluctant—might feel impelled to act, and the Port Authority, which in spite of its political strength was potentially the most vulnerable member of the road coalition because of its wealth and regional transportation mandate.

Meanwhile, the proponents of further aid to the rail system sought to develop an interim strategy—a comprehensive study of the transportation problem—which might effectively serve its long-range goals.

CHAPTER III

Strategy for Policy Innovation

During the early 1950s, the rail coalition devoted increasing attention to the need for an extensive study of the region's transport problems. This emphasis on "further study" was inevitable if the rail alliance was to make any progress toward its goals. For the present, political obstacles, including differing perspectives within the rail group, the strength of the highway interests, and governmental fragmentation, precluded more direct policy changes. An extensive study might help to overcome these restraints by providing a feasible plan around which all members of the rail alliance could unite. In addition, a study and the proposals for action growing out of it might attract other groups to the cause, enhancing the chances for success. Also, the passage of time might lend further impetus to the cause if rail service continued to deteriorate while the survey was being carried out. The use of a program of study for these several purposes is a frequent one in the development of policy for metropolitan regions and in other policy areas.[1]

The "further study" strategy had one other important advantage. Compared with the alternative, direct action, it entailed less political leadership, fewer funds, and less infringement on the independence of the road coalition members and the local areas. As a consequence, it might avoid the intense counterpressure from these forces which a direct-action campaign would arouse. In fact, some of those who were wary of policy change joined the rail alliance in favoring an extensive study. The Port Authority and the governors supported it in part as a delaying tactic: further study would reduce the pressure on them for immediate action.[2] The Authority also hoped that a study would support its position—that it should not become involved in the rail problem and that a separate transit agency should be established. In addition, state and local officials looked forward to such a study as helping to provide feasible lines of action when and if such action became politically imperative. The assistance of these groups, then, might aid the rail alliance in its efforts to obtain a study which could be used as a springboard to more direct action, including policy changes which its temporary allies (such as the Port Authority) might oppose.[3]

But those who were wary of change realized that an extensive study entailed dangers as well as advantages to their interests. Consequently, the rail interests soon found themselves under pressure from the road coalition and from those in both states who were suspicious of regional cooperation. Controversy arose during the 1951–54 period over whether there should be a study at all, the proper scope of any study, and what group should be responsible for carrying it out.

The members of the rail coalition overcame these obstacles, and by mid-1954 a significant measure of success had been achieved. In June, the bistate Metropolitan Rapid Transit Commission (MRTC) was created to study the transit needs of the New York region. Moreover, its members had set forth their intention to make the study a truly comprehensive one, embracing road as well as rail transport and freight as well as passenger services. This study, they concluded, should produce an "overall coordinated plan for transportation in the Metropolitan Area." [4] Those who opposed such overall coordination, and the shift in emphasis toward rail which it implied, had lost the first round.

PRELIMINARY STUDIES

Innovation begins, Huntington has argued, with the uncoordinated efforts of particular groups to meet an apparent need.[5]

The early efforts of the rail coalition to alter the region's transport policy illustrate this generalization. A wide variety of approaches were put forward by the railroads, central-city interests, and spokesmen for suburbia.

During the years 1951–54, however, the campaign for a major study gained momentum and came to dominate the rail coalition's efforts, and the focus of responsibility progressively narrowed. In 1951 and 1952 three spokesmen—the Regional Plan Association (RPA), the New Jersey Regional Planning Commission (NJRPC), and consultant L. Alfred Jenny—assumed major roles in defining the coalition's perspective and outlining a program of studies. Between 1952 and 1954 the center of activity was narrowed further as two parallel state commissions carried out a joint review of the problem. Their recommendations led directly to the creation of the MRTC. During these three years, the basic outlines of the studies desired by the rail coalition were developed, and some of the obstacles that would hinder the MRTC's study were first encountered.

Three reports prepared during 1951–52 warrant particular attention—an analysis made by Jenny for New Jersey state officials in early 1951, and brief reports of the RPA and the NJRPC during the following year.[6] In these reports the rail spokesmen raised three important issues which would divide the rail coalition from other groups in the region: the question of whether the study should extend to road as well as rail policy, geographic priorities, and the kinds of improvements in rail service which should be evaluated in the studies.

As to the first issue, the rail spokesmen viewed the expansion of highway facilities as a basic cause of rail service deterioration and argued that vehicular and rail developments should be studied together. From the proposed survey, they felt, should come recommendations for closer coordination of transport planning, and perhaps financial allocations from road to rail facilities as well.[7] On this issue a direct clash with the road coalition seemed likely, for the Port Authority and its allies argued that the development of road and rail policy should evolve independently, and that no overall study or coordination was required.[8]

A second issue concerned the geographic scope of the proposed studies: Should they focus primarily upon one sector of the region, or attempt to evaluate transport policy throughout the area? Here the preliminary reports were divided along predictable lines. The RPA, with members from all parts of the metropolis, called for a regionwide approach. The NJRPC and Jenny, representing New Jersey's suburban segment of the rail coalition, placed major emphasis on the trans-Hudson problem. Each alternative had advantages and disadvantages from the viewpoint of the rail alliance. The trans-Hudson emphasis would offer fewer technical and political obstacles to developing a concrete feasible plan. But it might be more difficult to obtain support for this approach at the state capitals, since a smaller proportion of the states' population would benefit directly.[9]

A final issue concerned the kinds of improvements in rail service that should be considered in order to halt or reverse the decline in rail travel. At least three possibilities might be considered: major additions to the system (for example, new rail tunnels under the Hudson), less expensive improvements (such as new railroad commuter cars and more frequent service), or no significant improvements at all (that is, merely providing subsidies to maintain service at existing levels). These alternatives were not mutually exclusive, of course; the studies might look carefully into all three policy approaches. Such an "open-ended" analysis was preferred by the RPA. But the reports by the NJRPC and by Jenny argued that primary attention should be given to studies of new rail facilities, and particularly to proposals for a trans-Hudson rail tunnel and connecting terminal. This approach would tend to insure a costly set of final proposals and consequently would heighten the concern of the

Port Authority and others who might be asked to help carry out the study group's recommendations.[10]

In addition to taking positions on the proper scope of the proposed studies, the three reports considered the question of which group should be responsible for carrying them out. The dominant view was that a new interstate commission or parallel state commissions be established for this purpose, although the RPA report also included the suggestion that the Port Authority might be given responsibility.

CREATING A BISTATE AGENCY

The third of the reports, that of the NJRPC in January, 1952, was a catalyst for further action. On the basis of the Commission's recommendations, bills were introduced at Trenton and Albany to establish state commissions to act jointly in developing plans for improving transit facilities. The bills called upon the two commissions to consider facilities for both passenger and freight traffic, and to give "special attention" to the NJRPC proposal for a new trans-Hudson rail tunnel and terminal. The bills provided appropriations of $50,000 from each state and asked that the Port Authority meet the remaining costs of the studies. In New Jersey, the measure readily obtained majority support in both houses and appeared to be headed for approval in mid-March.

However, the proposed studies were now challenged from two vantage points, and only with difficulty did this attempt to develop regional coordination move forward. First, the interstate approach of the studies conflicted with divergent state perspectives and priorities; and once these obstacles had been temporarily removed, the road coalition tried to modify the direction of the developing study to suit its own needs.

Problems of Interstate Cooperation. The first sign of difficulty appeared at Albany in late March. The New York bill was amended to eliminate references to a coordinated study with the New Jersey Commission and to a study of possible freight operations on any new transit project. The request that the PNYA pay for studies was also deleted, and the appropriation was reduced from $50,000 to $10,000. In this form the New York measure was passed by the legislature and signed by Governor Dewey on April 3, 1952.[11] There were several reasons for these changes: the lower level of concern in New York with commuter problems generally and especially with the problem of getting New Jersey's commuters into Manhattan, the feeling that an independent New York commission would give higher priority to intra-New York transit needs, and objections by the PNYA and its friends in the legislature to the Authority's paying for the study and to extending the new commission's jurisdiction to include railroad freight—a specific responsibility of the Port Authority under the 1921 compact.

The New Jersey legislators were unhappy with the New York changes and amended their bill to permit the New Jersey transit commission to act "either independently or jointly" with the New York agency. They also reduced the funds available from $50,000 to $20,000. The references to the use of PNYA funds and freight traffic were not changed. The New Jersey bill was then passed and was signed by Governor Driscoll on May 16, 1952.[12]

Two study commissions charged with taking a closer look at the metropolitan transit problem had now been established, but it could hardly be said that the drive for regional action had gotten off to an auspicious start. Differences in perspective among leaders in the two states seemed likely to complicate the efforts to solve an already difficult problem.

On August 1, 1952, the members of the New Jersey Metropolitan Rapid Transit Commission (NJMRTC) were appointed by Governor Driscoll. David Van Alstyne, Jr., chairman of the NJRPC, became a member of the new commission. Also appointed from the Planning Commission were Frank Scott, Jr., of Elizabeth, and Kenneth Hanau of Upper Montclair. The other two men named to the NJMRTC—Charles F. Krause of Weehawken and John F. Kraus of North Plainfield—had not served on the NJRPC. None of the Democrats on the NJRPC had been named to the new commission, and all five of Driscoll's appointees to the Commission shared the Governor's Republican affiliation.

The five commissioners were diversified in background and experience. Two, Van Alstyne and Krause, were very active politically. Van Alstyne had served as state senator from Bergen County, one of the state's largest and fastest-growing suburban areas, since 1943. Although he had chaired the NJRPC and endorsed its criticisms of Port Authority facilities, he was no enemy of the PNYA. He recognized the importance of the Port Authority's contributions, especially the George Washington Bridge, in the development of his home county. Van Alstyne was also senior partner in Van Alstyne, Noel and Co., a Wall Street investment firm.

Krause was mayor of Weehawken, in Hudson County. Long a critic of the PNYA, he had been engaged for more than a year in a battle with the Authority concerning construction of a third tube for the Lincoln Tunnel. The first two tubes had terminated in Weehawken, eliminating property from the tax rolls, and the township had thus far refused to give permission for the PNYA to use local property for the third tube.

Kraus, an engineer with the New York Telephone Company and a commuter from Somerset County, had been active in rail commuter organizations for many years; he also was a severe critic of the Port Authority. Kraus had been a member of the Raritan Valley Commuters' Association in the late 1930s and had served as chairman of the IMGBRS since 1945.

The final two commission members were New Jersey businessmen. Scott, from Essex County, was president of the Morey

Larue Laundry and Hanau, from Union County, was executive vice-president of the Wagner Baking Company.

On the whole, the appointments seemed to satisfy the standards of those who wanted a strong effort made to reverse the trend toward vehicular development and congestion. The Bayonne *Times*, for example, had suggested that those appointed to the Commission should have a

keen awareness of the need to carry people by common carrier, not by automobile. . . . The Commission should be made up of men removed as far as possible from the Port Authority's favorite idea of moving people one to a car, 50¢ per car.[13]

The New Jersey commissioners met for the first time in September, 1952, and elected Van Alstyne chairman, Krause vice-chairman, and Kraus secretary. Since the members felt that bistate cooperation was essential, especially on the trans-Hudson issue, they decided to postpone action until they could meet jointly with the New York commission. The New York members had not yet been appointed.

More than a year then elapsed before the two commissions were able to get together. First, two months passed before Governor Dewey appointed the five New York commissioners. He then named Charles H. Tuttle as chairman, Michael J. Madigan as vice-chairman, and Allen S. Hubbard, William Zeckendorf, and Carl Whitmore as the other three commissioners. All were Republicans, but Tuttle was the only one who had been prominent politically. He had been U.S. Attorney for the Southern District of New York from 1927 to 1930 and Republican candidate for governor in 1930, losing to Franklin D. Roosevelt. In 1913, he had been appointed a member of the board responsible for New York City's higher education system, and he had been reappointed by each succeeding mayor. He was senior partner of the leading Wall Street law firm of Breed, Abbott and Morgan. Although at seventy-two the oldest member of either Commission, Tuttle was extremely energetic and outspoken. His jousts with the Port Authority and with Robert Moses were an important part of later developments.

Madigan was a member of Madigan-Hyland, a New York City firm of consulting engineers which was frequently used by the City; Hubbard was also a Wall Street lawyer, with Hughes, Hubbard, Blair and Reed; Zeckendorf was president of the real estate firm Webb and Knapp; and Whitmore was a director and former president of the New York Telephone Company.

Even with the New York commission appointed, no further action was forthcoming for several months. The New York commissioners continually rebuffed efforts of the New Jersey agency to develop a joint attack on the problem, and they also failed to take any action on their own. Behind these delays were the continued reluctance of state leaders to have much effort devoted to the interstate problem, the desire of the New York commissioners and state officials to keep this problem separate from the current controversy over establishment of the New York City Transit Authority and the increase in subway fares, and the feeling on the part of some New York members that more funds would be needed before any useful action could be taken.

Finally, after increasing criticism of the inactivity of the two agencies from both sides of the Hudson, the termination of the subway fare battle, and a direct plea for cooperation from Governor Driscoll to Governor Dewey, the two commissions agreed to a combined effort in October, 1953.[14] Joint offices were established and a staff hired. As the New Jersey chairman noted, this was the first time that official bodies representing the two states had agreed to merge their efforts in seeking a solution to the region's passenger transit problem.[15]

Although now united, the commissions had little time to conduct their studies, for the New York agency was required to report to the legislature by late February, 1954. In the intervening four months and with the limited funds available, they could do little more than outline the problem, describe the possible solutions, and recommend further action in a combined report to the two states. The commissions hoped to use their joint report as a springboard for the more detailed regional study which they felt the problem required.

The Road Coalition and the Proposed Study. The approach which the two commissions would take and the kind of study they would recommend were of considerable interest to the highway coalition and especially to the Port Authority and to Moses. Concerned with the possible threat which the commissions' work might pose to their independence of action, the PNYA and Moses tried to persuade the two agencies to accept their own point of view of the transport problem. In a public hearing sponsored by the commissions during the fall of 1953 and in informal discussions, the PNYA agreed that an extensive study was needed but argued that the Authority was not responsible for the deterioration of rail service and should be excluded from any possible role in the rail transit field. Moses also disavowed any place for his agencies in aiding rail, argued that there was little need for new rail facilities, and concluded that each part of the region could best handle its problems by itself; a regionwide effort was not needed.[16]

In their meetings during the winter of 1953, the members of the two study commissions largely rejected the positions of the Port Authority and Moses and accepted instead the perspectives of the NJRPC, the RPA, and rail consultant Jenny. Rail and road developments were interrelated, they believed, and required coordinated study and, later, coordinated planning. A regionwide perspective was essential, they argued, and perhaps extensive new rail facilities would be needed. These views were incorporated in a draft report completed in January, 1954, and circulated to several groups for comment.[17]

The Port Authority now made a final and somewhat more

successful effort to influence the commissions' work. Authority officials found several phrases and sections in the report disturbing. They objected, for example, to the statement that "the losses sustained by the New Jersey railroads due to bus and automobile competition since the opening of the George Washington Bridge and the Lincoln Tunnel have been serious," and they were unhappy with a number of other direct or implied criticisms of PNYA facilities.

The problem of how to persuade the commissions to eliminate such criticisms, in spite of the known hostility of some of the transit commissioners to the Port Authority, was solved by the dual position of David Van Alstyne. Van Alstyne, chairman of the NJMRTC, had also been appointed in May, 1953, to serve as a commissioner of the Port Authority. At the suggestion of Authority officials, he recommended that several rephrasings drafted by the PNYA staff be adopted by the commissions, and some of these suggestions were ultimately incorporated into the final draft. For example, the phrase quoted above was altered to eliminate the reference to Port Authority facilities: "The losses sustained by the New Jersey railroads since 1930 have been serious." But in a number of other instances the transit commission majority insisted that their original wording, critical of the Authority, be retained.

Although not of great significance in themselves, these efforts to dilute the force of the joint report indicate the high level of PNYA interest in the work of the transit study group and suggest some of the differences in perspective that would later result in serious conflict between the two regional agencies.

The Bistate Commission. The final draft of the joint report was approved by the two commissions in late February and released to the public on March 5, 1954. The report began by noting the "critical importance and urgency" of the rail and road traffic problems and argued that an extensive study was required. Particular emphasis was placed upon the need to improve rail service and on the possibility of new facilities to overcome the trans-Hudson problem. But the perspective of the report was much broader. In opposition to the road coalition view, the report argued that the problems of rail and road transport and of people and freight were "inevitably intermingled," and it criticized the past emphasis on highway construction while rail service deteriorated. In contrast to the view that the problems of each part of the region could be considered by themselves, the report saw the New York area as constituting "one great metropolitan community." A comprehensive study was needed, the two commissions argued, this study to result in an "overall coordinated plan for transportation" throughout the region.

The report concluded that action should be taken immediately to consolidate the two commissions into one bistate agency and to provide the joint commission with at least $50,000 from each state. Such a sum would still not be sufficient for the extensive studies that were needed, but the question of the source of additional funds and the amount needed could be left in abeyance until the new commission had been created.[18]

Immediate reactions to the transit report were generally favorable. The New Jersey legislature's Joint Appropriations Committee passed a resolution the same day, expressing tentative approval of the $50,000 request. Governor Dewey was reported to be willing to take prompt action on the MRTC bill, and the region's newspapers asked that the two states "give this [bistate study commission] a trial." [19] Further deterioration of rail service within recent months had given additional emphasis to the need for action, and the steps called for in the joint report held some attraction to cautious state officials. Only a small amount of funds was required, and responsibility for devising a solution to the transport problem could be shifted, at least temporarily, to the new study commission.[20]

In fact, the only significant obstacle to state action on the joint report's recommendations came from those who favored a more direct attack on the PNYA. While the transit study bills were under consideration, New Jersey state senator Malcolm S. Forbes (R–Somerset County) introduced a resolution calling upon the Port Authority to finance an MRTC study "in whole or substantial part" and to refrain from starting any new construction projects until the new commission could complete a comprehensive study. An unusually direct challenge to the independence of action of the road coalition, the resolution temporarily diverted attention from the MRTC bill. Committee hearings were held in early April, and the Forbes proposal received the support of two rail commuter groups and two suburban railroads.[21] But in opposition, the Port Authority pointed out that the resolution would call for halting construction plans at PNYA waterfront and airport facilities in Hoboken and Newark, as well as highway developments. Such action would have an adverse effect on the economy of "all of Northern New Jersey," executive director Tobin asserted, and would require explanations to the men "who are expecting work in Hoboken, and to the men who are depending also on the increase of jobs and payrolls at Port Newark and Newark Airport." In addition, Tobin argued that legally the Authority had "no power to use its funds to pay the expenses" of the MRTC. Several other groups also opposed the resolution.[22]

Faced by economic, political, and legal obstacles, the Senate committee soon voted down the Forbes resolution and the legislature embraced the safer, more circuitous route to modifying the region's transport policies. The MRTC bill was passed in Trenton and Albany during the spring, and action was completed on June 14, 1954, when New Jersey's recently elected governor, Democrat Robert B. Meyner, signed the measure. On that date a new bistate agency, the Metropolitan Rapid Transit Commission, came into being. The Commission was to study "present and prospective rapid transit needs of the New York–New Jersey Metropolitan Area and develop, recommend and report as soon as possible measures for meeting such needs." Each state appropriated $50,000 for the Commission's use.[23]

As drawn up by their Republican sponsors, the bills did not include provisions for the appointment of commissioners. Instead, the joint agency was established by consolidating the two commissions "as now constituted." The members of the two agencies were thereby continued in office with indefinite tenure.

Thus, by June, 1954, the rail coalition had achieved an important measure of success in its campaign for transport policy innovation. A bistate study commission had been established, and this commission stood ready to carry out an extensive survey leading to improvements in rail service and to improved coordination of rail and road facilities.

CHAPTER IV

The Study Commission and the Port Authority

As David Truman has pointed out, interest groups tend to concentrate about any locus of power able to affect their goals.[1] The new Metropolitan Rapid Transit Commission now became such a locus of power and thus the object of a variety of pressures—from the rail alliance, from public officials in both states, and especially from the road coalition. Because of the great variety of actors and activities which focused upon the Commission during its five-year life, the events of this period are particularly useful in understanding the metropolitan political system.

As the MRTC began its work, those who wished to shape its program found a powerful lever at hand. The Commission believed that extensive studies should be made of the region's transport problems, requiring financing well in excess of the $100,000 appropriation from the two states. The donor of these additional funds could exert considerable leverage on the transit agency in the development of its studies and its final recommendations. The Commission's activities during these early months, therefore, can be interpreted in terms of two questions: Who would provide the needed funds? And what would be exacted from the Commission in return?

The MRTC first tried to obtain funds from those most in sympathy with its initial goals, the members of the rail coalition. But the financial weaknesses and divergent priorities noted in Chapter II were evident here, and neither the railroads nor the business and civic groups of the region were able to translate their professed concern into financial support. The Commission members turned to the states in the hope that the governors and other officials would show an increased willingness to support a major regional study. Again they were disappointed. Finally, the Commission found the Port Authority ready to extend financial aid, but for a price: restrictions upon the scope of the study and upon the selection of the staff which would undertake the surveys.

Eight more months of negotiations then followed, as the MRTC tried to reassert its independence of the Port Authority and as it negotiated for additional state funds. In September, 1955, the two states agreed to supplement the Authority's grant but not until New Jersey's Governor Meyner and the PNYA had wrung additional concessions from the study group. The five New Jersey members were replaced, and the study plans of the Commission suffered further restrictions. Thus, the "comprehensive" study which the MRTC once envisioned had been reduced to dimensions acceptable to the states and the road coalition. Finally, fifteen months after its creation, the MRTC had reached accommodations with the major political forces of the region and was ready to begin its studies.

THE MEAGER ALLIANCE

The members of the MRTC assembled for their first meeting on July 8, 1954. Charles Tuttle, former head of the New York commission, was elected chairman, and David Van Alstyne and John Kraus, both from New Jersey, were chosen as vice-chairman and secretary, respectively. Allen Hubbard of New York served as treasurer.

The commissioners had already agreed on the general nature of the transit studies they wished to undertake, and a brief outline of these studies had been included in the joint report of March, 1954. However, since the two states had provided only

$100,000 toward MRTC expenses, the first problem facing the transit body was to locate supplementary assistance. At this first meeting, the commissioners decided to confer as soon as possible with representatives of the railroads, business and civic leaders, and other interested groups, in order to determine what assistance might be available, including technical data, detailed plans which the Commission might support, and, most important, direct financial aid.[2]

The efforts of the MRTC might ultimately prove to be of considerable value to the rail coalition—providing a feasible plan for rail improvements and additional public support for effective action; but the ability of the coalition to capitalize on this opportunity rested in part on the willingness of its members to support the MRTC's work. The Commission's negotiations with the railroads and civic organizations during these early months illustrated the weaknesses of the rail group in the face of this opportunity.

During the summer and early fall, the MRTC held conferences with officials of most of the railroads in the New York area. The Commission noted that it was especially concerned about inadequate service between New Jersey and Manhattan and asked the railroads to suggest plans to meet this and other transportation problems in the region and also to weigh the possibility of financial assistance to the MRTC.

The answer of the railroads, presented in a joint memorandum on November 1, emphasized the differing priorities of the carriers and the MRTC.[3] The railroads argued that the New Jersey–Manhattan problem was not a separate matter but related to a more fundamental issue—the railroads' continuing financial losses on commuter service. The most important question for public consideration, in the rail carriers' view, was how to improve rail earnings; and the solution would probably involve some combination of tax relief and greater freedom for the rail lines to increase fares and curtail service.

With regard to the MRTC's primary concern, the memorandum suggested that a railroad loop connecting the New Jersey lines and Manhattan would be useful and that the Commission should also consider the possibility of an integrated regionwide rail system. The railroads indicated that they were ready to "cooperate" with the MRTC in studying the transit problem, but they were unwilling to commit either funds or substantial staff assistance to the Commission's effort.

During the fall the MRTC also turned to local business and civic organizations in the hope of assistance. Several of these groups had publicly supported the work of the two transit commissions during 1953 and 1954, and two of them—the Regional Plan Association and the Avenue of the Americas Association—had outlined specific plans for the Commission's consideration.[4] Hoping to obtain further aid, the MRTC met on October 18 with representatives of the New York and New Jersey State Chambers of Commerce, the RPA, and three major business groups from New York City. At this meeting, the private organizations agreed to join to form a Metropolitan Conference on Rapid Transit to cooperate in the transit studies.[5]

This cooperative effort was short-lived, however. There was disagreement among the members of the Conference as to what assistance they could offer, and two of the original members withdrew in early December. In fact, the only groups that seemed willing to give more than verbal support were the two state Chambers of Commerce, and at the end of the year even they had not yet agreed on what contribution they might make.

The region's civic and business groups suffered from several weaknesses. Their own financial and staff resources were limited, and they were reluctant to devote a major portion of these resources to the MRTC work. In addition, the organizations were not fully agreed in their views of the MRTC's plans. The Commission was primarily concerned with the need to improve access to New York City, especially from New Jersey. The New

York associations tended to support this position, but New Jersey's business leaders were divided. Some of them foresaw advantages for their own sector of the region in the existing difficulties of travel to Manhattan. One of Jersey City's newspapers expressed this view in a December editorial:

> Eventually, business executives will have to start thinking in terms of moving their plants and offices to North Jersey rather than face the daily headache of bringing their personnel to New York.[6]

The conflicts among different sectors of the region implied in this statement were later to develop into a major issue surrounding the Commission's activities.

A PLAN OF STUDIES

Observers of the regulatory process have noted the tendency of organized support for a new program to disappear once the enacting legislation is approved. The loss of broad public concern makes the new regulatory agency vulnerable to the pressures of the regulated groups, which are "well organized, with vital interests to protect against the onslaught of the regulators." Yet the agency usually begins its career in an "aggressive, crusading spirit." It tends to take a "broad view of its responsibilities, and some members . . . will develop a fair measure of daring and inventiveness in dealing with their regulatory problems." [7]

A similar pattern characterized the transit-study problem in the early months of the MRTC's existence. The support offered to the new commission by the railroads and business interests was minimal. Other members of the rail coalition were no more helpful: the commuter groups lacked the necessary financial and staff resources, and government leaders in New York City were preoccupied with the problems of the city's own transit system. By early November, it appeared that the MRTC would face the road coalition essentially alone.

Still, the MRTC pressed forward undismayed with its preparations for an extensive study. During the early fall, a survey was conducted of contemporary transit studies in ten other metropolitan areas, including San Francisco, Philadelphia, Toronto, and London. This review confirmed the Commission's position, for most of the other studies were regional in scope and embraced not only rail transit, but automobile and bus as well.[8] Then, in mid-October, Frank H. Simon was hired as executive director and given responsibility for "arranging and directing studies to be made for the Commission." Simon had been with the New York City transit system for eighteen years and had served from 1950 to 1954 as general manager of the Long Island Rail Road. Building upon the previous work of the Commission, Simon drew up an outline of studies and distributed it to the commissioners in late November.

Several facets of the proposed studies are worth noting:

1. They would be regionwide in scope. Population, employment trends, and travel habits throughout the region would be analyzed, and transportation planning for the metropolis would be based on the resulting projections.

2. The studies would include evaluations of possible new rail facilities, together with capital costs, financial results, and recommendations as to the type of organization which should operate any new rail line.

3. All modes of surface transport would be included in the survey. The studies of new rail facilities would not only assess passenger usage but would include the possibility of handling mail, express, and freight as well. Bus operations in the region would be coordinated with rail; in fact, the Commission would recommend a system of bus routes to feed any new rail facilities and might propose the elimination of some routes which would duplicate such rail lines (between New Jersey and Manhattan, for example.)

4. Finally, the MRTC would work with other agencies in

the region, including the Port Authority and the Triborough Authority, in order to develop a "general plan" for future bridges, tunnels, and major expressways. This plan would be "so coordinated with the proposed rapid transit system that the two networks would be complementary in the best public interest."

Simon's outline was consistent with the approach taken in the 1951–52 reports and in the March, 1954, report. It emphasized the importance of broad geographic and intermodal planning, and at the same time it referred to the need to consider construction of new rail lines, especially to overcome the trans-Hudson problem. The MRTC approved the outline on December 13 and allocated a small portion of its limited funds to the study of population trends which Simon had recommended.

THE PORT AUTHORITY OFFERS ASSISTANCE

The MRTC had now gone as far as it could without additional funds. Realizing the difficulty of obtaining adequate support from the rail coalition, it had already begun negotiations with two other possible sources of financing: the states and the Port Authority. These discussions resulted in a large grant to the MRTC in January, 1955. Before turning to the negotiations themselves, it should be helpful to outline the attitudes of these major actors relative to one another as the discussions got under way in October–November, 1954.

The MRTC, the States, and the Port Authority. The members of the MRTC saw their main goal as the development of a competent and detailed plan to improve rail service, and they expected that such a plan might well entail the construction of new facilities at heavy cost. Certainly an extensive and expensive study would be required in order to determine what plan should be adopted. The Commission was strongly committed to this approach, although it was not the only plausible alternative. Conceivably, the commissioners could have decided instead to review previous studies in a few months and then to work out a politically feasible program for immediate action with governmental leaders from both states; but for several reasons such an alternative was not adopted.

First, the prospects for immediate state action on any significant policy proposals seemed very dim. Also, while the MRTC was inclined to view its mandate broadly in other ways, its heritage and membership led it to follow tradition here. The assumption of previous regional study groups that fundamental and costly improvements were essential was readily embraced by the new agency.[9] Finally, it may be that a kind of natural selection operates in the choice of unpaid members of a transit study commission, whereby those inspired by the potential of dramatic and important results—and desirous of being associated with such results—are the men willing to devote their leisure to the study of transit.[10]

While the commissioners were committed to devising a rail-improvement plan, the questions of geographic scope and the proper relationship to road development were matters of debate within the transit agency. The dominant view, as noted above, favored a study and a set of proposals which would be comprehensive in geographic scope and encompass road as well as rail. But there was also some sentiment in the Commission for limiting the study to rail transit and to one geographic area, New Jersey–Manhattan. This position was supported by those who felt that rail improvements would in themselves attract many passengers and thus reverse the trend to rubber. Also, it was argued that the technical and political obstacles facing such a limited study would be far fewer.

From the viewpoint of the MRTC, state financing was preferable to obtaining funds from the Port Authority, for it was less likely that the states would try to direct the study in a way which would impair its "objectivity." It was uncertain, however, that substantial state funds could be obtained. Lack of a tradition of state responsibility in this area, combined with the demands of other programs, had in the past resulted in minimal state response except under conditions of dramatic crisis.

The existence of a continuing bistate commission might, however, alter the attitude of state officials. There were three possible approaches which the states could take toward the MRTC's work. One alternative was close state supervision to insure that the study and the resulting proposals were consistent with state policy. A second, as Banfield suggests, would be to insure that "all principally affected interests are represented, that residual interests (i.e., the 'general public') are not entirely disregarded, and that no interest suffers unduly in the outcome." [11] According to this concept, the states would be relatively neutral as to result, but would assure that the Commission considered all sides of the issues involved in transit planning.

The third alternative open to state leaders was to avoid any responsibility for the MRTC, allowing it to proceed with its current funds or to accept financial aid from the Port Authority or other donors even though such funds might significantly limit the Commission's freedom of action. This alternative had the advantage of requiring the least amount of money and of state officials' time. But it would also reduce the probability that the MRTC's recommendations would be helpful to the governors in resolving the transportation problem—unless the goals of the donor and state officials fortuitously coincided.

For most members of the MRTC, Port Authority financing was the least attractive alternative. During the previous two years, the Authority had demonstrated an interest in influencing the work of the two state transit commissions, and a grant from the Authority would probably entail some control over policy. But the Authority seemed as unlikely a source of funds as it was unattractive. Only a few months before Austin Tobin had

argued that his agency was legally barred from using its funds
to pay for studies by the MRTC.[12]

Meanwhile, the question of what position to take regarding
the MRTC was undergoing review at Port Authority headquarters. The Authority foresaw continuing deterioration of
the rail system in the New York region, leading to demands
for further public action. The PNYA would probably be called
upon again, as it had in the past, to take some continuing
responsibility in the transit field.

In this situation, the MRTC offered both an opportunity
and a threat to the Authority. An opportunity clearly existed,
for if the Commission were to carry out a definitive study of
rapid transit and conclude that the PNYA should not and could
not take on any responsibility in this area, and if its report led
to the formation of a separate agency with jurisdiction over the
rail transit field, the position of the Port Authority would certainly be strengthened.

Under some conditions, the PNYA might have been willing
to take advantage of this opportunity merely by granting the
needed study funds with no strings attached. For years, the
Port Authority had argued that an objective look at the entire
situation would support its contention that it must avoid involvement in rail transit, in order to safeguard its credit standing and its "nonpolitical" status. But if the Authority felt that
an objective study would confirm its own position, it did not
believe that a survey by the MRTC would do so. Some of the
comments in the March, 1954, report had been critical of the
PNYA, and the antagonism of several transit commissioners
toward the Authority was well known. An independent MRTC
study might reach conclusions which would be highly critical
of the PNYA, and thus provide a valuable weapon for those
who desired Port Authority action in the rail field or who would
otherwise curb Port Authority independence. In this sense,
then, the MRTC posed a threat to the Authority.

As the negotiations concerning study funds commenced, the Authority could count on considerable resources which could be used to achieve its ends vis-à-vis the study commission: a large and experienced staff, flexibility in the use of its financial resources, a high level of prestige with state officials, the press, and other institutions, and Van Alstyne's strategic location on the MRTC. Its position was also strengthened by the ambivalent attitude of state leaders toward the MRTC and, of course, by the high priority which the transit commissioners placed upon funds for an extensive study.

Negotiations Begin. By early November, 1954, the Port Authority had established contact with the Commission, and in the middle of November Austin Tobin asked the PNYA Board of Commissioners to agree formally to contribute to the MRTC study if a satisfactory agreement could be worked out. Tobin explained to the assembled Board members that the MRTC was a "most important asset to the Port Authority," that the rail transit problem had to be solved, and that he favored a substantial Port Authority contribution to the study. The Board agreed to contribute up to 100 percent of the cost of the surveys. The position taken during the previous spring, that the Authority had "no power" to aid the Commission, had been a useful strategy with which to counter legislative pressure for a forced contribution; but on reconsidering the question, the Authority found its discretion not so drastically limited.

The revised position of the Authority was met with a mixture of relief and alarm at the MRTC. In view of their inability to obtain aid from the railroads or from business groups, the general feeling of the commissioners was that they should take advantage of the Authority's offer and begin negotiations for the funds without delay. But one member warned that "any funds received from the Port Authority . . . should be without strings attached," and another commissioner argued that it would be wiser for the MRTC to make a further appeal to the states. After some discussion, the MRTC authorized its executive director, Simon, to negotiate with the Port Authority staff and report back to the Commission.

During the next several weeks, a few members of the MRTC who were wary of Port Authority assistance pressed for increased state financing. They spoke before several organizations in the region in an effort to alert the public to the importance of the rail problem and to the adverse impact which the PNYA and other members of the road coalition had had on the region's transportation situation. A state grant of $750,000 to $1 million was needed, they explained, in order to meet the MRTC's planning needs. The commissioners also appealed to local officials along the rail lines where service reductions had been most drastic. And they met with the governors and legislative leaders in both states and with the New Jersey Board of Public Utility Commissioners in an effort to generate further support for a large state grant.

These activities had some positive effects. The Bergen (N.J.) *Evening Record*, the Newark *Star Ledger*, and the New York *Herald Tribune* all supported the request for state funds; and the New York Board of Trade, after hearing chairman Tuttle make a vigorous appeal for a million dollars for a "comprehensive, coordinated and complete overall transit study," passed a resolution in support of the request. But as of early January, neither Governor Meyner, newly elected Governor Averell Harriman of New York, nor legislative leaders in the two states had given any indication that they would support the proposal.[13]

Meanwhile, Tobin and Simon were engaged in negotiations concerning the scope and cost of Port Authority-financed studies. Tobin and his fellow Authority officials found their relations with the MRTC disturbing in several respects. Some of the commissioners' public statements were highly critical of the PNYA, reinforcing the Authority's belief that some control over the Commission's work would be desirable. The scope of the studies approved by the MRTC on December 13 compounded the Port Authority's concern. Tobin and his aides objected to the Commission's plans to study the freight problem, since freight was explicitly included in the Authority's mandate under the 1921 compact. The proposal to study which bus routes to Manhattan should be discontinued would conflict directly with the Port Authority's activities, especially since the PNYA was then considering construction of its bus terminal near the George Washington Bridge. Finally, Tobin objected to the Commission's plan to join with the Port Authority, Triborough Authority, and other agencies in developing a general plan for future bridges, tunnels, and highways, to be coordinated with the proposed rail transit system. This was viewed as a major challenge to the road coalition's independence, especially since the Port and Triborough Authorities were then completing a year-long study concerning the need for expansion of the region's highway network—without any effort to coordinate it with rapid transit planning.

Coupled with these problems was one development in Tobin's favor. By mid-December, through its contacts at Albany and Trenton, the Authority had learned that neither state was likely to advance the funds needed by the MRTC in the immediate future.

The best strategy for the Port Authority, then, would be to conclude negotiations with the MRTC as quickly as possible. During the latter part of December and early January, Tobin and his assistants held a series of conferences with the MRTC's executive director; and by January 4 they had worked out a draft agreement labeled a "Memorandum of Understanding," which Tobin said the Authority would be willing to support. Although it seemed clear that the outline would face objections from some members of the MRTC, Simon agreed to present it to the Commission for discussion at its scheduled meeting the following evening.

The Memorandum of Understanding. The plan of studies which the transit commissioners were handed at their January 5 meeting was similar in some important respects to the outline they had approved on December 13 and to their March, 1954, report, but it also differed from these earlier plans in several ways.

Geographically, the proposed studies would be limited to the New Jersey–Manhattan sector rather than encompassing the entire region. Such a limitation was not inconsistent with the Commission's interests, however, since the MRTC viewed studies of the trans-Hudson problem as the most important and probably the most costly which they planned to undertake.

The kinds of rail improvements which would be studied were set forth in considerable detail in the Memorandum, and in general these specifications were consistent with the Commission's December outline. Several methods of bringing New Jersey rail passengers into Manhattan through trans-Hudson tunnels would be evaluated, along with less expensive ways of meeting rail problems in the bistate area. Costs of construction and equipment, gross revenues, and expenses would be assessed. Underlying these estimates would be studies of the future distribution of population and employment in the region, together with surveys of commuter travel habits. As a result of these extensive studies, "a financially and politically acceptable method" of meeting any deficits would be outlined, and the consultants would recommend the kind of agency which should administer the transit system.

The most significant differences between the Memorandum of Understanding and the expressed views of the MRTC concerned the problem of coordinated road and rail planning and especially the relationship of the Port Authority to future rail development. The March, 1954, report and the December 13 outline were critical of the past efforts and future plans of the PNYA and other highway agencies, and advocated integrated planning and perhaps financing of all surface transport facilities. In contrast, the Memorandum envisioned the continued separation of rail and highway development:

1. The draft excluded the MRTC from any significant role in road planning. All references to joint development of a "general plan" for rail and road were eliminated. And in contrast to past MRTC criticism of road development, the transit agency was now asked to subscribe to the view that there was "no conflict" between the effort to maintain adequate rail transport and current Port Authority–Triborough plans to extend the network of highways and bridges in the region.

2. The draft included a number of elements which, taken together, would make it very difficult for the studies to support a recommendation that the Port Authority be given any responsibility for passenger rail transit. The MRTC was asked to give "full recognition" to the view that the Port Authority could undertake only those transport facilities which could in the long run be self-supporting "in and of themselves." It was also asked to "recognize" that all previous Port Authority studies had concluded that the maintenance and improvement of rail transit in the New York region could not be self-supporting and that experience in almost every other metropolitan area was consistent with this conclusion. The possibility that freight revenues might help a proposed transit system to achieve self-support was foreclosed, since estimates of revenue would exclude "any attempt to convert the line into a freight operation."

The suggestion in the December 13 outline that the studies might recommend the elimination of interstate bus lines competing with a trans-Hudson rail project was omitted; instead the bus studies would focus upon the possibility of adding new bus lines where rail service would not be financially feasible. Having essentially excluded the Port Authority as a source of funds to meet any deficit, the studies would carefully evaluate other means of public assistance to rail transit, including the reduction of property taxes and other subsidies by the local communities.

3. Finally, the draft required that the MRTC cede partial control over the studies to the Port Authority. Consultants to carry out the studies were to be engaged "and their assignments clearly outlined" on the basis of "mutual agreement" between the MRTC and the PNYA. A project director would be engaged to coordinate the studies rather than using the MRTC staff to fulfill these responsibilities. Policy decisions on the studies would be handled jointly by the two agencies. These general controls enhanced the ability of the PNYA to safeguard its interests.

However, to reassure the skeptic who might question the objectivity of the resulting study, the Memorandum of Understanding included this guarantee: the two agencies would carry out "the most comprehensive studies ever undertaken" of the region's transit problem "without any preconceived conclusions as to the interstate transit requirements of the area, or the best means of accomplishing the objective of maintaining and improving rail transit service."

The MRTC Consents. When Simon distributed the draft at the MRTC meeting on January 5, he also explained that the Port Planning Committee of the Port Authority would meet the following day. Therefore, if the Commission were to approve the draft at this meeting, the PNYA Committee could ratify it on January 6, and the entire Port Authority Board would be able to complete action at its regular meeting, January 13.

Several commissioners objected to immediate approval. They noted that this was the first opportunity they had had to look at the proposed agreement and that it ran sixteen pages in length and was rather complicated. Thus, they could not favor such hasty MRTC action, even if the agreement seemed satis-factory on first reading.

In addition, they had several serious reservations concerning the draft. They strongly objected to the view that there was no conflict between rail transit improvement and the arterial pro-jects then being studied by the Port and Triborough Authori-ties. One of those projects, for example, a second deck on the George Washington Bridge, might well conflict with and weaken the self-support potential of a rail transit line in the same area. Also, they argued that one of the basic questions to be answered by the study was whether or not a self-supporting transit system might be devised. Yet self-support would be especially difficult if freight operations were to be excluded, as the Memorandum directed, and if no evaluation of competing bus operations were included. Finally, they vigorously attacked the paragraphs which gave the Port Authority equal control over the choice of consultants and over all policy decisions.

Other members of the MRTC felt that the studies outlined in the Memorandum, although not embracing all facets of the problem, would be very valuable. The draft did give careful attention to the matter of greatest concern—improvement of rail passenger service, especially across the Hudson River. And it was not clear to some of those present that the MRTC should expend its energies in the study of rail freight, bus service, or ways of coordinating road and rail facilities. Several commis-sioners believed that rail improvements would by themselves attract a large number of passengers and reverse the trend to rubber.

In addition, they foresaw important obstacles to extending the studies to these other matters. Such studies would take several years more than the rail survey, and would require con-siderably more funds. Political obstacles were also greater; little cooperation and perhaps obstructionism could be expected from the Port Authority, Moses, and, perhaps, state highway agen-cies. These commissioners were not persuaded that the MRTC

would ever be in a position to object effectively to the Port
Authority–Triborough arterial program. Thus, although a relatively broad outline had been approved by the MRTC on
December 13, there was considerable sentiment within the
transit agency for a more restricted set of studies.

With the Commission divided on the draft, it was suggested
that further discussions be held with the Port Authority before
the MRTC took final action. Possibly the governors and legislative leaders could be brought in on the problem too.

At this point, Van Alstyne, who served on both agencies,
indicated that the position of the Port Authority would have to
be made clear to the MRTC. The wording of the draft, he
advised, was such as to allow the Authority to proceed within
its framework; and it would be necessary to approve the draft
that night to insure that the Authority did not change its mind.
This put a different complexion on the situation. The commissioners realized that the possibility of substantial aid from
any other source was very slight. Acceptance of the draft as it
stood might, then, be the last opportunity for the MRTC to
develop any detailed studies of the region's transit problems.

One or two of those present felt that it would be better for
the MRTC to take its chances with the states than to accept the
Port Authority's offer under the stated conditions. But others,
more pessimistic with regard to the possibility of state funds
and more sanguine about the draft, strongly objected to any
postponement. At least two threatened to resign if the Authority's offer were not accepted. In support of immediate approval,
it was also suggested that once the draft had been ratified and
the PNYA was committed to aiding the MRTC, the transit
agency might press for more favorable terms.

Finally, after extensive discussion, the commissioners voted
5–1, Elder dissenting, to approve the Memorandum of Understanding. The seventh member present, Van Alstyne, abstained.[14]

Even with the Memorandum approved, a few members of
the MRTC tried to obtain the support of state officials for

broadening the scope of the studies and for increased MRTC independence. A meeting with Governor Meyner was arranged, but he was unsympathetic. The Governor was willing to approve Port Authority financing of any studies it was ready to support, but he was not greatly interested in lengthy studies or certain that they would help resolve the transportation problem. Elder also appealed to several New Jersey state legislators to help the MRTC "maintain its complete autonomy," and one senator, Wesley Lance (R–Hunterdon), finally responded by introducing a resolution which called upon the Authority to subsidize the MRTC study without controlling the use of its funds.

But Port Authority actions do not need to wait upon the slow unraveling of the many bills and resolutions which would affect the agency. Once the MRTC had approved the Memorandum, PNYA officials quickly obtained the support of Governors Meyner and Harriman; and, while the New Jersey Senate was weighing this latest attempt to offer guidance to the Port Authority, the Authority Board formally approved the terms of the grant.[15]

That afternoon, January 13, the MRTC and the Port Authority announced approval of the Memorandum of Understanding, under which the PNYA would finance extensive studies of the regional transit problem, at a cost of $500,000 or more.[16] Reactions to the announcement were strongly favorable. Governors Harriman and Meyner expressed their pleasure. The New York *Times* thought the step represented a "highly constructive turn in Port Authority thinking." The Bergen *Evening Record* hailed the agreement as "epochal" and "courageous":

Here is a study which starts without preconceptions or prejudices. . . . It is clear enough that we have turned a corner and that the community owes the Port Authority its thanks for a courageous decision made with the kind of sober forthrightness the emergency indicates.[17]

CHAPTER V

Conflict and Accommodation

The situation confronting the MRTC in mid-January contrasted sharply with that of the previous June. The Commission, which had been prepared to carry out a broad study of the region's transportation problems, now found itself constrained by an agreement that would narrow its aims to those acceptable to a major antagonist of the rail interests, the Port Authority.

However, as the Port Authority soon discovered, the Memorandum of Understanding did not provide the anticipated leverage in PNYA relations with the MRTC, and the two agencies engaged in an extensive controversy concerning the interstate surveys. During the spring of 1955, the Commission also found itself in conflict with New Jersey's Governor Meyner as it sought additional state funds for intrastate surveys. These controversies continued until September, 1955, when the three main participants finally agreed on policies and procedures which would govern the MRTC's activities.

THE COMMISSION VERSUS THE PORT AUTHORITY

The relationship between two organizations with overlapping spheres of interest may take a variety of forms. They may, on the one hand, agree on a range of common goals (although differing on other aims) and engage in a cooperative search for the most efficient ways of achieving their mutual objectives. At the other end of the continuum, there will be a wide area of disagreement concerning goals, and each organization will attempt to achieve its ends at the expense of the other. The first style of behavior may be designated as cooperative problem-solving, the second as bargaining. Among the characteristics of a bargaining process, as March and Simon point out, are "acknowledged conflicts of interest, threats, [and] falsification of position."[1]

As viewed by the Port Authority, the Memorandum of Understanding established a relationship between the Authority and the MRTC in which cooperative problem-solving would predominate. The PNYA believed that the two agencies had agreed upon all the major goals which would guide the transit study. Henceforth they would join forces in assembling information which would permit them to achieve the objectives set forth in the Memorandum with maximum speed and efficiency.

The dominant position within the MRTC was quite different. The commissioners had accepted the Memorandum under duress; they now wished to limit its impact on the Commission's independence of action as much as possible. The aggressive spirit of the past year and the desire to engage in comprehensive transport planning had not yet been purged from the MRTC. Within a few weeks after the Memorandum had been approved, the MRTC demonstrated its intention to return to its previous position as a major spokesman for the pro-rail, anti-highway coalition. Eight months of vigorous conflict with the Port Authority then ensued. The events of this period emphasize the deep divisions in goals and procedures which separate the more aggressive members of the road and rail alliances and illustrate the variety of tactics available to a powerful institution like the PNYA in gaining its ends.

The MRTC Attacks. The first step which the MRTC took to reaffirm its independence was a separate search for candidates for the post of project director for the joint studies. During the latter half of January, the MRTC executive director prepared a list of possible candidates for this position, and in mid-February the Commission selected De Leuw, Cather and Company, a Chicago engineering firm, as its choice.

On February 18, Simon wrote to Tobin, explaining that the MRTC, after conducting a "comprehensive investigation" of possible candidates, had "unanimously resolved" to recommend the De Leuw firm as project director. In deference to the Memorandum, Simon then noted that the project director must be mutually acceptable to the two agencies and that he was "submitting the choice of this Commission to you for consideration."

The Memorandum of Understanding was all but forgotten, however, in the campaign which the MRTC launched during the same month. In an interim report to the states in late February and in a series of speeches by individual commissioners in February and March, the MRTC attacked the past efforts and "grandiose plans" of the Port Authority and its fellow road-building agencies and argued that future highway construction must be carefully coordinated with rail planning. The Commission's report took particular note of the joint Port Authority–Triborough announcement of arterial plans issued in late January. The result of a year's study of vehicular needs, this announcement had called for construction of a second deck on the George Washington Bridge, a bridge across the Narrows (joining Staten Island and Brooklyn), and a new bridge across the East River. The total cost of the facilities and connecting highways would be $570 million.[2] It was this set of major proposals which the PNYA had sought to remove from the MRTC line of fire by inserting in the Memorandum the paragraph that asserted there was "no conflict" between rail improvement and the effort to provide new bypass arterial routes.

In sharp contrast with the Memorandum, the MRTC now argued that the arterial plans of the Port and Triborough Authorities "will, in all probability, tend to generate additional

traffic to further choke the streets of Manhattan." The interim
report suggested that perhaps no further Hudson River crossings should be constructed "until it is determined whether
future crossings should be designed to encourage rail or vehicular traffic." Similar views were expressed in speeches by Commissioners Tuttle, Kraus, and Elder; and in mid-March Commissioner Elder called for defeat of the bills which would
authorize the Port Authority to construct the second deck of
the George Washington Bridge and the Narrows bridge.[3]

The Port Authority Responds. Officials at the Port Authority
followed these developments with growing concern. The
MRTC campaign conflicted directly with the Memorandum of
Understanding, and the strong emphasis on the view that the
road coalition suspend further construction went beyond previous MRTC criticism. The Commission now seemed to have
allied itself with the more extreme anti-road groups, whose
activities a year earlier had included Senator Forbes' abortive
effort to stop the Port Authority from commencing any further
projects until the MRTC had completed its study.

The MRTC attacks were especially objectionable because
they tended to offset the major public relations success which
the PNYA and Moses had achieved with the announcement in
January of their multimillion-dollar bridge-building plans. The
New York *Herald Tribune* had characterized the Port Authority–Triborough program as a "triumph of regional planning,"
and Governor Meyner had congratulated the two agencies for
their "bold approach." Most eloquent in its praise was the New
York *Times*, which saw this "dramatic, indeed spectacular,
program" as opening "new vistas for the planning and development of the New York metropolitan area." [4]

But the recurrent MRTC attacks in February and March
were reported prominently in the press, and a few newspapers
showed sympathy for the MRTC position. The New York

World-Telegram & Sun and the Staten Island *Advance*, for example, agreed with the MRTC's demand for "integrated planning." The Bayonne (N.J.) *Times*, concurring, argued that the Port Authority–Triborough program, "grand and inspiring as it is, involves us in a vicious circle from which there is no escape."[5] In time, the MRTC campaign might lead to additional opposition to the PNYA in the state legislatures, raising obstacles to current and future Port Authority projects. Also, if the transit study were controlled by those who were presently attacking Authority projects, the conclusions might well be unfriendly to the PNYA; and it now appeared that January's Memorandum of Understanding would not provide the expected safeguards.

The Port Authority sought ways of effectively neutralizing the renewed MRTC threat. One approach would be to have the offending members removed from the transit agency. But while the Authority knew that at least Governor Meyner was concerned about the "holdover" Republican membership, neither he nor Governor Harriman had indicated that they planned any immediate steps to depose the incumbents. However, another strategy was available to the PNYA: the selection of a project director who could be relied upon not to join the "anti-Port Authority" members of the MRTC and who would be competent to handle policy questions as well as technical supervision, thus preparing the way for a reduction in the policy-making role of the transit commissioners.

The Port Authority thereupon selected Ralph J. Watkins, director of research at Dun and Bradstreet, as its preferred nominee, and on March 30 submitted his name to the MRTC. Tobin's letter to MRTC chairman Tuttle outlined Watkins' experience in conducting transportation and economic surveys and concluded by suggesting, "You and I should meet as promptly as possible to discuss the retention of Dr. Watkins in order that the rapid transit survey may get underway at the earliest possible moment."

In dispatching this letter, Tobin was employing tactics similar to those used effectively in early January. A Port Authority position had been established; all alternatives were now to be eliminated and the need for a prompt decision emphasized. Tobin's letter did not refer to the MRTC's earlier nomination of the De Leuw firm, nor was the Commission expected to propose any alternatives to the PNYA nominee. And the meeting should take place "as promptly as possible" so that the survey could be started "at the earliest possible moment," although Tobin had just taken six weeks to reply to the MRTC letter of February 18.

In its January negotiations with the MRTC, the Port Authority had used the threat to withdraw financial support to achieve its objectives, but now this tactic could not be used. Such an approach would obviously violate the policy of joint control established by the Memorandum and lead to further public criticism of the Authority. Also, coupled with the recent series of MRTC and editorial attacks, this step might generate substantial pressure within the legislatures to force the Port Authority to provide funds "without strings" or to authorize state funds for an independent study. Either alternative would weaken the Authority's position. Thus, the PNYA found itself enmeshed in a network of constraints it had fashioned for the Commission.

Being aware of these limitations on the Port Authority, the MRTC found Tobin's letter unpersuasive. Meeting in early April, the commissioners decided to bypass the PNYA nominee and to develop a list of additional candidates to be presented to the Authority.

The MRTC's assaults against the road coalition continued unabated during the next several weeks. Elder leveled an

attack on "the propaganda for more unnecessary highway building," and Tuttle complained that "private enterprise . . . by
rail" was being "choked to death by the irresistible competition
of vast tax-exempt and toll-charging public facilities for automobiles." Public support for the Commission's position also
continued to grow. Even the Bergen (N.J.) *Evening Record*,
long a staunch friend of the Port Authority, thought that Elder's
criticisms were "sound" and chastised the Authority for attempt-
ing to build more highways and bridges before the MRTC
could develop a "master plan" for all transport facilities.[6]

The Port Authority now tried a new tactic, in the hope of
redirecting public criticism from itself to the Commission and
of ending the impasse concerning selection of a project director.
On April 27, the Authority released to the press a statement
which attacked the MRTC for failing to act on the Authority's
March 30 nomination of Watkins as project director and therefore for delaying the start of the transit study. "The Port Authority Commissioners," the statement asserted, "feel the public
and the press are entitled to have all the facts as they have
developed" concerning the delay, and the PNYA urged that
the two agencies meet as soon as possible "to get this . . . study
off the ground." The statement failed to mention the MRTC's
recommendation of De Leuw in mid-February or the intervening delay in Port Authority action.

Although the MRTC responded immediately with a statement which referred to the earlier correspondence and which
said that the Commission had already planned to take further
action in early May, the Port Authority succeeded in achieving
its immediate goals. Most news articles and editorials were
critical of the MRTC, and the Authority was commended for
its efforts to get the study underway.[7] Also, negotiations were
resumed within the next two weeks, although that may have
been the MRTC's plan in any event. The price the PNYA paid

for this success was increased hostility on the part of the transit commissioners.

A Project Director Is Chosen. With the metropolitan press now agitated by the extended delays in beginning the study, the two agencies found it expedient to work out a compromise. The MRTC forwarded to the Port Authority a list of four candidates it considered acceptable and offered to permit the Authority to make a final choice from among the four. After seeing the list, the Authority accepted the offer and selected Arthur W. Page, a seventy-one-year-old New York business consultant who was well known to several members of the PNYA. On May 23, representatives of the two agencies met with Page and persuaded him to accept the post of project director.

Page had been a vice-president of the American Telephone and Telegraph Company from 1927 until he retired in 1947. Since then he had maintained offices in downtown Manhattan as a business consultant, and during 1954–55 he had served as director of the Working Group of the Presidential Advisory Committee on Transport Policy and Organization (the Weeks Committee). Page was known to be sympathetic toward the problems of the railroads, but at the same time he was an admirer of the Port Authority and its efficient, businesslike approach.

After four months, an important obstacle to proceeding with the studies had been removed; only formal resolutions of approval by the two agencies remained. The MRTC could feel satisfied that it had won this battle, for the Port Authority had acquiesced in one of the MRTC choices. At the same time, Authority officials were not unhappy, since some of them were well acquainted with Page and knew of his admiration for Port Authority achievements.

But the MRTC could not resist a final slap at the Port Authority. Meeting on June 6, the full commission "unanimously and cordially" invited Page to accept the appointment in a resolution which omitted any reference to joint action with the Authority.[8] Once again the Commission had rejected the fundamental tenet of combined Port Authority–MRTC control as set forth in the Memorandum of Understanding. At this point, however, developments from another quarter put an end to the conflict and prepared the way for a return to the "cooperative problem-solving" approach long desired by the Port Authority.

THE STATES AND THE MRTC

In February, 1955, the MRTC had made another appeal for state funds, this time for studies of transit problems wholly within New York and New Jersey. Since the Memorandum of Understanding had focused on the trans-Hudson problem, the Commission now hoped that the two states would be willing to support surveys in other parts of the region, including Westchester, Long Island, and the Newark area. The MRTC asked that each state provide $150,000 for such intrastate surveys.[9]

The Commission's latest plea received a more favorable reception in New York than had its earlier requests. In part, this was because of fortuitous circumstances—the problems of New York City's transit system and of the Long Island Rail Road, which had absorbed the attention of local and state officials in 1954, had been temporarily resolved. Also, the intrastate problems were of greater concern to the New York suburbs and some central-city interests than were the difficulties of New Jersey–Manhattan transportation, and the responsibility of New York State for financing studies in these areas was clearer. New York City's major business and civic groups gave active support to the MRTC's request. Mayor Wagner also praised the MRTC for "recommending a careful study of the rapid transit problem in the whole metropolitan area" and approached Democratic legislators and Governor Harriman to enlist their support for the transit agency's request. Only the railroads withheld active assistance, preferring—as they had explained to the MRTC in the fall—to devote their attention to such immediate legislative interests as tax relief for the rail lines.[10]

As a result of the widespread backing for the intrastate grant, the New York bill was passed unanimously by the Assembly on March 24, and a few days later the New York Senate agreed, also without a dissenting vote. In late April Governor Harriman signed the measure, making $150,000 available to the MRTC for intrastate studies conditioned on New Jersey's appropriating a similar sum.[11]

Governor Meyner and the Transit Commission. The intrastate-studies proposal faced a more difficult situation in New Jersey. Governor Meyner was reluctant to support the MRTC's request, and the legislature was divided on the measure. The problems encountered by the MRTC during this new controversy illustrate some of the continuing difficulties which confront independent agencies in trying to develop adequate political support at the state capitals.

It was clearly of great importance for the MRTC to maintain friendly relations with Governor Meyner. The immediate reason was obvious: his signature would be needed on the intrastate-study bill. A satisfactory working relationship was also crucial in the long run, for the MRTC would have to call upon the Governor for political leadership in support of its later recommendations.

Yet in the spring of 1955 several obstacles stood in the way of a close working relationship. First, Governor Meyner was not particularly interested in the rail transport problem, as he devoted his main energies to education and other areas of traditional state concern. Also, in so far as he was concerned about the transit issue, Meyner inclined to the view that his own executive agencies should have primary responsibility for policy development within the state. In contrast, the MRTC believed it should have a central role in devising a coordinated regional policy, covering problems that were essentially intrastate as well as those which crossed state lines. Finally, differences in political party separated the Governor and the MRTC.

It was the last of these three problems that formed the basis for the most direct conflict between the Transit Commission and Governor Meyner. Having taken office in January, 1954, after ten years of Republican control, Meyner was sensitive to the problem of holdover Republican appointees and had determined to replace them with men of his own choice. Even where no real difference in outlook between Meyner and the appointee existed, replacement often seemed desirable to assert the Governor's position as master in his own house.

The MRTC represented a particularly annoying case of the holdover problem, for its New Jersey members, all Republicans, had been appointed by the previous governor for indefinite terms. Possibly Meyner could remove them anyway, but this might involve a court test, which he preferred to avoid. Or, conceivably, the legislature could be persuaded to pass a bill providing that the members serve at the Governor's pleasure, but it was unlikely that the Republican-controlled houses would take such action.

From Meyner's point of view, the best solution would be for the New Jersey commissioners, realizing that they did not have the Governor's full confidence, to resign voluntarily. Thus, in a conference with MRTC spokesmen in January, Meyner had suggested that he should have some representation on the agency if he were to give it his full support. But the MRTC's immediate response—that there was "no objection to increasing the size of the Commission by one additional member from each state" to allow the present governors to make appointments—was unsatisfactory to Governor Meyner.

The MRTC's request for state funds seemed to offer another route to the Governor's goal. Meyner was far from certain that $150,000 should be added to his budget for a transit study by a bistate commission. Other items appeared to have higher claims against limited state resources, and a solely intrastate study might better be carried out by an agency of the state government. In any event, the Governor was definitely opposed to allocating this sum if the study were to be conducted by the "holdover" Republicans.

In early May, Governor Meyner and his aides met with the leaders of the State Senate and Assembly and asked that the bill providing intrastate study funds be amended to stipulate that the members of the MRTC serve at the pleasure of the Governor. But the Republicans, a majority in both houses, refused to accept the amendment.[12]

The Democratic minority then tried to defeat the bill as it came to the floor of each house. Some attacked the indefinite nature of the commissioners' appointments, others demanded the Port Authority provide the extra funds, and a few outspoken critics of the Authority, led by Hudson County assemblyman William V. Musto, argued that the PNYA should be required at once to construct and operate rail transit facilities throughout the Port District.

The Republican majority favored the intrastate-study bill, however, and it was passed in both houses during May. Many of the suburban legislators who supported the measure gave particular weight to the pleas from mayors, other local officials, and commuter groups, who asked that their local transit problems be given as much attention as the interstate issue. They also noted that the Port Authority had shown no inclination to provide intrastate funds and that the possibility of forcing it to do so was slim.

With the bill on his desk for signature, Governor Meyner now applied pressure directly upon the MRTC. During late

May and early June, the Governor and his aides met with the
New Jersey members on several occasions. The Governor
insisted that he should have the right to name the entire New
Jersey membership of the agency. The commissioners were
also informed that unless they resigned, the appropriation bill
for intrastate studies would not be signed. The Governor and
his aides also questioned the need for the intrastate funds in
any event, and at one meeting Tobin was on hand to support
the Governor's contention. Tobin took the position that intrastate studies were included in the PNYA-MRTC study, making
the $150,000 appropriation unnecessary.

Although the New Jersey commissioners understood the importance of obtaining gubernatorial support for the MRTC's
work, they had previously been very reluctant to resign. They
had already devoted many months to the transit study, and they
had hoped to guide it through to a successful conclusion. But
any further effort to oppose the Governor might be made at the
cost of the intrastate studies. Finally, on June 13 all five members
submitted their resignations. As one of the commissioners explained the following day,

We've been stymied for a year for lack of funds. . . . Now, with
an appropriation for an important task in sight, we learned that
Governor Meyner feels he is out of touch with the commsision and
should be represented on it. . . . So we figured we might as well
settle that issue by resigning, so that the commission may get on
with a job of tremendous importance.[13]

The region's newspapers sought to interpret these latest
developments for their readers. As the Newark *Evening News*
saw it, the Republican members had been frozen into their
jobs. "Governor Meyner was justifiably resentful of this en-
croachment on the executive prerogative" and understandably
withheld his signature from the bill. But to the Bergen *Evening
Record*, it was "a pretty high price to pay, this sacrifice of five
men to the sullen gods of party politics." The *Record* viewed

Meyner's actions as motivated by the desire to end Port Authority influence on the Commission (by removing Van Alstyne), and to put in "his men" so that he could "dictate" Commission policy.[14]

In part the *Record* was correct, for political concerns had motivated the Governor. But had the five Republicans remained on the Commission, there would have been little chance of active gubernatorial support for any later MRTC recommendations. The resignations at least insured that the transit agency could move ahead with its studies, and that it would have a more harmonious relationship with the Governor's office in the future.

As to Meyner's relationship with the Port Authority, the *Record* had somehow missed the mark. The PNYA would strengthen its position substantially if such anti-Port Authority spokesmen as Elder and Kraus could be removed, and it was pleased to assist the Governor in forcing the resignations of the transit commissioners.

The Meyner Appointments. A month later, on July 5, Governor Meyner announced the names of his five MRTC nominees. Those chosen were Edward J. O'Mara of Jersey City, John A. Kervick of Short Hills, William F. Young of Ridgewood, John F. Sly of Princeton, and Thomas J. Harkins of Roselle Park.

Two of the appointees, O'Mara and Kervick, were important members of the state Democratic party. O'Mara had been state senator from Hudson County for twelve years (1941–53) and was currently a counsel for the Pennsylvania Railroad. Kervick was vice-president of a New York construction firm and served also as treasurer of New Jersey's Democratic State Committee. A third member, Young, had attended Columbia Law School with Meyner, was a Democrat, and was now assistant vice-president of the New York Life Insurance Company.

Sly, a Republican, was professor of politics and director of
the Princeton Surveys at Princeton University. He had been a
commissioner of the Port Authority since 1951, a post from
which he said he would now resign. Sly also served Meyner as
chairman of the Commission on State Tax Policy. The final
member, Harkins, was assistant grand chief engineer of the
Brotherhood of Locomotive Engineers and an independent
politically.

Thus, Meyner had put together a group of widely varied
backgrounds and perspectives. Politically, there were three
Democrats, one Republican, and an independent with a labor
union background. Three of the five brought considerable experience in transportation matters to bear on their work, though
from very different perspectives—railroad management, railroad
labor, and the Port Authority—and the other two were trans-
Hudson commuters. Even a geographical spread had been obtained: five counties in the New Jersey sector were represented.

The reactions of North Jersey editors were strongly favorable to the selections. The *Jersey Journal* thought them "excellent," and the Elizabeth *Daily Journal* spoke of "balanced
qualification." Even the Bergen *Evening Record*, which had
earlier attributed the changing of the guard to "the sullen gods
of party politics," commended the Governor:

Cynical people could and did say that the Port Authority would
want a survey biased in favor of the automobile. . . . They could
and did say Governor Meyner would want a survey biased against
anything that any authority wanted. Mr. Meyner's appointees are
men of character and diversity enough to warrant dismissal of any
apprehension.[15]

The Port Authority was not displeased with the outcome,
either. PNYA officials were not sure of the attitude toward the
Authority held by some of the new men, but they could be certain that Sly would take a position on transit problems compat-

ible with the interests of the Authority and that he would present his views effectively.

Only the deposed transit commissioners and the Senate Republicans who had supported them against Meyner were unhappy. The Senate was reluctant to take immediate action on the nominations, but finally, in two sessions in late August, the appointments of the five new commissioners were confirmed. During the summer, one change was also made in the New York membership. The resignation of Michael Madigan allowed Governor Harriman to make his first appointment to the MRTC, and he named Ernest W. Williams, associate professor of transportation in the Graduate School of Business, Columbia University. Williams had served with Page on the Working Group of the Weeks Committee on Transport Policy in 1954–55 and as a transportation consultant to the Office of Defense Mobilization since 1951, where he had worked for a time with Harriman.

New Jersey Funds for the MRTC. Meanwhile, in early August, Governor Meyner announced that he would sign the bill providing funds for intrastate studies. However, the statement accompanying his approval severely limited the use of state funds. It also emphasized the differences in perspective which separated Meyner and the MRTC.

The MRTC's responsibilities, asserted the Governor, must be limited to interstate problems and closely related intrastate questions. Study of a "purely intrastate problem," in the Newark or Paterson area, for example, was "not within the purview of the Commission." This position contrasted sharply with the transit agency's broad interpretation of its mandate to study "rapid transit needs of the New York–New Jersey Metropolitan Area." Having limited the MRTC to the bistate problem, the Governor then noted that the Port Authority grant already covered this issue, rendering state financing unnecessary. Therefore, although he would sign the bill so that the money would be available "if actually needed," Meyner asked the New Jersey members to "refrain from expending the funds . . . unless it appears that a second study is actually necessary." [16]

Thus, Governor Meyner had worked out a formula which would allow him to have his cake and eat it too. By signing the bill, he had taken a progressive stand in favor of metropolitan studies. If he had vetoed the measure, after Harriman had approved the New York counterpart, Meyner would have been vulnerable to charges of parochialism and obstructionism. However, he so restricted the use of the appropriation that it probably would never be spent. His reluctance to support the Commission's work was due in part to his feeling that policy-making within the state should be controlled by agencies responsible to the Governor. The advantages of coordinated regionwide policy-making were of much less interest to him. In addition, Meyner feared that funds allocated to a regional agency might then be pooled and used for studies outside the state; for example, the New Jersey allocation might be utilized in part for studies in Westchester or Long Island. "New Jersey," the Governor emphasized, "is not interested in spending money to solve problems which affect only New York." The problem is a recurring one in regional efforts: the development of closer regional cooperation was hindered by a fear that funds from one tax jurisdiction might be used to benefit another.

Governor Meyner was widely commended for approving the study funds, but the reactions of the metropolitan press to his statement revealed contrasting views of the New York region. The Bergen *Evening Record* argued that the "fundamental" transit problem was "how to move people between New York and New Jersey." Therefore, the *Record* found Meyner's demand that the MRTC limit itself to this problem "comprehensible and judicious." The MRTC had shown a regrettable interest in expanding the study to include the problems of West-chester and Fairfield counties, complained the *Record*: "No horizon is too distant; no problem is secondary or deferable." Thus, the *Record* and Meyner agreed on the proper focus of the Commission's work, although they had reached this conclusion via different routes. The *Record*, located in the county with the highest percentage of commuters to New York City of all New Jersey counties, had mirrored its readers' concerns. For the Governor, with his single-state constituency and perspective, MRTC emphasis on the interstate issue would diminish the threat which the Commission presented to state funds and to gubernatorial control over intrastate policy.

The Newark *Evening News* took issue with the Governor and the *Record*. It argued that the distinction between interstate and intrastate problems

seems unimportant if, indeed, one can be drawn at all. If the metropolitan area is . . . a single economic unit, it is doubtful if any part of the transit problem can be isolated. . . . What we need is an all-embracing look and a program that will cover the whole situation.

Such an all-embracing look would, of course, entail studies of transit problems in the Newark area as well as other local regions.[17]

ACCOMMODATION

Shorn of half its membership, the MRTC remained dormant throughout the summer. With the confirmation of Meyner's new appointees in late August, however, the Commission was able to resume its efforts. Two tasks confronted the members immediately: the reaching of a *modus vivendi* with the Port Authority and the still unfinished business of appointing the project director.

The new commissioners from New Jersey had discussed the recent MRTC–Port Authority conflicts with officials of both agencies, and they were in general agreement that greater harmony between the two organizations was needed if the studies were to be completed expeditiously. One way to promote harmony, they felt, would be to reduce the initiative and authority of the present chairman, Charles Tuttle, since he (together with former commissioners Elder and Kraus) had been in the forefront of past controversies. The New Jersey members finally concluded that the best solution would be to elect co-chairmen, one from each state, a change that would also symbolize the equal status of both states in MRTC activities. At the September meetings, the full Commission agreed unanimously to the selection of co-chairmen, and Tuttle and O'Mara were elected to the posts. Young of New Jersey was chosen as secretary and Hubbard of New York as treasurer.

The appointment of co-chairmen struck a responsive chord among New Jersey interests who were sensitive to their state's relations with New York. As Hudson County's *Jersey Journal* pointed out, in an editorial entitled "Full Partner,"

It is a good way for the Transit Commission to start—recognizing that New Jersey's stake is quite as important as New York's. It means, too, that in this commission New Jersey will not be a tail wagged by a dog, nor will it be a tail trying to wag a dog. It will be a big dog just like the other big dog.[18]

The MRTC also decided to alter its previous position on the project director in order to mollify the PNYA. In June, the Commission had planned to hire Arthur Page on a unilateral basis rather than jointly with the Authority. But at its September 7 meeting, the Commission adopted a new resolution requiring that the MRTC work with the PNYA in completing arrangements for employing a project director.

These developments were received with satisfaction at the Port Authority. But this was not the first time that a reconciliation with the MRTC had ostensibly been achieved, and the PNYA decided to insure that the reconstituted Commission fully accepted the basic tenets of the Memorandum of Understanding and that the surveys would go forward on that basis. It was essential, Tobin explained to the Port Authority commissioners at the September 15 meeting, that the "entire conduct of the study [be] governed by the principles and detailed specifications set forth in the Memorandum." Tobin then recommended and the Board approved a resolution approving Page as project director for the study "to be made in accordance with the Memorandum of Understanding . . . *provided, however*, that his approval shall be effective only upon the adoption by the [MRTC] . . . of a resolution confirming its prior approval of . . . the said Memorandum." [Emphasis in the original.]

On September 20, the MRTC met to complete action on hiring Page. First, however, the Commission would have to reaffirm the Memorandum. At this point, one of the new appointees, William Young, raised anew the issue of MRTC independence. He was opposed to relying on the PNYA for funds and to the limitations contained in the Memorandum. Some discussion followed, but it now seemed clear to the other members that there would be no interstate study without Port Authority funds and no Port Authority funds without MRTC concurrence in the January agreement. Finally, the Commission performed the obeisance required by the Authority, "approving and reaffirming" the Memorandum. Favorable action on hiring Page followed immediately. For the present, at least, the relations between the PNYA and the MRTC had returned to the "cooperative problem-solving" approach which the Authority preferred.[19]

On September 25, 1955, the two agencies announced that a project director for the transit study had been chosen and that the study would begin "without delay." Interviewed at his office that afternoon, Page underscored the renewed optimism of the sponsoring groups: "We should finish our survey possibly by the end of next year. . . . If our plan is any good, and it is adopted, it ought to help take care of the bi-state transportation problem for the next twenty years." [20]

The reaction to the announcement was one of satisfaction and of relief that the study was at last going to get under way. As the Bergen *Record* commented,

The Survey . . . is an apparatus of immense size and importance, but it appears at last to have gotten its awesome bulk off the ground, and there seem to be substantial grounds for assuming that we are on our way to a solution of our most serious common problem.[21]

More than fifteen months had now elapsed since the MRTC came into being. The events of these months illustrated the great difficulties which confront an organization advocating policy innovation in a metropolitan region. The power of the interests which supported—and were in turn supported by —existing transport policies, together with the differing perspectives and priorities of state officials, had by the fall of 1955 substantially diminished the ability of the transit agency to challenge the *status quo*.

The adroitness with which the PNYA steered its way around and through the various obstacles in its path, and thus achieved its major goals, was especially marked. The financial resources and capable staff of the Authority, its high level of prestige with state legislators and the press, its access to the governors, and its well-developed tactical skill—all these were effectively employed to gain the MRTC's consent to the Memorandum of Understanding and later to insure that the Commission would concur with the Authority's philosophy. Rarely, Banfield has observed, are public organizations able to demonstrate a high degree of "rational" behavior; their goals are complex and often inconsistent, and they lack the time, staff and other resources to identify and select alternatives which will maximize their goals.[22] But the Port Authority, as its behavior in 1954–55 illustrates, must be allotted a rather high position on a "rationality" continuum. Its goals are relatively clear-cut and consistent, and it lays out courses of action to achieve these goals with great skill.

The minimal level of gubernatorial and legislative interest in the regional transit problem facilitated the Port Authority's success in dealing with the MRTC. In his 1949 study of the governors of New Jersey and two other Eastern states, Wood suggested that "the chief executive office faces every major functional decision through the filter of metropolitan life." He becomes, in effect, a "metropolitan partisan." [23] The characterization seems to fit neither Governor Harriman nor Governor Meyner in 1954–55, at least in so far as it implies a motivation toward positive action on transit. Governor Meyner viewed the transit problem primarily from the vantage point of his state constituency and political strength. The desire to eliminate Republicans from positions of power and to safeguard gubernatorial prerogatives and state "fiscal integrity" in the short run took priority over any interest in exerting guidance on policy development in metropolitan transportation. Even Banfield's concept of the political leader as an umpire—insuring all interests an opportunity to be heard—was disregarded by the two governors.[24] They acquiesced in Port Authority control over the MRTC's goals and failed to appreciate the limitations that this shackle might place on policy development generally and on their own freedom of action as the transit crisis worsened.

In the New Jersey legislature the PNYA confronted a small but vocal group of critics—the only important source of criticism of the Authority other than the MRTC members during this period. Yet the PNYA never found the legislators a significant threat. The Authority could often act with such speed that legislative interest was barely aroused by the time the matter was decided. In January, 1955, for example, the New Jersey Senate had just begun to consider a resolution asking that the Port Authority provide funds to the MRTC without controls, when its efforts were rendered purposeless by the joint announcement of the Memorandum of Understanding.

Even when the Authority's pace was slowed, the process of building a legislative consensus in opposition to the PNYA was far too time-consuming to be effective. For instance, after the conflict between the MRTC and the Port Authority over the choice of a project director became known, a campaign was begun at the state capital to bring pressure upon the PNYA to "cooperate" with the transit agency; but by the time a Senate committee had been created to look into the matter, the two agencies had already agreed upon Page.[25] Thus, the legislators found themselves constantly in the position of observing a *fait accompli*. Of course, the Authority's political strength during this period was such that it was doubtful whether even a more timely and vigorous legislative campaign would have been effective.

In the face of the Port Authority's onslaught and lacking effective political support at the state capitals, the MRTC found it impossible to hold to its original plans for a study embracing road as well as rail. Its capitulation to the Authority was caused basically by the MRTC's inability to build a constituency which would support the agency against the forces favoring the *status quo*. Such a constituency would have been able to agitate within the region and at Trenton and Albany for more adequate funds and discretion for the MRTC. Lacking such political support, the Commission drifted toward the classic state of immobility described by Norton Long: a "forlorn spectacle, . . . possessed of statutory life . . . yet stricken with paralysis and deprived of power." [26]

Then, by drawing upon the financial resources of the Port Authority, the MRTC was able to salvage part of its original plan, an extensive study of rail passenger problems per se. Here the interests of the Authority and the Commission overlapped, although they did not coincide. The PNYA viewed the MRTC study as midwife to a new locally financed rail organization, permanently eliminating the Authority from pressure to take action. The Commission was more interested in extensive physical improvements in the rail system, especially to overcome the trans-Hudson barrier. As the study progressed, these two aims might well become incompatible, causing renewed conflict between the two agencies. But in the fall of 1955, the MRTC and the Port Authority were willing to include both aims in the transit study.

Several factors made it impossible for the MRTC to build a constituency adequate to its broader goals. First, the several groups forming the rail coalition were divided in their aims and meager in political resources, as the early MRTC contacts with railroads and business interests illustrated. Only briefly, when a few New Jersey mayors and commuter spokesmen and several New York City business groups agitated for passage of the intrastate-study bills, was there any significant organized effort. Second, the complexity of the transit issue made it difficult for even the well-informed observer to understand what was happening; for example, were the statements contained in the Memorandum of Understanding helpful guidelines or fatal restrictions? Even some of the transit commissioners themselves seemed unclear as to the limitations in that document. Third, the lack of a dramatic crisis in rail service handicapped the building of wider support. Finally, the skill and prestige of the PNYA were so great that its actions and opinions on regional transportation tended to be accepted as "in the public interest." It was difficult to generate political support for a comprehensive study of road and rail if the acknowledged expert in the field said such a study was unnecessary.

While complex regional issues provide the press with an opportunity to educate the region's public and build support for more effective policies, the activities of the press in the

New York area during 1954–55 suggest not so much the role of educator as that of a faulty Greek chorus or a well-constructed weathercock. The editors were constantly alert to the latest developments in the transit-study issue, ready with compliments and condemnation, and frequently warning of difficult trials ahead. Vigor of style and decisiveness of interpretation substituted for understanding of underlying issues. Thus, the praises heaped upon the Port Authority for its part in the January Memorandum of Understanding were undiluted by any clear comprehension of the implications of that document for the MRTC's freedom of action; and while some newspapers did alert their readers to the importance of the issues raised by Elder and his colleagues during the spring, the press was ready to disregard those issues as soon as the next "highly constructive" action was announced.

The interest of the press in the overt events relating to the transit problem was not matched by any strong or well-organized concern in the region at large. The local economic and political groups which would be affected by the policies carved out by the MRTC, the Port Authority, and the states were largely inactive during this period. Later, faced by concrete recommendations and by identifiable benefits and costs to specific groups, these regional interests would bring the plans of the Commission and the Authority for a locally financed regional transit system crashing down in ruins.

But now, in September, 1955, the scene was more pacific. The MRTC and the Port Authority were about to turn their attention to the problems of choosing engineering and financial consultants to carry out the studies and of molding the results of these studies into a set of proposals for public action. Even with the limitations inherent in the Memorandum of Understanding, these transit surveys would be of more than technical interest. The interstate studies might threaten the PNYA, and the intrastate surveys would challenge the independence of action long enjoyed by Moses' New York empire.

The conflicts that arose during the consultants' studies, and the processes through which compromises among the interested parties were achieved, suggest a number of implications concerning the role of expert consultants in the formulation of public policy, as well as extending our understanding of the behavior patterns of regional organizations in the transportation field.

CHAPTER VI

The Transit Surveys: Professional Standards and Political Pressures

Until the fall of 1955, the shaping of rail transport policy in the New York region was characterized primarily by avowed conflicts of interest and public bargaining among many participants. During the transit survey period, however, a different political style predominated. From the fall of 1955 through the end of the surveys in 1957 the major actors were few in number and agreed as to their main goals, and their activities were largely insulated from external political forces. Cooperative problem-solving rather than bargaining prevailed.[1]

The basic units around which this transit study subsystem was constructed were the MRTC and the Port Authority. The system was elaborated through the development of a small staff under Arthur Page and the addition of a number of consultants to carry out the detailed studies. There was general acceptance among these participants of the need to seek extensive rail improvements and a new transit agency to carry them out. The Port Authority, it was generally acknowledged, would be excluded from any role in rail projects, and no effort would be made to study the possible advantages of coordinating rail and road policy.

Agreement on goals within the study group was combined with relative isolation from other regional interests that had important stakes in transport policy. The study group did come into conflict with Moses, a member of the road coalition with whom no accommodation had previously been achieved. Negotiations with the railroads were resumed, and the rail lines' interest in public action to meet existing passenger deficits was ultimately integrated into the survey. And there were sporadic contacts with commuter groups and business associations in the region, as well as occasional discussions with elected officials at the local and state levels. Throughout the studies, however, major norms established in the fall of 1955 were retained and, in fact, went unchallenged by any significant cluster of regional interests. The transit study subsystem during this period resembled the relatively well-integrated pattern of urban renewal politics which Kaplan has identified in Newark, an integrated pattern being one in which there exists "a common set of norms, a high degree of interaction among the actors, clearly defined and stable roles, role differentiation, resistance to deviation from the norms, and socialization of new members." [2]

THE INTERSTATE SURVEYS ARE BEGUN

According to the Memorandum of Understanding, the consultants for the interstate studies, as well as the project director, were to be chosen on the basis of mutual agreement between the MRTC and the Port Authority. In the spring of 1955, Simon and Tobin had begun canvassing possible candidates for the various studies. During the fall the two executive directors worked jointly with Page and completed negotiations, and on October 18 the two agencies announced the names of the consultants chosen and their assignments. To provide a basis for determining the future demand for mass transit, the RPA and Charles E. De Leuw would analyze the future distribution of population and employment and other relevant factors. De Leuw would also conduct studies of the engineering and economic feasibility of trans-Hudson rail tunnels and several other major proposals for improving interstate rail service.

Coverdale and Colpitts was to study less expensive methods of improving rail passenger service, and Ford, Bacon and Davis would analyze the role of bus service in meeting interstate travel needs. Finally, William Miller was asked to study various financial and administrative devices which could be used in the operation of any recommended transit system. The total cost of the contracted studies ran well above the $500,000 originally allocated by the PNYA, and the Authority agreed to provide up to $800,000 for the interstate work. This was to be the last significant financial commitment of the Authority to rail transit until the 1960s.[3]

All the consultants appeared to be well qualified in their fields. The RPA had been making studies of the New York region since 1929. De Leuw, Cather and Company, of Chicago, had taken part in transit studies in Cleveland, Detroit, Chicago, and other cities. Coverdale and Colpitts, a New York firm, had made several surveys of rail service problems, including a 1949 study for the Port Authority, and Ford, Bacon and Davis, also from New York, had undertaken bus studies for the PNYA and several bus companies in the region. Miller, a government consultant with offices in Princeton, had previously served as an adviser to the New Jersey State Tax Policy Commission, which was chaired by MRTC member John Sly, and had assisted in drafting the legislation creating the New York–New Jersey Waterfront Commission in 1953.

The work of the consultants was begun immediately, under the direction of Page and a small staff; the project director's organization was given the title of the Metropolitan Rapid Transit Survey (MRTS). It was expected that the surveys could be completed and a report to the MRTC prepared within about eighteen months.[4]

A CHALLENGE TO ROBERT MOSES

With the trans-Hudson studies underway, the MRTC turned its attention to intrastate studies. Governor Meyner reaffirmed his reluctance to have the New Jersey funds expended, and the MRTC limited its initial planning to studies within New York State. During the latter part of 1955 and 1956, the Commission reviewed transportation problems in Staten Island, Long Island, and Westchester, and consultants were engaged to evaluate several proposals for improved rail service in these areas.[5]

In contrast with its Port Authority-financed interstate surveys, no accommodation with the road interests was required before the New York studies were begun. The MRTC drew upon its state appropriation and developed its studies alone. Consequently, and perhaps inevitably, one of these studies conflicted directly with Moses' policies and plans. The Triborough chairman and the MRTC were soon engaged in a controversy which underscored the conflicting values of rail and road interests and the different perspectives of operating agencies and study groups. The attitude and tactics used by a regional agency sensitive to any infringement on its independence of action were also illustrated.

The name of Robert Moses has been connected with a number of large and dramatic projects. One such project—perhaps the most dramatic with which his name has been joined—is the Verrazano-Narrows Bridge. Construction of this span, which connects Staten Island and Brooklyn, had been recommended in the joint Triborough–Port Authority report of January, 1955, and Moses was ecstatic:

It will be the longest suspension bridge in the world, and the tallest. . . . It will be the biggest bridge, the highest bridge, and the bridge with the greatest clearance. It's all superlatives when you talk about this bridge that will cross the Narrows.[6]

But many obstacles remained before this monument would be completed. First, there was the question of financing. The Triborough Authority's borrowing capacity was not sufficient for it to finance the bridge immediately, and a cooperative venture with the Port Authority was required. The project would be financed and constructed by the PNYA, operated and maintained by Triborough, and later purchased by Triborough. Ultimately, then, all costs would be borne by the Moses organization.

Other problems to be resolved included the questions of state and federal funds for the approaches to the span, the problem of relocating the people in the way of the approaches, and—the issue which brought the MRTC and Moses into conflict—the question of rapid transit on the bridge. The plans of the Triborough and Port Authorities excluded rail transit facilities from the Narrows span. Since such facilities would link Staten Island to the subway system of New York City's other four boroughs, providing added impetus for the island's growth, the Authorities expected some objections to their decision. They attempted to meet any criticisms in advance by explaining their reasons in the initial announcement of the project. A rail line on the bridge, they noted, could be joined with the city subway system only if it could feed into the Fourth Avenue Line in Brooklyn. But, "according to the New York City Transit Authority," this line was already operating at capacity. Therefore, an entirely new subway line would be required in Brooklyn to accommodate rail traffic coming across the bridge. To allow such passengers to continue into Manhattan, additional tunnels under the East River would also be necessary. The Triborough–Port Authority report reasoned that the "enormous costs" of the total program would present an "insurmountable burden" and therefore there was no advantage in constructing the bridge line.[7]

During the spring and summer of 1955, the plan to exclude rail was attacked by the Staten Island Chamber of Commerce and several other groups. Then, because of the potential importance of rail service on the bridge to the development of Staten Island, the MRTC decided in the fall in 1955 to include a study of the problem in its intrastate surveys. A prompt and thorough analysis was needed, the Commission believed, so that if a need for rail transit were found, the bridge could at least be constructed so as to allow tracks to be added at a later date.

Learning of the MRTC's plans and hoping to forestall this further challenge, Moses wrote to the Commission in January, 1956. He pointed out that it would cost $10 million to strengthen the bridge so that rail service could later be added. He reiterated the position that the Fourth Avenue subway was operating at capacity, requiring a new subway line "at a cost of roughly $750,000,000." Thus, he thought the development of rapid transit to Staten Island "most improbable" and the cost of strengthening the Bridge a "waste" of public funds.

The transit commissioners had learned the advantages of caution from their encounters with the Port Authority. They talked with officials at the Transit Authority and learned that the Fourth Avenue subway did have additional capacity which could be used by Staten Island passengers. They approached city and state governmental leaders and obtained their support for an objective study of the question, regardless of "any stand taken by Mr. Moses." The Commission then wrote to Moses, pointing out that his information on the Fourth Avenue subway was in error, and that the MRTC would undertake the needed study. A few days later, the Commission announced that Day and Zimmerman, Inc., would study the feasibility of a transit line on the Narrows span.[8]

The MRTC study represented an important challenge to Moses' independence in policy-making. If he were to wait until the study were finished before completing plans and awarding contracts, considerable delay might result. Moreover, the Commission might reach the conclusion that the bridge should carry rails, particularly in view of its known preference for rail. The Triborough Authority might then be expected to absorb the extra cost, an expense that highway-builder Moses was loath to undertake for the benefit of a rail project. Rather than await-

ing the results of the consultant's study, therefore, Moses took
the offensive. In a radio interview in early April, he called rapid
transit over the Narrows a "preposterous" idea and said he had
no confidence in an "overhead" organization like the MRTC.
A few days later, the New York *Times* chided Moses and defended the Commission. The question of rails on the bridge
needed "thorough, professionally skilled exploration," said the
Times, and the MRTC could be relied upon to provide it.
Moses then countered with a letter to the *Times* criticizing the
proposal to build "extravagant Staten Island connections." He
asserted that the total cost would rise from $750 million to
"a billion dollars" if all related subway extension costs were
included.[9]

By this time, Moses was thoroughly annoyed with the MRTC
for stirring up the controversy. It did not greatly surprise the
Commission, then, to find difficulties in its path when it tried
to carry out studies relating to another of Moses' domains. One
of the intrastate studies involved an analysis of travel patterns
of Long Island motorists, including users of the state parkways,
which were under the jurisdiction of Moses' Long Island State
Park Commission. As in Westchester County and other areas,
the MRTC asked for permission before conducting the Long
Island surveys, but found its request denied. As Moses explained
in a letter to the Commission in late April, "We cannot permit
the distribution of your questionnaire cards . . . because of
the exceptionally heavy traffic with consequent congestion, and
delays, littering and other nuisances, irritation to drivers, etc."

The transit commissioners considered Moses' reasons carefully, weighed against them the fact that no significant "littering . . . etc." had resulted from the MRTC surveys in Westchester nor from the Triborough's own survey a year before, but
finally decided, at a meeting in early May, to take "no further
action in this case."[10]

Meanwhile, in the latter part of April, Governor Harriman

took up the defense of the MRTC's study of rapid transit across the Narrows. In a letter to the two Authorities, Harriman said he hoped that no action would be taken which would preclude rapid transit on the bridge until the Commission's survey was completed.

Moses' reply to the Governor illustrated his highway–bond-holder perspective and his commitment to his own version of the situation. He argued that a "thorough investigation" of the cost and need for rapid transit on the Narrows span had been made before the 1955 Joint Report was released. This investigation had led to the conclusion that such a facility "would not be required" and that the cost of strengthening the bridge for rail "should not be subsidized through increased tolls" paid by motor vehicles. Moses then reasserted that the Fourth Avenue subway could not accommodate trains from the bridge, requiring a billion-dollar expenditure by the Transit Authority. In fact, Moses argued, the $10-million cost of strengthening the span in itself "would be prohibitive." The Authorities could not finance the bridge at all, Moses maintained, if this additional sum were added to the original cost of construction, estimated as $220 million. In conclusion, Moses emphasized that he and his fellow commissioners had not only a "public trust" but also a "responsibility for businesslike administration to the bondholders. . . . They cannot conscientiously recommend substantial expenditures for which they can expect no direct or indirect return."

Governor Harriman and his staff were not fully convinced by Moses' arguments, and they asked the MRTC for its comments. The difference in approach between the MRTC and Moses was apparent. The transit agency pointed out that there was little evidence of a "thorough investigation" of the rail question. The Commission had been unable to find any definitive studies, and the Triborough–Port Authority Joint Report "devoted only one paragraph . . . to rapid transit and does not mention at all whether there is a need for rapid transit." The Commission also reviewed the question of the capacity of the Fourth Avenue Line and attached a letter from the Transit Authority supporting its contentions on excess capacity. Finally, it asked that consideration be given not only to questions of "businesslike administration" but to broader issues:

The desirability . . . of rapid transit across the Narrows Bridge cannot properly be weighed . . . without considering the over-all values, indeed the possible necessities (imposed by the City's growth in population and economy) of the mass movement of people by rapid transit between Staten Island and the rest of the City.

At this point, state and city officials and the MRTC agreed that the best way to resolve the controversy was to complete the survey as soon as possible, and the engineers were asked to expedite their work.

The report from Day and Zimmerman, submitted in November, 1956, was an anticlimax. The consultants concluded that the Fourth Avenue line could accommodate Staten Island traffic for ten to twenty years, but that such a line would not save passengers much time compared with existing ferry service to Manhattan and would run at a yearly deficit of more than $2 million. These results were disappointing to some members of the MRTC, but they decided that the cost of providing rapid transit on the bridge was "not warranted by the benefits to be received" and that the city should consider bus service instead.[11] The transit commissioners were satisfied, however, that their objective and professional analysis of the problem was far better, in terms of the overall interests of the region, than the preconceptions and narrow perspectives applied by Chairman Moses.

COMPLETING THE INTERSTATE STUDIES:
SOME SELF-CONFIRMING PROPOSITIONS

During 1956 and early 1957, the consultants engaged in the interstate surveys continued their work under the supervision

of Page, his staff, and representatives of the MRTC and the
Port Authority. These studies would permit the transit commissioners to move from conjecture to firm recommendations
on the major questions before them: What changes in regional
transport policy were needed, especially with regard to the
trans-Hudson problem? Would the proposals result in a self-
supporting rail system, and if not, how would deficits be met?
Finally, what kind of organization should be given responsibility for carrying out the needed changes?

The search for answers to these questions was not entirely
disinterested. Before the surveys began, the Port Authority and
the MRTC had agreed upon a set of guidelines which would
govern the studies; and as the consultants' work progressed,
these standards were effectively implemented. The guidelines
represented a composite of the highest-priority interests of each
of the two agencies.

At Port Authority headquarters, the primary objectives were
to guarantee that no studies of integrated rail and highway
planning be conducted, and that the Authority be excluded
from any role in rail transit. Eliminating rail-highway studies
from the Memorandum of Understanding had adequately safeguarded the first interest. The exclusion of the Port Authority
from rail responsibilities was less fully guaranteed as the studies
began, but the two agencies had agreed in the Memorandum
that the Authority could only take on responsibility for self-
supporting projects, that rail transit would almost certainly
operate at a deficit, and that studies were needed of other
sources of financial aid. There was a strong presumption, then,
that the PNYA would not be given rail responsibilities and that
a new agency would be established to take on rail duties in the
region. If such an agency were created, the pressure that had
long been directed at the Port Authority could be permanently
transferred to the new organization; at least, so the Authority's
officials believed.

For the majority of MRTC members, the matter of primary

concern was the careful study of major trans-Hudson rail improvements and how such improvements could be effected. The extensive surveys being carried out by De Leuw and by Miller were directed toward meeting these goals.

By the start of the interstate studies, the PNYA and the MRTC had come to accept the position that the major goals of each could be pursued, and hopefully attained, without sacrificing the primary aims of the other. Improvements in rail service could be achieved, the MRTC implicitly agreed, even though deficits would result and even though its rail plans would not be coordinated with highway developments. The need for new sources of public aid to rail and for a new rail agency, the PNYA felt, could be linked to the MRTC's extravagant plans for new rail projects without fatally contaminating the Authority's main goals.

Only one further step was required in order to make these contrasting priorities compatible: The general public, it might be assumed, would be willing to accept the whole package, absorbing from general tax resources the costs required to meet the combined demands of this new rail-highway alliance. Or, if the public were to resist, each faction hoped that its own goals could be extricated from the joint program and accepted by the region. The MRTC majority would hope to secure major improvements, using Port Authority funds to help in meeting any deficits if the public so demanded; the PNYA would try to salvage the scheme for a separate rail agency, sacrificing the new rail projects if expedient.

While the consultants labored on the interstate studies, the MRTC and the PNYA pressed for public acceptance of the conclusions they believed would emerge from the surveys. The main public relations campaign was carried out by the members of the MRTC. Aware that the region would have to be alerted to the seriousness of the problem and to the possible need for major improvements and public financial support, the commissioners devoted their energies to a series of public addresses and informal discussions with various groups in the region.

Co-chairman Tuttle led the campaign. He praised the plan then under consideration in the San Francisco region, which called for a $1.5-billion transit system. "Surely," he declared, the New York region "will not shrink from their example." The MRTC interim report published in March, 1956, echoed Tuttle's plea: "The choice is between a continuing worsening of what we have or going all out for the best." Led by Tuttle, O'Mara, and Sly, the commissioners also emphasized that the "cities and towns and villages" of the region should expect to help pay for improved rail service.[12] The MRTC was gratified to encounter some favorable responses. "If we . . . want satisfactory rail transportation," the Bergen *Record* agreed, "we shall have to shell out." The Newark *Evening News* and the Ramsey *Journal*, a Bergen County weekly, concurred.[13]

Members of the MRTC also held informal discussions with committees of New York's Commerce and Industry Association, the Queensboro Chamber of Commerce, and other business groups in the region. They kept in touch with the organizations of suburban mayors and commuters which were protesting service reductions and fare increases on the West Shore, Susquehanna, Erie, Lackawanna, and Jersey Central Railroads and connecting ferries, and they met several times with a liaison committee on regional transit problems appointed by Mayor Wagner.

Preferring to remain in the background, the Port Authority left the public education efforts largely to the MRTC. Occasionally, however, the PNYA utilized the MRTC study to fend off criticism of its own inaction in the rail field. For example, in October, 1956, the Northern Valley Commuters Organization wrote to Meyner and Harriman, asking that the Authority be directed to acquire and operate trans-Hudson ferry services. In response, Tobin explained to the governors that he was "of

course . . . sympathetic" with the commuters' problems but
that the issue had been assigned by the states to the MRTC for
study. Tobin also took the opportunity to quote a "pertinent
. . . guiding principle" from the Memorandum of Understanding,
outlining the PNYA's inability to undertake deficit operations
and the probability that rail improvements would yield substantial deficits.

The activities of the MRTC and the PNYA could not, however, be limited merely to public relations. The desire of the
Commission majority for extensive rail improvements would be
satisfied only if they were shown to be feasible from an engineering, economic, and political standpoint. And the primary
aims of the Port Authority could be achieved only if any such
improvements yielded deficits and if financial and administrative solutions other than Port Authority action could be identified. The two sponsors might, of course, have adopted the approach of the MRTC toward the Verrazano-Narrows Bridge
study, permitting the consultants to reach their own conclusions
without close guidance. But the interests of the PNYA and the
MRTC were too deeply involved in the interstate surveys to
permit this luxury, and substantial efforts were devoted to safeguarding their interests as the studies proceeded.

Major Rail Improvements: A Deficit Is Likely. In his study of
the trans-Hudson problem, De Leuw concluded that the most
efficient solution involved the construction of one or two rail
tunnels under the Hudson, using these tunnels to run subway
trains between Manhattan and the terminals of the New Jersey
railroad lines. Four alternative plans were outlined, varying in
cost from a minimum of $246 million to a maximum of
$474 million, depending mainly upon whether one or two
tunnels were constructed and upon whether or not a new subway line through Manhattan were added. (One of these proposed subway loops, known as Plan 2, is shown by the heavy line
on Figure 3; this was the plan later adopted by Page.) [14]

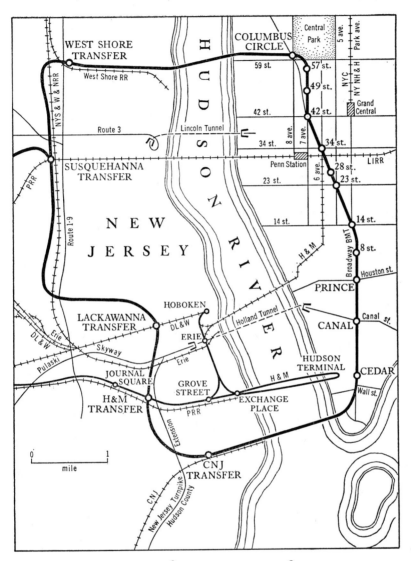

FIGURE 3. DE LEUW PLAN 2
Source: Report of the Project Director, Metropolitan Rapid Transit
Survey, pp. 8–9

De Leuw then turned to the financial results which could be expected on the four systems. Here he and his staff were confronted with significant constraints, implicit and overt. They were familiar with the position agreed to by the study's sponsors—that all previous Port Authority studies had shown that rapid transit projects in the New York area "could not be economically self-supporting." In fact, it was more than a general familiarity that confronted De Leuw; the contract to which he and the other consultants had agreed in undertaking the study required that his survey be made "in accordance with the Memorandum of Understanding." In addition, De Leuw believed that a relatively low fare structure would be advantageous in terms of attracting passengers and that the benefits to be obtained from trans-Hudson rail service would justify outside financial assistance. He therefore felt it appropriate to assume a trans-Hudson fare of only 25 to 30 cents per passenger in calculating the revenue which the system would yield. Consequently, all four plans under consideration would yield sizable annual deficits during the early years of operation, ranging from $2.6 million to $7.4 million.

This conclusion was entirely satisfactory to the Port Authority and acceptable to the MRTC, but it was not the only possible outcome. The deficit projected by De Leuw ranged between 3 and 8.5 cents per one-way trip, depending on the plan chosen. In addition, a fare structure higher than 25 to 30 cents would not have resulted in a significant loss of passengers according to De Leuw's calculations. "Any reasonable variation in fares from those assumed herein," De Leuw concluded, "is not likely to materially change the estimated use of the system." Therefore, a fare structure of 30 to 40 cents might well have produced a self-supporting trans-Hudson system.

While this conclusion was implicit in his data, De Leuw did not include this more optimistic result among the alternatives listed in his report. Based on the constraints which guided him, he limited his discussion to deficit operation and briefly defended his choice of the fare structure that yielded these deficits. An outside subsidy would be needed, the report asserted, unless one were to assume "a fare schedule substantially higher than we deem reasonable and proper."

Even without a "substantial" increase in fares, a self-supporting system might have been held out as a possibility, for, as he acknowledged in his report, De Leuw had excluded several important revenue sources in estimating the financial results of the system. No income from mail and other goods was included, because of the difficulty of estimating potential revenues from these sources, although he noted that there were "real possibilities in connection with the handling of mail and express." Also, no income from intrastate New Jersey trips was included under one plan because of complications in the fare structure; De Leuw said only that a "modest increase" in revenue would result from such passengers.

These estimates referred only to the early years of loop operation, however, and De Leuw was willing to paint a brighter long-term future for the new system. In a draft of his final report, De Leuw estimated that passenger traffic on the loop would increase continuously, reaching in 1975 a point 20 percent higher than initial traffic. At this time, even based on a 25-to-30-cent fare, the deficit might drop to "less than $500,000." Ultimately, De Leuw conjectured, one might perhaps see the "elimination of annual deficit financing."

De Leuw's comments on future traffic were not entirely pleasing to the Port Authority. If the Authority's plan to avoid involvement in rail transit were to be successful, any references to a potentially self-supporting system would have to be eliminated. The PNYA thereupon brought its considerable resources, especially its staff expertise and its general prestige, to bear upon the problem. Its experts argued that accurate forecasts of future traffic on the new system were not possible and that optimistic forecasts were especially questionable in view of the decline in rail passenger service throughout the nation in recent years. According to one story, perhaps apocryphal, a PNYA staff member suggested that De Leuw's report might discuss the effect on the deficit of a 20 to 30 percent decline in traffic rather than the effect of a 20 percent increase.

Realizing that forecasts of future rail traffic were difficult to determine with certainty, De Leuw finally agreed to eliminate these estimates. The "Forecasts" section was retitled "Provisions for Future Traffic," and no specific figures nor financial results were included. Readers of the final report of February, 1957, found only the large deficits based on initial operation and a few vague statements on future traffic.

Paying the Bill: The Port Authority's Views Confirmed. De Leuw's findings now went to Miller, who was charged with studying financial and administrative devices which could be used in connection with any recommended transit system. De Leuw's conclusions met the standards of the two sponsors, and Miller was therefore asked to base his analysis on these recommendations.

For the Port Authority, this was the crucial study. Fortunately for the PNYA, Miller was not an antagonist. He believed that the Authority was an important contributor to the region's progress and that its financial strength and independence should be protected. Also, he was inclined to feel that a greater degree of public control and flexibility in rail transit planning could be obtained if some source other than the PNYA were utilized. These assumptions, combined with the results of the other studies, provided the basis for Miller's recommendations for public action.[15]

Two questions considered by Miller are of primary interest: how large would the rail-system deficit be, and how would it be financed? Although De Leuw had already submitted a tentative estimate of the deficit, Miller reviewed the financial results of the four plans and concluded independently that a deficit of $2 million or higher was likely. But the limited vision which affected De Leuw was found in Miller's analysis as well. Miller's estimated deficit was based on a number of assumptions which could have been altered, and a self-supporting system could reasonably have been included among the alternatives forwarded by Miller to Page and the sponsoring agencies.

In fact, while the estimate of $2 million or higher was emphasized in the summary section of Miller's report, it was not the only estimate found in the text. At one point, Miller suggested that the deficit might be as low as $400,000 if the states were to provide repayable advances similar to those granted to the PNYA and several other state authorities in the past and if special assessments were used to finance the cost of station construction. Both of these assumptions, Miller believed, were "reasonable." In addition, these financial results excluded the interest from investment of the debt service reserve, yet this interest would probably total $500,000 or more per year. Also, a $6.5-million annual payment to the New York City Transit Authority for use of its facilities was included under one plan (Plan 2), but Miller thought it possible that this amount could be reduced significantly. Although he did not analyze the results of these alternatives in detail, Miller was inevitably led to conclude that given certain assumptions, "there could be no deficit on Plan 2." But a more conservative estimate was stressed: a deficit of $2.0 million to $6.3 million, depending on the plan chosen.

If Miller had been willing to reevaluate the fare structure assumed by De Leuw, the possibility of a self-supporting system would have been even more likely. Under some assumptions, all of the plans could have been made self-supporting if the fare were increased by as little as 1 to 7 cents per one-way trip. But Miller joined De Leuw in accepting the 25-to-30-cent fare as "reasonable" and argued that higher fares would cause more loss of traffic to private automobiles than was desirable. The disadvantages of such traffic diversion were not, however, carefully weighed against the possible advantages—in terms of political feasibility and other goals—that might be obtained from a self-supporting loop system.[16]

Using a working assumption of a $2-million-to-$6-million yearly deficit on the proposed trans-Hudson project, Miller then turned to the questions of how to finance the deficit and what organization should have responsibility for constructing and operating the new service. First, the state and federal governments were eliminated as major sources of funds because of political and other obstacles. Then, Miller considered the possible contributions which could be made by five existing public authorities in the New York region—the New Jersey Turnpike Authority, the New Jersey Highway Authority, the New York State Thruway Authority, the Triborough Authority, and the Port Authority. The first four agencies were unable to contribute to rail transit because of the nature of the resolutions under which their bonds had been issued. With one or two minor exceptions, these resolutions limited the agencies to the financing of vehicular facilities. Adding rapid transit to their responsibilities would subject the bondholders to risks they could not have expected and therefore would violate the obligation-of-contracts clause of federal and state constitutions.

Miller then considered the Port Authority as a potential source of funds for the project. His reasoning reflected the limited perspective from which he viewed the problem—a perspective that assigned higher priority to safeguarding the Authority's goals than to full exploration of the question. Miller's analysis warrants close attention, since it is the only detailed consideration of the relationship of the Port Authority to the rapid transit problem in any of the reports to or by the MRTC.

Miller began by noting that, unlike the other authorities,

the PNYA could legally finance rapid transit projects. But the Authority had always limited its investments to projects which "may reasonably be expected to become self-supporting eventually." This policy is appropriate for the PNYA, Miller argued, because of "two basic factors":

1. The Authority's ability to acquire funds for its "important public undertakings" depends on the confidence of the investor that its revenues will provide "sufficient reserves" to meet any emergency, and a deficit rail project might raise doubts on this score.

2. "Were it to follow the practice of undertaking deficit projects which do not eventually become self-supporting, its earnings from other projects would be permanently drained off and further expansion of its services to the public would be prevented."

Actually, under some of the assumptions discussed above, the loop might reasonably be expected to achieve self-support, but Miller did not emphasize this point or note its implications for Port Authority action. Even if one assumed that the rail loop would be a permanent deficit operation, however, Miller's arguments were incomplete, illustrating the lens of Port Authority protection through which he saw the issue. For example, in view of the substantial net income on other PNYA facilities, it seemed likely that the Authority could have accepted responsibility for a rail system with an annual deficit of several million dollars without any loss of confidence on the part of PNYA investors and without preventing expansion of other PNYA services. This was, in fact, an argument to which the Port Authority would accede in 1960, but Miller failed to explore this possibility.[17]

Also, Miller's arguments were focused on the question of whether the Port Authority could fully undertake the proposed rail improvement itself—that is, plan, finance, construct, and operate the loop. He did not pause to consider an alternative role for the PNYA; it might have been asked only to provide a specified amount of funds to assist another agency in meeting deficits. Bypassing these questions, Miller instead emphasized his own firm conviction that the PNYA be permitted to continue uninhibited along its traditional path:

It seems . . . essential, that the Port Authority should conserve its borrowing power . . . in order to be able to apply it to the success-ful consummation of the huge improvement program . . . which the Authority itself has outlined.[18]

With the Port Authority excluded from any contribution to rail transit, Miller turned to the major remaining source: the local communities of the region. In 1954, Austin Tobin had asserted that "We must have public acceptance of the fact that the suburban communities themselves will have to meet the cost of existing fixed rail service (to say nothing of any im-provements)." [19] Miller was now faced with the responsibility of analyzing the economic and political feasibility of Tobin's suggestion.

Miller first considered the question of whether the local gov-ernments could safely add the rapid transit debt to the existing debt structure. After a careful review, he concluded that "it . . . appears that the metropolitan area as a whole could readily stand the added burden" of financing the proposed trans-Hud-son project. In order to tap these available resources and carry out the improvements, Miller proposed that a bistate Metro-politan District be created and that it be empowered to "plan, construct, finance and operate trans-Hudson rapid transit facil-ities and services in the region." The deficits from District operations would be allocated among the twelve counties west of the Hudson and New York City on the basis of population, tax ratables, and extent of trans-Hudson travel.[20] The District would be governed by a council whose members would be selected by the governing boards of the western counties and the New York City Council.[21]

Thus, Miller had effectively met the issues of fiscal capability and administrative technique. But feasibility involves another factor of major importance, as Miller realized: Would the benefits to be received by those paying the bill be sufficient to attract their support for the plan? Miller argued that the costs would be more than offset by resulting benefits. New York City and Boston were cited as illustrating the economic benefits of rapid transit. "Thoughtful leadership on all sides" was found to favor tax subsidies for rail transit: Miller cited the views of Luther Gulick, Walter Blucher, and Austin Tobin. But he did not attempt to identify the specific benefits which the proposed trans-Hudson facility would offer.[22]

Miller's report must be read in conjunction with De Leuw's study of the four plans, however; and in that report a number of benefits directly related to the project were spelled out. For commuters, time savings of about 12 minutes per trip, new rail cars, and other conveniences of the loop were noted. Also, De Leuw held forth the possibility that "railroad managements would discontinue their almost constant pleas for permission to curtail or abandon service," although this optimistic conjecture was not supported by any detailed analysis.[23]

Advantages for noncommuters were also listed. They would benefit on their occasional rail trips to Manhattan, of course, and those who traveled into Manhattan by automobile or bus would find a "modest" reduction in traffic congestion (perhaps 1 to 10 percent) in their trans-Hudson trips and in Manhattan. In addition, De Leuw asserted, the loop would stimulate the growth of New Jersey's suburban areas because of improved access to New York City. But he presented no solid evidence to support this assertion, and he did not explore the issues suggested by his argument—issues which would be raised by opponents of the loop plan in the near future. For example, would improved access to Manhattan from New Jersey have adverse effects on business centers in Newark, Jersey City, and other large New Jersey cities? If so, why should such areas assist the new project through tax assessments?

The combined reports of De Leuw and Miller thus supported the MRTC's hope that several trans-Hudson projects were practicable from an engineering perspective and the Port Authority's view that all were likely to yield substantial deficits and that the Authority was unable to meet such deficits. The reports also confirmed the joint expectations of the two regional agencies that the local communities would obtain sufficient benefits to warrant their supporting the new facility. But except for the question of engineering feasibility, all these conclusions were based on questionable assumptions and incomplete information.

The Neglected Studies. Not all the interstate studies supported the preferences of the two sponsors, however. Two studies—of less expensive trans-Hudson projects and of bus service improvements—led to rather different conclusions, and the fate of these studies underscores the limited perspectives which guided the interstate work.

Coverdale and Colpitts was assigned the responsibility of evaluating four relatively inexpensive methods of replacing trans-Hudson ferry service. By the mid-1950s, the ferry services of the New Jersey railroads were operating at a combined annual deficit of more than $3 million, and most of the rail lines had petitioned the ICC for permission to abandon them. The main proposals studied by Coverdale and Colpitts involved methods of redirecting ferry passengers from the Central of New Jersey, Erie, and Lackawanna Railroads to the H&M. In late 1956, the consultant's report was forwarded to Page and the MRTC. The proposals to shift ferry passengers to the H&M were found to be feasible; but construction of one track to bring travelers from the Central to the H&M station would cost $13.4 million, and the additional passengers would overload the H&M during peak hours, requiring some passengers to wait 4 minutes for a train.[24]

These were relatively modest improvements at relatively low cost. They did not meet the standard of the MRTC, "going all out for the best," and none of the proposals would be needed if any of the grander De Leuw projects were carried out. The MRTC decided to take no further action on the report at that time, and the possibility of achieving such partial improvements faded from sight as far as the activities of the Commission were concerned.

The challenge to the transit commissioners' expectations which was posed by the Ford, Bacon and Davis study of bus service was even more direct. Ford, Bacon and Davis had been assigned to study means of improving bus transportation "where new investments in rail lines do not appear justified or in cases where continuance of existing railroad commuter service is found to be economically impracticable." From October, 1955, until May, 1956, the firm investigated all possible areas where buses might be used in place of rails, including their potential use for trans-Hudson commuting. But in May, 1956, De Leuw completed his preliminary studies, which showed that several rail projects across the Hudson were feasible. Page then consulted the MRTC and the Port Authority and told Ford, Bacon and Davis to eliminate studies of trans-Hudson bus service from its investigations. All its future work, Page directed, should be "premised on the construction and operation . . . of a trans-Hudson rail rapid transit system."

Ford, Bacon and Davis then concentrated on the role of buses to replace passenger service on lightly used railroads in New Jersey and concluded in its final report that travelers on several of the smaller lines could be handled on buses feeding into the proposed trans-Hudson rail loop. But Ford, Bacon and Davis was not fully satisfied with the restrictions placed on its studies. Its preliminary surveys suggested that improved bus service across the Hudson might, in conjunction with the H&M, be able to handle all trans-Hudson traffic. If this were feasible, the need for new rail tunnels, at a cost of $246 million to $474 million, would be thrown into serious question. But neither Page, MRTC, nor the Port Authority were willing to allow further consideration to be given to this alternative before they committed themselves to the rail loop. Finding no support for their position, the engineers had to be content with a few hints of their heretical findings in their final report. They noted that bus service has a "distinct advantage" over rail for travel between a single terminal area and widely dispersed suburbs, and that the combination of highway expansion in New Jersey and double-decking of the George Washington Bridge would increase the "potential usefulness of interstate buses" entering upper and midtown Manhattan. As to downtown Manhattan, the report suggested that ferries could be replaced by bus service if a separate bus lane and a bus terminal in lower Manhattan were added. In this case, Ford, Bacon and Davis noted, "buses operating in interstate service could transport the 26,500 peak-hour rail-ferry passengers across the Hudson River." The major capital cost for such a bus-service alternative to the rail loop would be a $20-million investment for the bus terminal.[25]

Why were the two regional agencies unwilling to allow Ford, Bacon and Davis to expand their promising initial studies into a detailed exploration of this less expensive alternative? For the MRTC, personal and public commitments to rail were the basic factors. "The Commission," the 1955 interim report had proclaimed in bold-face type, will give "strong consideration to mass transportation by rail." An improved rail system, the 1956 Report declared, "must create an attractive position in relation to the private automobile or the bus." The MRTC had, of course, agreed on bus transportation in place of rails over the Verrazano-Narrows Bridge. But if it were now to come forward with trans-Hudson bus service as its major recommendation for solving the region's transport problems, its position would be awkward, to say the least. The MRTC was not inclined to do this, however, and the probable advantages of the loop over bus service in terms of speed and comfort, as well as the feeling that the region would be willing to accept a high-cost project, led the Commission to reject any detailed study of the bus alternative.

What of the Port Authority, a firm supporter of the bus and builder of two bus terminals in Manhattan? Several reasons appear to have led to its decision not to press for the bus substitute. First, the MRTC would be unlikely to accept such a proposal. Second, an MRTC plan for additional bus service would not justify the creation of a new agency; instead the PNYA would be expected to construct a downtown bus terminal and a third tube at the Holland Tunnel in order to provide a separate bus lane into lower Manhattan. It was doubtful that the extra tube would be a self-supporting project, however, and the Authority was not eager to build it. Also, if a new rail agency did not result from the MRTC's efforts, the PNYA would continue to be the object of attack from those who wanted more vigorous regional action to save existing railroad services. In sum, a bus alternative might or might not have been of benefit to the New York region; but it certainly did not seem to be of benefit to the Authority, and no attempt was made to press for further consideration of the proposal.

The Problems of the Railroads. The transit study group operated essentially as a self-contained unit. The PNYA, the MRTC, Page, and the consultants generally agreed on goals and procedures, and outside interests were unable to penetrate. At one point in the study, however, a new goal—responsibility for taking action to meet current railroad problems—was accepted by the group.

In the original discussions between the MRTC and the rail carriers in the fall of 1954, a difference in priorities had been evident. The Commission was concerned primarily with new facilities and the railroads with reducing their financial losses from current passenger services. During the next two years, the two groups pursued their separate paths. In 1955 and 1956 the railroads pressed their drive to curtail service before state regulatory commissions and the Interstate Commerce Commission. The Susquehanna had petitioned to eliminate all passenger service, the Erie and the West Shore had taken steps to end their trans-Hudson ferry routes, and reductions in service on several other roads were also pending.

Page was disturbed by this continuing deterioration of rail service. Any recommendations for improving service across the Hudson would be of little value if passenger travel to the new facility were eliminated. Also, it seemed unreasonable to Page for the private railroads to absorb continuing economic losses in providing commuter service. His recent work with the President's transport study committee had made him aware of the weakened financial condition of the Eastern roads and of their need to end the economic drain of commutation services. Thus, Page was, in effect, a representative of important elements in both the rail and road fields. His admiration for the Port Authority was matched by his concern that rail service be maintained but without the railroads' absorbing the financial burden.

In the fall of 1956, Page met with representatives of the MRTC, the PNYA, and the railroads. After some discussion, it was agreed that the MRTS should include a study of the extent of the deficits incurred by the New Jersey railroads in providing commuter services and of ways to reduce these losses. Thus, the MRTC ended the divergence in perspective that had separated it from the railroads and took the first step toward incorporating the rail lines' goals with its other objectives.

In February, 1957, a consultant's study of rail deficits was completed. The report concluded that current losses were approximately $12.6 million and that changes in fares and services might readily reduce this deficit to $8 million.[26] This report was immediately forwarded to Miller, and he was asked to evaluate means of meeting these losses. In Miller's final report, he estimated that there were "ample resources" in the region to support this annual rail deficit as well as the loop deficit and outlined the statutory powers that would be required if Page and the MRTC wished the Metropolitan District to encompass these additional responsibilities.[27]

A $400-Million Transit Program. In early 1957, Page and his staff began preparations for their report to the MRTC. Originally, the Commission had expected Page to limit his report to a factual summary, with the commissioners then deciding upon policy recommendations. As the studies came to a close, however, an alternate strategy was adopted by the MRTC: Page would include his own recommendations in his report, and public hearings would be held on these proposals. Having tested public sentiment in the region, the Commission would then decide upon its final program of action. The MRTC also decided to have Page limit his report to the problem requiring most immediate public attention, that of the interstate rail network. Later a report on the intrastate surveys would be prepared by the Commission's own staff.[28]

This arrangement was eminently satisfactory to the Port Authority. The Authority was much more confident of the kinds of policy recommendations that Page would produce than it was of the MRTC's eventual product—both because of Page's known admiration for the PNYA and because the Authority had been closely involved in the work of the transit survey. Once Page had publicized recommendations which, the PNYA anticipated, excluded the Authority and advocated a new rail agency, the MRTC would find it difficult to do otherwise—particularly since these conclusions would be based on the MRTC's own expert studies.

On May 23, 1957, the Page report was released to the public. The report called for creation of a permanent Metropolitan District which would construct a $345-million bistate transit loop and in addition assume responsibility for passenger service on existing North Jersey railroads. The deficit from these activities would total $12 million per year, and the District would apportion this cost to New York City and to the twelve participating counties west of the Hudson.[29]

Immediate editorial reaction to the report was generally favorable. "It is the most comprehensive and searching examination of the trans-Hudson problem ever made," declared the New York *Herald Tribune*, "and the recommended program of action is equally thorough and constructive." "It seems to promise . . . a splendid improvement," asserted the New York *Times*, and at a "dollar cost so moderate that even the commission chairman, Charles H. Tuttle, exclaimed at it." The Newark *Star Ledger* ascribed the virtues of "boldness and imagination" to the plan, and the *Jersey Journal* found it a "frank and clear attack upon a basic problem." [30]

The program outlined by Page was a composite of the proposals presented by De Leuw and Miller, together with the results of the belated study of railroad deficits, and it was shaped by the same assumptions that guided the consultants' studies. Page discarded the modest alternatives considered by Coverdale and Colpitts in favor of De Leuw's Plan 2. He also accepted the fare structure recommended by the consultants, added $60 million to construction costs to compensate for inflation during the construction period, made a few other changes in the consultants' estimates, and calculated a yearly deficit of $3 million for the rail loop. This result was even higher than Miller's primary estimate for Plan 2 ($2.6 million).

Again, were it not for the selective goals that shaped his work, Page too might have entertained the possibility of a self-supporting loop system.[31]

In addition, consistent with his own preferences as well as the views of the Port Authority and some influential MRTC members, Page recommended that the public accept responsibility for maintaining and improving rail passenger service between New York and New Jersey. Responsibility for meeting existing railroad deficits would be taken from the rail carriers, and a $55-million program of replacing and modernizing rail cars and improving railroad stations would be carried out. The deficit from this suburban rail service program alone would total $9 million a year.[32]

How would these extensive costs be met? Page accepted Miller's recommendation that a bistate district construct the loop, maintain railroad service, and meet the combined annual deficit of $12 million ($3 million from the loop, $9 million from the railroad program) through a tax levy on the local communities. No mention of any possible role for the Port Authority was included in the project director's report. Page thought that the total deficit would not be "an unreasonably heavy burden on the tax resources of the benefited area," an opinion which would not meet with unanimous acceptance in the region during the coming months. The project director's analysis of benefits was built directly upon those of De Leuw and Miller and contained the same limitations as did those earlier reports.[33]

RESULTS OF THE STUDIES

The transit study phase thus ended as it began—the central participants forming a relatively well-integrated subsystem, dominated by the goals of the Port Authority and the MRTC. The aims of the two sponsors were largely accepted by the other participants throughout the period, although in a few cases threats to the main priorities of the agencies had arisen. On these occasions—for example, in De Leuw's projections of future traffic and Ford, Bacon and Davis' views on interstate bus service—the behavior patterns paralleled those found by Kaplan in his Newark study. Conflicts were settled informally, "not through overt attacks or public agitation." [34]

The more fully a social system is integrated, one may argue, the more likely it is to succeed in achieving its goals. An integrated structure can identify and pursue objectives more efficiently than a loosely knit complex or one marked by significant internal conflict.[35] In this sense, the transit study group may be termed successful. A number of studies of complex problems were initiated and completed within a relatively short time, and the studies yielded a set of concrete proposals for public action which were consistent with the objectives of the sponsoring organizations.

But there are other aspects of success which warrant consideration: Was the transit group successful when measured by the standards publicly proclaimed by its sponsors? Was it successful in providing a set of proposals that would meet the test of political feasibility?

Before, during and after the transit study, the MRTC and the Port Authority drew the attention of the public to the standards which assertedly governed the study. The surveys would be carried out, the Memorandum of Understanding declared, "without any preconceived conclusions as to the interstate transit requirements of the area, or the best means . . . of maintaining and improving rail transit service." The approach that "must be used here," Tuttle proclaimed in early 1956, is "study by the best engineering and technical brains . . . who will go about their task courageously and disinterestedly, impervious to political and self-interested pressures."

"The eminent Director of that study," asserted the Port Authority in 1958, "and the distinguished consultants . . . were, it should hardly be necessary to say, completely free to reach their own conclusions." [36] In reality, however, the internal and overt constraints which governed the work of the survey group tended to insure that the prior conclusions of the two sponsors would result. With the exception of the Verrazano-Narrows Bridge study, the "self-interested pressures" of these two organizations shaped the outcome of the surveys. The guidelines publicly proclaimed by the sponsors tell us more about the ways in which expert studies may be used than about the functioning of those studies.

This is not to suggest that the behavior of the members of the study group could have been very different from what it was. The Port Authority's activities were aimed at seeking a way to maintain its independence and financial strength. Its use of the transit survey to achieve its goals was predictable. The MRTC's commitment to rail was well publicized; and, given the lack of alternative financial support, it could pursue its aims only in conjunction with the Authority. The consultants, once they had agreed to the contracts and consequently had consented to carry out the studies "in accordance with the Memorandum of Understanding" and under the supervision of Page and the two sponsors, were largely bound into the system of selective perceptions.

It might be argued, of course, that important questions of professional responsibility are raised when an expert accepts the role assigned to the MRTS consultants. As Bryson has argued, the adviser has a

responsibility to protect himself against being used to justify decisions already made. . . . If the expert accepts the role of rationalizer, he may destroy his own integrity; he can often detect the hidden invitation to serve as mere helper in the formulation of the question he is asked to advise on.

The MRTS consultants might well have seen that invitation; surely their names and reputations were used to justify results significantly shaped elsewhere; but, as Bryson concludes, "No rule will suffice to guide the consultant here; he is the keeper of his own conscience." [37]

What of the political criteria of success? The insulation of the transit study subsystem from external political forces has been noted. Such insulation gave rise to two mechanisms which tended to reduce the political feasibility of the system's output. First, the lack of guidelines offered by outside political leaders permitted the study group to engage in logrolling, adding all the major priorities of its members together and presenting the results as a single program. Huntington has noted a similar pattern in the military:

If . . . the limits permitted by superior executive authority are broad or undefined, logrolling enables each service to obtain what it considers most important. In "Operation Paperclip," Army, Navy, and Air Force proposals are added together and called a joint plan.[38]

Perhaps the tendency is inevitable; surely it is easier to aggregate priorities—rail tunnels, new commuter cars, large deficits, a new agency—than to engage in the bargaining (perhaps leading to the breakdown of the integrated system) which would result if a reduction in the total bill were sought in the interest of a vaguely defined "political feasibility."

The second impact of isolation was to maximize the tendency of the system's members to view the environment as consistent with their prior assumptions, that is, to engage in selective perception. The survey members communicated primarily with each other, thus emphasizing the acceptability of their mutual goals. In addition, in their relatively limited contacts with outside points of view, they perceived a situation favorable to their objectives. Perceptions that were "discordant with the frame of reference" previously adopted were "filtered out." [39] The support given the MRTC's call for local tax support by the Newark *Evening News*, Bergen *Evening Record*, and other regional newspapers was viewed as providing a strong presumption that a major program would be accepted. Comments of a group of local officials—that when the Page report was submitted, "there will be much for [us] to evaluate and possibly implement"—were seen in the same light. Occasionally criticisms of the transit survey did arise, particularly in Hudson County, but to the study group these appeared to be a negative minority rather than straws in the wind.[40]

Isolation thus permitted a pyramiding of the desires of the MRTC, the Port Authority, and the project director and provided no effective way to assess the political feasibility of the results before publication of the Page report. Now, however, the willingness of the public to accept the proposals would be tested. During the summer and fall of 1957, spokesmen for many interests in the metropolis, long unorganized and excluded, would raise a number of important questions concerning the assumptions and conclusions of the transit study phase: Were expensive trans-Hudson improvements needed? Should the Port Authority be exempted from involvement? Would the local areas actually receive sufficient benefits to warrant the proposed tax burden?

CHAPTER VII

Reactions to the Surveys: Diversity and Conflict in the Metropolis

Upon publication of the Page report, the search for transit policy partially emerged from the insulated policy-making environment of the previous eighteen months into a broader political arena. During the next eight months, the MRTC obtained the views of a wide variety of regional interests, assessed the political feasibility of Page's recommendations, and prepared its final report. The MRTC was now formally autonomous; the two-year alliance with the Port Authority had ended, and the MRTC was able to complete its investigation independently and reach its own conclusions.

The first five months were devoted to a series of public hearings sponsored by the MRTC and to a number of additional Commission meetings with business and civic associations, commuter organizations, and public officials in the region. In past years admonitions concerning the need for a "plan of action" and "close cooperation" to meet the region's transport problems had evoked general approval. But now that a concrete program had been suggested, each group turned instead to a careful calculation of how its own interests would be affected. The arguments advanced by most groups reflected this narrow concern, and few looked to the needs of the region as a whole. The difficulties of obtaining a broad regional consensus on specific recommendations for policy change were clearly illustrated.

While the transit issue became the subject of extensive discussions during these months, its emergence into the broader public arena was only partial, for the MRTC retained control over the content of the report that followed these discussions. Not until January, 1958, would political institutions which normally act on regional problems, in this case the two state legislatures, take responsibility for action. And while the MRTC sought to present proposals which were politically feasible, the pattern of assumptions that had directed the search of past months could not be cast off. Some changes in Page's recommendations were made as a result of the public discussions in 1957, but the basic approach of his report was retained in the MRTC's final recommendations of January, 1958. A Transit District was proposed, and local financing of rail improvements was emphasized. No contribution by the PNYA was suggested. Page's $400-million improvement program was altered upward to a $500-million package. The MRTC found itself unable to shake off the constraints built into the transit-study alliance during the previous two years.

THE REGION'S MANY VOICES

Normally, as Dahl has noted, "most citizens are indifferent about public matters." [1] Certainly indifference and inaction characterized the attitude of most citizens in the New York region where rail policy was concerned, especially during the 1955–57 period. But Page's specific and dramatic proposals for changes in the transit network and the governmental system of the region stimulated interest among a wider variety of regional groups than had heretofore been involved. During the summer and fall of 1957 these groups debated the issues within their own ranks and argued their positions before the MRTC and in the press. These months provided an unusual opportunity to obtain the perspectives of a large number of interests on a major regional issue. In addition, this phase was important in terms of the development of the Commission's final report and as background for the debate on that report during 1958.

Those who favored the Page proposals hoped that they could obtain a wide measure of approval within the region. Support might be forthcoming from much of the rail coalition—that loose alliance of suburban commuter groups, business and civic associations, and rail corporations which desired changes in transport policy and whose concern had led to the creation of the MRTC in 1954. State and local officials concerned about the crisis might also give assistance, now that a concrete plan was at hand. The member of the road coalition most directly involved, the Port Authority, would support the recommendations. Other road interests might criticize the proposals, but most would remain neutral, since the plan did not involve a direct attack on their policies or independence of action. Criticism could be expected from local government officials and businessmen wary of tax increases to support rail needs, but Page and his supporters expected that the favorable voices would outweigh those in opposition.

The region's response was a distinct disappointment to those who took this optimistic view. Individual members of the transport coalitions and most other regional spokesmen reacted to the transit proposals in terms of their own narrow self-interest. The major lines along which these interests divided and regrouped were related to their perspectives of the region and to their views of the urgency of the rail problem. The resulting responses can generally be classified into four fairly distinct positions—first, those in Manhattan and across the Hudson who viewed Manhattan as the center of the region and who saw the rail problem as urgent; second, others with a Manhattan orientation but with less of a feeling of urgency concerning the rail issue; third, spokesmen from Newark and other large cities in the western zone who saw their interests as competitive with those of Manhattan; and finally, those who favored action in the eastern sector of the region instead of or concurrent with improvements in the western zone. Overgeneralizing somewhat, we might say that the reactions were a composite of two conflicts: eastern versus western sectors, and the central city versus the region's competing cities.

The strongest support for Page's recommendations came from those who shared the Manhattan business district orientation that dominated his report and who believed that immediate action was needed. Although Page foresaw advantages for the entire region, his report emphasized that Manhattan business and the New Jersey suburbs with large numbers of New York-bound commuters would be the primary beneficiaries. Major trade groups in New York City, such as the Commerce and Industry Association and the West Side Association of Commerce, were largely favorable to the proposals, and the New York *Times* and other New York daily newspapers concurred. Several of these spokesmen emphasized the direct advantages to New York business that would result from improving access for workers and shoppers from New Jersey. A few also defended the Page plan in terms of a broader regional perspective. The Citizens Budget Commission, for example, viewed the report as contributing to "the concept of the Metropolitan Region as a social and economic unit, which it is in fact." [2]

The Manhattan spokesmen were undismayed by the proposal to use tax resources to aid the rail lines. Having lived under this policy in New York City for many years, most agreed with the view expressed by the City's Chamber of Commerce—an adequate rail system was essential, and, since private enterprise could not provide it, governmental action was required. [3]

West of the Hudson, the proposals were most favorably received by spokesmen in Bergen County and adjacent Rockland County. Both areas were composed primarily of small residential communities, and they ranked first and second among the western counties in percentage of employed labor force working in Manhattan (20 percent in Bergen, 12 percent in Rockland). Both expected continued population growth, with increased trans-Hudson commuting.[4] In addition, rail services in these counties were in a precarious position in 1957, with the West Shore's Weehawken ferry and all Susquehanna passenger service in danger of abandonment in the immediate future.

Therefore, leaders in Bergen County viewed the loop plan as "very promising" and advocated construction as soon as possible. The Page program "stresses the suburbs' case," the Bergen *Evening Record* proclaimed; we must "hurry it into reality." A realtor in the area declared that the rail loop would have "an excellent effect on the future development of housing in Northern New Jersey," and Rockland's Board of Supervisors praised the Page proposals as likely to "greatly increase" the attractiveness of the county as a place to live.[5] The recommendations were also supported by the chairman of Bergen's Board of Freeholders and by several municipal-commuter groups in the two counties.[6]

As others viewed it, the problem of maintaining and improving rail services in New Jersey and into Manhattan was important but not important enough to justify the use of local tax resources. This position was taken by joint committees of municipal officials and commuters in the suburbs of Union, Morris, Passaic, Middlesex, and several other counties, by the Boards of Freeholders in some of these counties, and by New York's Mayor Wagner. In general, these spokesmen favored construction of the rail loop and public aid for the railroads, but they sought an alternate financial solution, with Wagner suggesting the states and the New Jersey groups arguing that the Port Authority should take responsibility.

The New Jersey counties represented by these spokesmen were in a different position from Bergen and Rockland. They contained important employment centers, such as Paterson, Clifton, and Elizabeth, and a lower percentage of Manhattan-bound commuters (between 4 and 9 percent of the working force of each county). And while the commuter groups from these areas fought continuously with the railroads over fare increases and service reductions, their rail services were not in imminent danger of collapse. There was still time available, they felt, to work for an alternative solution which would preclude the need for local tax support.[7]

In addition, this central New Jersey region was the home of the Inter-Municipal Group for Better Rail Service (IMGBRS), which had long been critical of the Port Authority's bridge-and-tunnel emphasis and of its avoidance of transit problems. The IMGBRS chairman, John Kraus, was one of the MRTC members who had engaged in a running battle with the Authority before being forced to resign in 1955. Once the Page report was released, Kraus and his colleagues began a campaign for PNYA action and thus reopened the conflict between rail and road interests, which had been muted during the study phase. It was a campaign that would gain adherents and ultimately force the Authority to reverse its traditional position.

During the summer of 1957, the IMGBRS leaders persuaded several other municipal-commuter groups to join forces in pressing for Port Authority responsibility, and at a MRTC hearing in September the IMGBRS counsel spoke for the combined suburban organizations in asking for a radical reversal of MRTC thinking. The MRTC should recommend, he urged, that the PNYA take immediate steps to continue all existing rail and ferry services and that it construct and operate a new trans-Hudson rail system. Most of the deficit would be met out of profits from other Authority operations, with trans-Hudson automobile tolls being raised, if necessary, to absorb any losses.[8]

Mayor Wagner's position contrasted with the views of most business and civic groups in New York City. While noting that improved transit in the region would be beneficial, Wagner argued that the "primary responsibility" for financing should be assumed by the two states and that it was "premature" to judge whether the proposed District was the best organizational solution. Here the Mayor was responding to two sets of pressures which did not operate upon the city's private organizations. First, his direct responsibility for the city's budget made him wary of proposals that might put additional pressure on the city's tax resources. In addition, within the past year he had initiated a new regionwide organization of elected city and county officials, the Metropolitan Regional Council (MRC). The development of cooperative efforts through this group might be jeopardized if a competing district agency were established. Also, if Wagner were to favor regional transit proposals opposed by a number of his New Jersey colleagues, cooperation on other problems would be endangered.[9]

Still another view predominated in the major retail and industrial centers of New Jersey—in Newark, Paterson, Elizabeth, and other large cities. Spokesmen from these areas doubted that they would benefit from improved access to Manhattan for workers and shoppers. As one Passaic businessman told Page, "What you are asking is that the industries of the county . . . support a plan that would help transport employees from New Jersey to New York." The president of Bamberger's, a Newark department store, argued that the loop "presents a definite threat to the retail market of the county," since "it appears possible that Jersey people in suburban communities will be able to get to Manhattan faster than they can get to Newark." These spokesmen favored neither local tax aid nor Port Authority action to provide a new trans-Hudson rail system. Instead, they emphasized the need to make New Jersey "more attractive to large offices and industrial plants and provide local employment and local ratables."

Representatives of these larger New Jersey cities challenged the position that the entire New York region is a single economic and social unit. As Kresge-Newark's president commented, the MRTC had focused on the "greater New York area" and had bypassed the Newark region: "What is good for one isn't necessarily good for the other in its entirety. . . . The problems of metropolitan Newark are peculiar to itself." The Perth Amboy *Evening News* asserted the doctrine of separatism in even more vigorous fashion. "There is no more logic in expecting Middlesex [to help pay for the loop]," the *News* asserted, "than to ask this county to make a contribution to improve the transit system of Pittsburgh." [10]

Actually, these business centers had an important stake in the retention of existing rail services, since their offices, plants, and shops were served by these lines. But most of the publicity had focused on the dramatic loop plan, and as these spokesmen evaluated the Page report, the proposals for maintaining existing services were largely disregarded. Also, the rail services of most of these cities were still generally adequate, in spite of slow attrition, and public financial aid was not seen as an urgent necessity. Finally, Page's rail service proposals as well as his loop plan faced a strong New Jersey antipathy toward subsidizing transport facilities. As a major spokesman for Newark business explained, in opposing the Page plan,

We have first and foremost predicated all of our thinking on financially self-supporting facilities. . . . We believe that the willingness of the user of transportation to pay the costs of the system is a real measure of its worth.[11]

This viewpoint, based on experience with private rail and bus services in New Jersey, which received no direct subsidy, was in marked contrast to that of New York groups, which had long accepted direct public assistance to New York City's transit system.

The fear of domination by Manhattan was found in an extreme form in Hudson County. The first reactions from the county and its major center, Jersey City, were encouraging to the plan's supporters. In late May, the *Jersey Journal* viewed the Page report as a "frank and clear attack upon a basic problem" and urged that it be read from "the same wide perspective" from which it was written. Jersey City commissioner Bernard J. Berry thought the loop plan was "a terrific idea," and Mayor Charles S. Witkowski said that at first glance it looked to be of "great advantage." [12]

A closer look soon convinced most Hudson County leaders that the loop had major drawbacks from the local point of view, however beneficial it might be from a "wide perspective." During the summer, vocal and vehement opposition developed throughout the county. The campaign was led by the Jersey City Merchants Council, which saw the loop as a major threat to the city's retail area. The Council was acutely aware of the vulnerable position of a city and county which had been losing population almost continuously since 1930. It feared the new rail facility would hasten the decline of the area by offering a faster ride to Manhattan, thus diverting potential customers from its shops to New York stores. "This is not a loop," exclaimed the Council's spokesman, Morris Pesin, "it is a noose around our necks!" Pesin could see no advantage for Jersey City under the plan, "only chaos and despair." Jersey City commissioner August W. Heckman agreed, predicting that the loop would make the city a "transit valley" between Newark and New York City. It would "decrease our tax ratables and in time would reduce Jersey City to a ghost community." By September most business leaders, newspapers, and public officials in Hudson County had expressed opposition to the loop and to the tax support plan.[13]

Finally, a few speakers commented from the vantage point of the eastern half of the region—the Westchester and Long

Island areas which were excluded from the proposed Transit District and from Page's other proposals. In the MRTC's view, this exclusion was a question of priorities and of funds: action on the trans-Hudson issue was more urgent, and more money had been made available for studies of this area than of the eastern zone. An official of Brooklyn's Flatbush Chamber of Commerce disagreed with this emphasis. "Let's get rapid transit improvements in Brooklyn first," he exclaimed, "before we furnish it in another state." The president of another Brooklyn business group characterized the Page proposal as "a foreign aid program for the people of New Jersey," and a Long Island commuter representative said that his group was "anxiously awaiting" an MRTC report on Long Island transit problems. Even the New York City organizations which favored the Page proposals urged that the MRTC broaden its perspective in the final report. They asked that the Transit District be expanded to include members from Westchester and Long Island and that final plans for trans-Hudson construction be postponed until proposals for the eastern sector could be prepared. The problems of coordinating these plans and the total cost should be known, it was argued, before construction in one part of the region was begun.[14]

Although reactions to the Page report tended to divide into these four geographic clusters, the pattern was marked by a number of exceptions. In a careful calculation of self-interest, some groups necessarily found themselves in opposition to the dominant attitude in their subregion. Thus, while most Hudson County spokesmen were vigorous critics, one city, Bayonne, saw itself in a position to prosper through the improved access to Manhattan which the loop would offer, and its representatives were among the strongest supporters of the Page plan. As the Bayonne *Times* commented, the loop would speed travel between Bayonne and Manhattan, and a loop extension through

Bayonne to Staten Island (a future possibility noted by Page) would open "limitless" prospects for the community. Bayonne industries would then be able to draw upon an expanded labor market, and the city would be "so attractively located that it would become a dormitory for men and women who work in New York." [15]

In Bergen, where sentiment was predominantly favorable to the Page proposals, the county Chamber of Commerce finally decided to oppose the plan. The Chamber of Commerce noted its concern with "unpredictable operating deficits . . . the costs of which must be raised by taxation in order to serve a small minority." Also, two New York business associations and one Bergen-area commuter group identified specific threats to their interests among the proposals and asked that these portions of the report be rejected by the Transit Commission. Page had suggested that the district purchase and modernize the Hudson and Manhattan to supplement loop service. But the uptown (33rd Street) branch of the H&M, which would partially duplicate the loop's route, would be abandoned. The 23rd and 34th Street–Midtown Associations both opposed this recommendation, fearing that merchants in the vicinity would be harmed by loss of the branch. The project director had also proposed that passenger service on the lightly used Susquehanna and on the Newark branch of the Erie Railroad be eliminated. The Susquehanna commuters' group at once took issue with this recommendation. The Page report generally deserved "widespread public approval," a spokesman explained, but the proposal to end service on these two lines was "a distressing blow." The MRTC was urged to "disavow, disclaim and repudiate" this section of the report.[16]

Narrow self-interest also determined the reactions of transportation interests. Although industry members generally divided along rail-versus-road lines, Page's proposals led to a temporary regrouping. Most of the railroads were favorable toward the report, and especially toward the proposal that rail passenger deficits be met from public funds. But the H&M opposed the loop plan, since this project entailed abandonment of the 33rd Street branch and therefore purchase of the railroad by the District at a reduced price. The H&M called instead for public purchase of its entire system and full use of its facilities, thus avoiding the "high cost and heavy subsidy" of the new loop.[17]

The road alliance was also divided internally, with the bus companies and Robert Moses attacking the Page plan, while the Port Authority maintained a benevolent silence. President J. F. Symington of Public Service Coordinated Transport, a major interstate bus company, argued that the new system "could well mean a breakdown of the present widespread bus system of Northern New Jersey," since a large number of current bus passengers would be diverted to the loop. Symington suggested that more highways and river crossings, plus improved bus service on these roads, would be a far better way to meet regional transit needs than additional, deficit-producing rail facilities.[18]

Moses was more caustic. He had followed the work of the MRTC since their clash concerning the Narrows Bridge a year before, and in September, 1957, Moses released his own evaluation of the Commission's efforts. The Page report, he concluded, was

another one of those long-winded and unrealistic studies of commuter transportation with which we are all familiar. . . . No doubt, there are . . . things that can be done [for rail transit], but they are not going to be the result of huge, cash subsidies based on arbitrary local assessment by a super-duper regional commission.

Moses suggested that partial tax exemption might help, and he offered rail officials a measure of free advice:

These railroads have got to be more ingenious. . . . And they can't just wish their problems on a new regional taxing commission, . . .

on the assumption that bailing out busted, lazy and backward private enterprise is the business of government.

Moses also pointed out that subsidizing rail service was not the only way to take care of mass transportation needs: "A great deal of passenger traffic consists today of car-pools," he explained, an "immeasurably more convenient" and cheaper system than rail.[19]

In contrast with the traditional pro-road and anti-rail positions of the bus operators and Moses, the Port Authority said nothing. The Authority was pleased with the proposal for a new agency to handle regional transit problems, but it had decided to deemphasize its crucial role in the survey and to avoid any public expression of satisfaction with the results. Silence by the PNYA would facilitate an image of the study as objective and also help to keep attention focused away from the PNYA as a possible source of transit financing. Consequently, the Page report was released to the public by the MRTC alone, rather than jointly with the Authority, and the PNYA neither participated in the MRTC's hearings nor took a public position on the transit proposals during 1957. For the present, the strategy was generally successful, and the Page proposals held the region's attention. Only a few voices in New Jersey were raised in protest, as John Kraus and his commuter group tried to divert the region's attention from the proposed Transit District to the PNYA—the agency with "the obligations and the qualifications required to solve this problem." [20]

While most spokesmen tended to defend their own immediate interests, something more should be said of three groups in the region—elected officials, business organizations, and newspapers. Elected officials tended to be the most negative of all the groups. Having direct responsibility for raising funds for any transit improvements and being wary of changes in governmental power, public officials were major opponents and infrequent advocates of the Page proposals. When opposition in

a local area was strong, elected leaders were often in the van-
guard, calling the loop plan "a projection into the realm of
fantasy" and the cost "excessive and unreasonable." The allocation of representatives on the District council was also attacked
by New Jersey officials as giving too much power to New York.
And in New York City and Bergen, where vigorous support for
the Page plan developed, elected officials were relatively inactive, leaving the brunt of the campaigning to newspapers,
business associations, and commuter groups.[21]

At the state level, occasional criticisms were issued by legislators in New Jersey, but most officials were silent. Governor
Harriman declined to take a position, and Governor Meyner
also demurred, explaining, "This is something put on view for
the public to examine. I think there should be a wide discussion of the plan and a full discussion of alternatives." [22] Even a
campaign for gubernatorial and legislative offices in New Jersey
during the fall of 1957 failed to develop much partisan attention toward the Page proposals. For the present, state officials
and candidates preferred to leave responsibility for the complex
transit issue with the MRTC and with the local interests directly affected by the problem.

In Chicago, Banfield found that the elected political leader
—whether mayor, governor, or county official—is inclined to
"let a civic controversy develop in its own way without interference from him." He will "hide" any personal views on the
issue, "especially if they are negative." The leader waits for
"the community to agree" upon a position and then carries the
agreement into effect.[23] The behavior of political leaders in this
study during 1957 only partially confirms Banfield's conclusions. The passivity of the governors and other state leaders is
consistent with his thesis. However, the activities of some local
elected officials suggest another generalization which might be
coupled with Banfield's: the more direct the perceived threats
to his own position and his own constituency, the more likely it

is that the leader will take a public stand in the early stages of a developing controversy. Faced, for example, with threats of increased local taxation and changes in governmental organization, he will try to shape the attitudes of his constituents. If the threat to the local area is clear enough, he may speak with confidence that newspapers and private associations will support him. Thus, elected officials in Hudson, Somerset, Passaic, and other New Jersey areas were among the early critics of the Page proposals. As one county leader expressed a common concern, "We are naturally highly disturbed, because we get excited over thirteen thousand, let alone twelve million dollars. And when you put the word deficit alongside of us, why, we are practically all out of office." [24]

Banfield also found that business and civic associations in Chicago were unlikely to take positions on controversial problems; "almost without exception they were split down the middle" on the issues studied, and inaction was the price paid to safeguard internal unity of the organizations. In addition, the statements of civic association leaders were full of "plausible-sounding but essentially empty generalities." [25]

The evidence from this study suggests that a rather different situation may exist on some regional issues in the New York area. Most of the major business and civic associations in the three largest cities devoted several weeks to consideration of Page's recommendations and then took explicit positions on the proposals. The Commerce and Industry Association, the New York City Chamber of Commerce, several other city groups, and the Regional Plan Association supported the key recommendations for creation of a bistate agency and local tax support for rail services. And where these organizations differed with Page and the MRTC (primarily on whether proposals for the eastern sector should be completed immediately), their views were presented carefully and in detail. The positions of the major business groups in opposition—Newark's Chamber of Commerce and Economic Development Committee and Jersey City's Merchant Council and Chamber of Commerce—were also clearly and persuasively argued. Whatever else may be said of them, Jersey City's Morris Pesin and many of the other spokesmen for business and civic groups can hardly be said to have dealt in "empty generalities." [26]

In previous years, the region's newspapers had generally supported the need for forward-looking action and closer cooperation in the region. Similar sentiments guided the initial reactions of some editors to the Page report, but where opposition developed from local business and political leaders, most newspapers were soon found in the "local interest" camp. Thus, Hudson County's *Jersey Journal*, which in May had urged that the report be read from a "wide perspective," altered its position after a series of attacks on the plan from other county spokesmen. "North Jersey businessmen ask why they should pay taxes to subsidize taking customers from their doors," complained the *Journal* in July. "Municipalities ask why they should levy heavy taxes to solve New York City's transit problems." The Elizabeth *Daily Journal* had commented just after the report's publication that the "big thing about this blueprint is not the bigness of the estimated cost, but the hope for ultimate relief," but by the end of the summer it too had joined those criticizing the proposed subsidy. The New Brunswick *Daily Home News*, the Passaic *Herald-News*, and other papers expressed similar concern for local interests.[27]

It is more difficult to evaluate the reactions of the New York City and the Bergen press. Public opinion in these areas was generally favorable toward the Page plan. In taking the same position, the New York newspapers and the Bergen *Evening Record* did not have to choose between local sentiment and defense of a regional outlook; the Page proposals appeared to satisfy both interests. Yet one may still question the breadth of the regional perspective which these papers assert to be their

guide. Their editorial pages made no serious effort to analyze
the issues raised in Newark, Jersey City, and Paterson. Praise
for the Page plan as helpful to "the region" was unmixed with
any attempt to consider the complexities of the metropolis and
the differential impact which the proposals might have in its
various local parts.[28]

On the other hand, both major dailies in Newark chose
regionalism over local attitudes on the transit issue. When
Newark business interests attacked the Page Report, the *Evening
News* demanded that negative criticism and the "myriad of
local transit problems" not stand in the way of action on a
crisis that "only a far-sighted, bold program can alleviate." And
while Newark leaders criticized any subsidy to rail, the *Star
Ledger* argued that assessing rail deficits against the benefited
area was a "sound suggestion." [29] In these cases, a readership that
extended into the suburbs of northern New Jersey and a general commitment to a regional perspective prevailed over home-
town sentiment.

PREPARING THE FINAL REPORT

The MRTC had hoped that the region would respond favorably to the Page proposals, and the highly critical tone of many
of the reactions was a distinct disappointment. But the commissioners now had the opportunity to make use of these comments
in shaping their final report: unable to obtain ready acceptance
of the Page plan, they could alter the proposals to overcome
the critics' objections. The question was how far the MRTC
members could depart from the pattern of assumptions and
selective perceptions that had governed their previous efforts.

In theory, the commissioners might have reviewed the region's transportation problems anew. Freed from two years of
indentured service to the Port Authority and armed with a wide
range of public comments, they could have reconsidered the
kinds of transit improvements needed, whether the PNYA

should be excluded, and the possible need for closer rail and road planning. In fact, during the public discussions the MRTC suggested that such a basic review was possible. The Commission had "not yet arrived at any decisions," it announced in a public statement in September. Many proposals, co-chairman O'Mara emphasized in October, were still under consideration.[30]

But organizations are rarely free to engage in basic reassessment of their goals. Past choices and ingrained habits of thought limit the ability of any group to strike out along new lines and direct it, instead, along familiar paths. So it was with the MRTC. Yet, while constraints inherited from the past circumscribed action, the MRTC still had several choices to make. Here differences in goals and perceptions were evident, and a number of compromises were required in deciding final policy.[31]

Constraints on the MRTC. The work of past years limited the MRTC in several ways. It would have been difficult for the agency to avoid proposing that a new rail facility be constructed across the Hudson. Its consultants had concentrated on this question and had reached results that were apparently positive. The MRTC itself had proclaimed its intention of "going all out for the best" and had shown little interest in minimal rail improvements or bus alternatives.[32] These factors provided a thrust and an MRTC perspective that could not easily have been rejected in these few remaining months.

Over the years, the MRTC and its predecessors had been much less concerned with the problem of deteriorating service on existing rail lines than with the need for new facilities. But in view of the current railroad crisis and the Page proposals, the Commission would have found it difficult to turn its back on this problem.

On several other issues facing the MRTC, the reports from the study phase also provided important limitations. These reports had emphasized the probability of large deficits, had placed primary responsibility for absorbing these deficits on the region's taxpayers, and had recommended against any contribution by the PNYA. It would have been difficult to reject these conclusions, particularly since the MRTC had sponsored the surveys and had referred to the importance of these expert studies in the development of its own recommendations.[33] An MRTC proposal that the PNYA contribute, for example, would be attacked as contrary to the conclusions of its own studies, based upon $800,000 worth of research and several years of work. Any MRTC effort to advocate closer coordination of rail and road planning would be even more devoid of support from the studies. And the Commission had neither time nor funds to pursue additional lines of inquiry.

Divergent Perspectives. The development of the MRTC's final recommendations was significantly shaped by these constraints. In addition, public reactions to the Page report and the varied perspectives of individual commissioners affected the outcome. Agreement was readily achieved on several major questions, but bargaining and compromises among the members were required before the final report was completed in late December.[34]

Meeting in October and November, the commissioners soon agreed to recommend creation of a bistate Metropolitan Transit District as the agency which would be responsible for regional action on transit problems.[35] The alternative proposed by some New Jersey critics, assigning full responsibility to the Port Authority, was rejected as politically and financially unfeasible. The commissioners also agreed to request immediate legislation only for the creation of the District. The questions of constructing the loop and absorbing railroad deficits would be deferred for further consideration by the new agency. Here, on a matter of political strategy, the public discussion phase had its most significant impact on the MRTC's work. In the Page report, the

District proposal had been closely linked to the loop and the railroad service program; but as criticism of the latter proposals mounted, it had become clear to the MRTC that the District would have to be cut loose from the other proposals if any legislation were to be obtained in the immediate future. By early autumn the members were generally agreed that the District should be created first and given only the powers to negotiate with other groups and to prepare general and emergency plans. The following year the District governing council could return with a concrete program of action and ask for legislation to permit it to "acquire, construct and operate facilities" and to obtain needed funds.

Finally, the commissioners decided during their early meetings to limit their recommendations to the interstate problem. The need for action was especially pressing here, and the MRTC's interstate studies had been more extensive than its intrastate efforts. In addition, to advance proposals now concerning the transit needs of Westchester, Long Island, or other areas might involve the MRTC in further political conflicts, jeopardizing chances of success for the District proposal. This position ran counter to the views of the agency's Manhattan supporters, who had asked that the total program be made known promptly. But since legislative action was to be limited to the District, which could then prepare proposals for the eastern zone during the following year, it seemed likely that the Manhattan groups would support the Commission's decision.[36]

With these questions decided, several important issues still remained: Should the MRTC take a position in favor of a specific plan for trans-Hudson rail facilities, and if so, which plan? Should it argue in favor of Page's plan to aid existing railroad service, or leave that question to the District? Must deficits be considered inevitable under any transit program, or could the possibility of a self-supporting system be projected? And if there were to be deficits, who would be expected to pay them? On all these questions, significant differences of opinion existed within the MRTC, and several meetings were devoted to resolving these differences.

The commissioners did not divide neatly into two groups on these issues, but there were two different sets of priorities represented. On one side were those who felt that the main job of the MRTC was to find a way to overcome the trans-Hudson barrier. They asked that the final report place primary emphasis on the District and on a specific trans-Hudson rail project. Their preference was Plan 1, the most expensive alternative, but the one offering the greatest advantages in terms of rider appeal and capacity for traffic increases. (Plan 1 required construction of a new subway in Manhattan; Page's choice, Plan 2, would use an existing subway line for the Manhattan leg of the loop. The capital cost of Plan 1 was $500 million; of Plan 2, $345 million.)

It was clear, however, that the loop proposal would face difficult political obstacles if it were part of a broad program carrying a large annual deficit. Those favoring this project offered several suggestions as to how the deficit which would be absorbed locally could be reduced or eliminated. A self-supporting loop could be projected through increased fares and other options discussed or implied in the consultants' reports. The possibility of a deficit-free operation had even been acknowledged publicly by Page as he fended off rising criticism during the summer.[37] Also, railroad losses could be offset by fare increases, and the District need not follow Page's suggestion of absorbing all remaining deficits. Finally, the emphasis on local tax resources to meet any deficits could be reduced by listing several sources of funds, including the states, the federal government, and the Port Authority.

Admittedly, the deficit to be paid by the region could be

reduced only by sacrificing several goals, including those of greatest concern to the railroads and the PNYA. But the proposals for a District and a transit loop would then be more likely to gain public approval.

Other members of the MRTC took a different position. They assigned highest priority to the problems of maintaining existing railroad services and protecting the financial health of the railroads and the Port Authority. The District, tapping local tax funds to support essential rail commutation, could effectively meet these needs. These members therefore favored an emphasis in the report on the District's role in meeting the railroad crisis. They also tended to oppose several recommendations put forward by the first group of commissioners: They preferred that the final report avoid explicit support for Plan 1 or any specific loop project. Such a dramatic proposal might be highlighted by the press, and criticism directed toward it would harm chances for approval of the District bill. They also objected to any suggestion in the final report that a deficit-free program might be attainable. Such a position would run counter to the consultants' conclusions as well as experience in other regions and would be subject to attack as unrealistic. Furthermore, a District that gave high priority to achieving self-sufficiency would be inclined to leave much of the current passenger deficit in the hands of the railroads, and it was argued that the public should expect to assume responsibility for absorbing these losses. In addition, any mention of a self-supporting program would increase the demand for PNYA action, and this was objectionable to those MRTC members who opposed burdening the Authority with rail problems.

These issues were discussed at several MRTC meetings in November and December, and in late December a final draft of the report was at last completed and accepted by the Commissioners.

A Program of Action. The making of military strategy
involves a process of negotiation among spokesmen for conflicting military interests; the resulting policy statements must
frequently be vague and ambiguous in order to obtain acceptance by all committee members.[38] The MRTC final report was
marked by these same characteristics.

The report recommended the creation of a Metropolitan
Transit District "as a first step and a base for the general program." New York City and twelve counties of the region west
of the Hudson would be included, and the District council
would be selected by the governing bodies of the participating
counties. Once established, the agency would review the recommendations of the MRTC and other groups, and prepare specific plans for construction or other operations. The District
could not carry out any such plans, however, until specific proposals were authorized by concurrent legislation of both states.[39]

The MRTC also proposed construction of a trans-Hudson
rail system, but it was ambivalent as to the specific plan. At one
point the report stated that "Plan 1 serves best as a base" for
meeting the region's needs; but elsewhere Plan 2 appeared to be
preferred, and the reader was also reminded that many other
proposals were available to the District "for consideration in
whole or in part." Thus the report presented the range of view-
points found among the MRTC members.[40]

The problem of maintaining and improving existing rail
services was treated even more hesitantly. No mention of this
question was included in the letter of transmittal, where the
District and loop proposals were first outlined. Several references to the issue in the body of the report were ambivalent as
to whether the District was expected to act in this area. Yet at
other points the report sounded a note of alarm:

The urgent nature of the problem is found in the pending requests
. . . for permission to cut back on service or to abandon lines entirely. Of particular concern is the plight of the Hudson and Man-

hattan Railroad. . . . It is problematical how long it can continue service without public financial assistance. The Commission stresses the need for prompt attention to this problem.

Thus, the MRTC phrased its views so as to satisfy both those who felt that little if any action should be taken by the District in this area and those who believed that this should be the primary concern of the new agency.[41]

By emphasizing that final decisions on the loop and the rail-service issue would be left to the District, the MRTC had tried to allay criticism of its work, but it then made a series of decisions which were likely to have the opposite effect. First, the MRTC decided to hold open no possibility of a self-supporting District program. This position was generally accepted once the members had agreed to propose Plan 1, with its higher scale of probable deficits. Having stated that a deficit was inevitable, the commissioners then felt impelled to answer the question of how the District would meet such losses. Extensive federal or state aid, they agreed, could not be expected. The possibility of a Port Authority contribution was debated at some length, but it was finally decided (on a split vote) to exclude any reference to the PNYA from the report. Only local tax funds remained, and the final report concluded, as had Page, that the "best method of providing the necessary subsidy" was support by the "benefited areas." [42]

With other sources of financing eliminated, the District and local tax support were inevitably intertwined. "These areas," Page had said, "should be represented in the determination of how their funds will be spent. To afford this representation the new metropolitan district would be created." The MRTC concurred, and carried this rationale into the draft legislation for the agency. The two states were asked to "find and declare" that the District "could not provide such [transit] facilities in this area without an income deficit" and that the agency would "employ the fiscal resources of the region for such public support as may be voted by local representatives." [43] Thus, the District, apparently rendered politically innocuous by the exclusion of powers to undertake costly projects, was still of considerable political consequence. At a minimum, the District bill would provide a clear legislative commitment to the principle of local tax support for regional transit facilities.

On January 6, 1958, the MRTC released its report and called for immediate steps to carry out its recommendations. This is a "guidepost for direction," the Commission declared, "the moment for action is now." [44] As a guide to action, however, the report had several important weaknesses.

First, as previously noted, ambiguity pervaded the document. This result was typical of the work of study commissions, "policy-making" committees, and other groups which do not face the immediate task of implementing their recommendations. When the responsibility for action is lacking, higher priority is likely to be given to satisfying all factions through logrolling and vague phrasing than to making hard choices among concrete alternatives.[45]

The multiple recommendations which this committee process produced also conflicted with the goal of political feasibility. A $500-million loop project with substantial deficits, a railroad service program with losses that might reach several million a year, and taxpayer support of the entire program—when combined, these presented a large target for the MRTC's critics. Had the MRTC been able to focus its report on the priorities of only one group—those favoring the loop, or those preferring action on rail service—its efforts would have been less vulnerable to attack during the ensuing months.

The hope for acceptance of the District plan lay in persuading the region and the state legislatures that this proposal could be divorced from the other MRTC recommendations and that the District itself was a worthy goal. But it was uncertain whether the MRTC could convince the critics on these points. Because the District and other proposals had been closely joined in the Page report and in the final report, the MRTC would spend much of the next year trying to convince the public that the attempted separation was meaningful. Even if this point were won, however, acceptance of the District was not assured. Municipal-commuter groups in several New Jersey counties had called for PNYA action instead of a new agency, a Newark spokesman had opposed any agency with potential access to tax resources, and Mayor Wagner had been reluctant to endorse the District. The MRTC's own assessment—that there was "practically unanimous" regional support for the District—reflected less the reality of the situation than the tendency of organizations to filter out perceptions that are discordant with the accepted frame of reference.[46]

There was one factor, however, which would be of great benefit to those favoring the District scheme. Debate on the Page plan had taken place almost entirely within the New York region. With publication of the final report, responsibility for action now devolved upon the two state legislatures and the governors. Consequently, the fate of the District bill would depend not on majority sentiment within the region but on alliances fashioned between metropolitan and outstate officials at Albany and Trenton. This was the environment in which the MRTC and the PNYA fought for the creation of the District and nearly succeeded, before going down to defeat in the winter of 1958.

CHAPTER VIII

A Regional Transit Agency?

In the absence of political institutions organized on a regional basis, the contest over regional policy must be resolved in whatever substitute arena is available. Because of its legal powers and geographic scope, the state capital frequently serves as that arena. This was the situation facing the proposals of the MRTC in January, 1958. After several years of intraregional policy development and debate, the MRTC, its allies, and its opponents would now appeal for a decision on regional transport policy to the lawmakers at Albany and Trenton.

In New York and New Jersey, as in most states, state action on metropolitan problems is shaped significantly by those not accountable to the regional electorate. Thus, at Albany a majority of legislators in both houses represented areas not included in the proposed Transit District. In New Jersey, representatives from the ten District counties held a majority in the Assembly but they were outnumbered in the Senate, where rural regions were overrepresented by a one-senator-per-county formula.

The nature of rural dominance in state legislatures and its impact on metropolitan interests have been the subject of a number of studies. Normally, the analysis has been framed in terms of rural-urban or metropolitan-outstate conflict. In order to understand legislative behavior on some issues involving a large metropolitan area, it may be more useful to view the legislature as divided into three geographic groupings—rural, suburban, and urban. The making of policy on a metropolitan problem is then likely to involve alliances along party lines, with urban Democrats ranged against suburban and rural Republicans.[1] The difficulties of establishing firm policy are increased when the relative influence of the rural, suburban, and urban components varies in different legislative houses and when the Governor is of a different party affiliation from that dominating one or both houses of the legislature. All these factors affected the efforts of the states to resolve the New York region's transportation problems in 1958 and in subsequent years.

Although the shift of focus from the region to the state capitals brought these additional factors into play, there were several continuing themes. Almost all the interests involved in the state arena viewed regional problems primarily in terms of their own self-interest, narrowly conceived. Consequently, each sought a solution which would minimize costs and maximize benefits, as measured from this vantage point. Most local officials objected to the Transit District bill with its implication of local funds and responsibility and supported a counterproposal that would assign the job to the Port Authority. Even the Metropolitan Regional Council, which had been founded to promote coordinated action on regional problems, was unable to develop a consensus in favor of a concrete, positive role for its membership. Similarly, the PNYA opposed the bill which would designate it as the responsible agency and urged that a Transit District be created. The railroads objected to absorbing passenger deficits and called for action by a new District, by the Port Authority, or by both. State legislators from the District area generally joined with local officials from their counties in opposing the new agency. The governors, and legislators from outside the District, were reluctant to propose that the state take action and, viewing the District as a way to shift the burdens of finding and paying for a solution to the region, favored that approach.

In addition, past traditions of governmental policy on the

rail issue and interstate jealousies affected the development of policy at the state capitals, as they had during the intraregional debate.

In brief, the events of 1958 were these: The District bill was supported in New York State by Manhattan business interests and Republican legislators from the city. In the absence of contrary pressures, it was passed by the state legislature at Albany in March. Belated objections from the city administration did not prevent Governor Harriman from signing the bill a few weeks later. In New Jersey, the MRTC proposal faced growing criticism during the spring, but an alliance of regional and outstate legislators finally secured Senate approval in June. Now the New Jersey Assembly became the center of attention; of the four legislative bodies to consider the measure, only the Assembly—with majority representation from the District area—was responsive to the widespread local forces opposed to the MRTC measure. The opposition developed a counterstrategy, a bill to require Port Authority action. The battle between these two factions was fought through the fall and winter of 1958. By December, both bills had been lost, and the effort to resolve the transit problem through a single regional institution was at an end.

The outcome of the 1958 legislative battle was twofold: First, it indicated that several proposed solutions to the region's transport problems were not politically acceptable. Second, it suggested that feasible policy goals could not easily be identified or carried out through intraregional efforts nor through cooperative bistate action. As a result of these largely negative findings, leadership in solving the region's transit problems would devolve in future years upon state officials, acting primarily on a state-by-state basis rather than in a regional framework.

NEW YORK STATE APPROVES THE DISTRICT BILL

The District proposal had met with generally favorable reactions in the New York sector of the region during the autumn of 1957, and the same response greeted MRTC support of the scheme in its final report of January, 1958. A number of major business and civic organizations in Manhattan endorsed the District plan, and they were joined by several city newspapers and by spokesmen for the commuting suburbs of Rockland and Orange Counties. In late January, bills to carry out the proposal were introduced in the state legislature by two Manhattan Republicans, Assemblyman John Robert Brook, a law partner of Charles Tuttle, and Senator MacNeil Mitchell.[2] These proponents of the District accepted the implication of local tax support contained in the bill, for it was consistent with established state and city policies toward the Long Island Rail Road and the city's transit operations. In addition, those favoring the District anticipated substantial economic benefits to the central business area if the District were to finance improved trans-Hudson service.[3]

Spokesmen for these regional interests were joined by the railroads and the PNYA, which met with friendly legislators in order to win support for the District plan. Only the union locals of the H&M dissented. Fearing that the Transit District might accept Page's proposal that part of the H&M be abandoned, they mounted a limited campaign against the bill. New York City officials, their attention directed primarily toward the city's own transit problems, took no position during the early months of 1958. Representatives of the eastern zone of the region—Long Island, Westchester, and Fairfield County, Connecticut—finding their localities not directly involved, generally remained silent during this period.[4]

If the Albany legislature were primarily responsive to New York City political leadership when city interests were directly involved, the legislative leaders at Albany might have delayed in bringing the District bill to a vote until city officials had decided upon a course of action. But the state legislature was not highly sensitive to city interests. Although New York City contained more than half the state population, its legislators were in the minority in both houses (25 of 58 in the state Senate and 65 of 150 in the Assembly were from the city). Moreover, the city delegation was predominantly Democratic, while a combination of suburban and upstate Republicans controlled both houses.[5] In this situation, several factors favored the District bill in spite of the lack of city support. The interests in the city with access to the Republican leadership—spokesmen for business and the Port Authority, and the small contingent of Republican legislators from New York City—supported the bill. Also, the measure would shift responsibility for solving the complex transit problem and financing a solution from state to local officials, while leaving the state with a veto power over District plans. In addition, the bill was consistent with previous state efforts assisting rail services. Finally, prompt action on the bill was facilitated by the traditional tendency of the New York legislature to complete its work by March or April of each year. It was not surprising, therefore, that the Republican leaders in both houses were ready to bring the bill to a vote by mid-March and that they expected it to be passed without difficulty.

At this point, a series of events dramatized the need for action. On March 12, the New York Public Service Commission authorized the New York Central to discontinue passenger service on its little-used Putnam Division, which served about 500 passengers a day in Westchester and Putnam Counties. During the same week, the New York Central was granted a 7 percent increase in commuter fares on its other Westchester divisions, the Long Island Rail Road announced a 6 percent fare rise, and the president of the Central of New Jersey announced that on the basis of present trends his line would soon be in bankruptcy. "Commutation is getting worse," lamented the *Herald Tribune* on March 18. Soon "passenger trains will simply give up the ghost." The *Herald Tribune* called for immediate passage of the Transit District bill. "It is only a beginning, but at least this is action. And action is what the commuters must have." [6]

The following day the New York State Assembly endorsed the District legislation unanimously, and five days later the Senate ratified the bill 50–3. The only dissenting votes were from upstate. Lacking guidance from City Hall, the city's Democratic delegation joined the Republicans in voting for the bill.

Belatedly, with the measure on the Governor's desk, the city decided to oppose the District plan in its present form. In a memorandum released in late April, Mayor Wagner expressed the fear that the bill would foreclose state financial assistance for regional transit, placing the entire burden on local taxpayers. He also argued that any new agency should include the eastern zone of the region.[7] Governor Harriman rejected the plea of his fellow Democrat, and signed the bill on April 24, 1958. He was not attracted to the purely negative action of a veto and, having relied on the MRTC for guidance during the past three years, had no available alternative to offer. Also, the advantages of shifting responsibility for finding and financing a solution away from Albany were not lost at the Governor's office. In a message accompanying his approval of the District bill, Harriman noted that the measure had the support of many business associations, the Port Authority, and the railroads, and that it could later be expanded to include the eastern part of the region. "I do not believe we should wait for another year," he concluded, "to get started on the practical task of assuring continued and improved transportation . . . between New York and New Jersey." [8]

NEW JERSEY DEBATES ALTERNATIVE
TRANSPORT POLICIES

The situation confronting the Transit District bill in New Jersey was very different from that in New York. In the Empire State, only the central city and two suburban counties would be part of the District. The New Jersey sector, however, included ten counties with several large cities and adjoining suburban areas; here were found a greater range of perspectives of the region than in New York and a greater diversity of views on the need for various rail improvements. Throughout most of northern New Jersey, the Page report had proved to be a catalyst which precipitated vigorous opposition. Much of the criticism was directed toward Page's physical and financial recommendations, however, and the MRTC hoped that by limiting its legislative proposal to the District it would obtain a more favorable response. Such a shift in attitude was of critical importance, for in contrast to New York, legislators from the District counties held a majority of votes in the New Jersey Assembly and almost half in the Senate.

The MRTC's strategy was essentially unsuccessful. A few groups which had initially been critical of the Page report regarded the District as a potentially useful institution, and these interests joined the MRTC camp in 1958. But the continuing debate also gave the opposition time to expand; and while the direct threat of the District legislation was less than that contained in the broader Page program, the narrow perspectives of regional interests and their wariness of future entanglements made the attacks of 1958 as vehement and nearly as broadly based as before.

Support for the Transit District proposal was concentrated in Bergen County, where Arthur Page's recommendations had also been widely hailed. Soon after the release of the MRTC report, the Bergen *Evening Record* announced that it favored creation of the District. Other local newspapers and the County's commuter organizations expressed similar views during the winter and spring. Bergen's state senator, Walter H. Jones, introduced a bill in late January to carry out the MRTC proposal. Outside of Bergen County, the Newark *News* and the Bayonne *Times*, which had been generally favorable toward the

Page report, also supported the District. A few spokesmen who had criticized the Page plan were won over to the District—for example, the Passaic Valley Citizens Planning Association and the Passaic *Herald-News*. To these groups and the Bergen interests, the new agency was viewed as a badly needed mechanism for obtaining organized regional action; the District might, they felt, accept or reject the loop and the local subsidy provisions of the Page plan.[9]

Hostility to the Transit District scheme was concentrated in those areas which had been most vigorous in their opposition to the Page plan: in the areas represented by the IMGBRS and in other central New Jersey suburbs, throughout Hudson County, and in other industrial and commercial centers in northern New Jersey. These critics attacked the District bill from a wide range of perspectives.

A number of spokesmen expressed the fear that passage of the bill would entail definite acceptance of the loop and railroad-service proposals, and local financing of these projects. This concern, sparked by the close relationship between the proposals in the Page report and the MRTC report, was heightened by the efforts of several groups which sought to defeat the District. An especially effective tactic in expanding the opposition to the bill was a booklet issued by the New Jersey Motor Bus Association, whose North Jersey members feared the impact of the Transit Commission's program on private bus service in the region. The association asserted that the District, if created, "will recommend the construction of a rapid transit system at a cost of over $500,000,000" with a deficit of "over $12,000,000 per year." It then set forth the county-by-county allocation of a $12-million deficit, based on the Page formula, and itemized the percentage of the deficit payable by each town.[10] The pamphlet was distributed to all municipal, county, and legislative officials in the North Jersey area in February, and it led to a spate of newspaper editorials and statements by local officials opposing the District legislation and its "mandatory" charges on the counties.[11]

The MRTC and its supporters were kept busy answering these attacks, and although they were largely successful in convincing close observers of the transit problem that the District bill did not enact all the proposals of the Page report, numerous groups in the region continued at the end of the year to view the two as inseparable.[12]

Other objections to the Transit District legislation withstood a close reading of the bill itself and were less readily countered by the MRTC. The issue of local financing received the most attention. Public officials and business spokesmen noted that the bill called for the use of "the fiscal resources of the region" to meet the transit problem. In addition, the MRTC report had concluded that substantial assistance could not be expected from any other sources. Could the new District reject these conclusions and develop an alternative financial plan? The local spokesmen doubted it, especially since the District would have limited study funds and would have to act quickly to meet the current rail crisis.

Similarly, a number of local groups argued that the District would find it necessary to adopt a physical plan much like those preferred in the Page report and the final report. Mayor William Dill of Montclair expressed a widespread concern:

The District council is only going to have $300,000 and how rapidly is it going to have to act. . . . Is it not going to . . . necessarily have to come up with an operable plan that will embody many of the aspects of the Page report and probably the financing scheme of the Page report?

"One of the things that scares the elected officials," explained Nutley's mayor, "is this Page report and the shadow that it has put on the whole complexion." [13]

A further issue raised by local spokesmen concerned the representational features of the bill. The debate on this question emphasized several conflicts that affect regional policy development—interstate hostility, metropolitan versus outstate, city versus county, antagonisms among regional organizations, and conflict between rail and road interests. Several critics, for example, expressed concern that New York representatives on the District council could obligate the North Jersey region to pay for extensive rail improvements without the consent of such large counties as Essex and Hudson. They pointed out that under the bill decisions would be made by straight majority vote and New York City itself would have a near majority of the thirty-two seats. "I am fearful," one Essex township committeeman explained, that the District's plan "may represent the thinking of 14 New York [City] members plus the thinking of certain members of New Jersey counties." [14]

To counter this criticism, supporters of the District bill pointed out that New Jersey's interests would also be safeguarded by the state legislature, which would have to ratify any plan approved by the District council. But a number of elected officials from the region were skeptical of the protection that this would provide. The state Senate, with a majority of its members from outside the District area, was the main object of attack. "Too often . . . ," said Essex freeholder Ralph Jacobson, "the taxpayers of Essex County are sold down the river. . . . We don't have adequate equal representation in the Senate . . . and our wishes are frequently not respected." [15]

The Metropolitan Regional Council raised two additional issues concerning representation. The MRC asked that the agency be tristate from the beginning, so that funds would be committed and plans carried out only after the needs of the entire region had been considered. It also objected to the selection of District council members by county officials. "Several cities indicate they object strongly to county domination over transit," the MRC explained, in arguing that further study should be made of ways to give cities a more direct role. A few members of the Council suggested that the Transit District be made responsible to the MRC itself.

A final criticism of the District legislation concerned the problem of rail-highway coordination. The District bill would establish as the policy of the two states the position that the planning and financing of mass transit and vehicular facilities should be handled separately. The MRC critics resurrected the debate of earlier years by asking that further consideration be given to pooling all transportation revenues and to integrated rail and highway planning in the region.[16]

Many of the critics focused only on weaknesses in the Transit District approach. But a number of commuter-area spokesmen, recognizing a need for an alternative solution, argued that the Port Authority should take action. During the Transit Commission studies and the 1957 debate on the Page proposals, the PNYA had largely been able to avoid criticism of its hands-off attitude toward rail transit. But in 1958, with the MRTC proposals under attack, the Authority became the most prominent alternative "solution" to the problem. The campaign to involve the PNYA was begun by Hudson County Democratic Assemblyman William V. Musto. In late January, 1958, he introduced Assembly Bill 16, which would direct the Port Authority to "develop, improve and coordinate" rail passenger facilities in the New York region. Within the next few weeks, the IMGBRS and other municipal-commuter groups in northern New Jersey reaffirmed their belief that the PNYA should take responsibility, and endorsed A-16. During the spring, county officials in Middlesex, Passaic, and Hudson announced that they favored this bill. The Port Authority bill won support as a way to avoid local financing and as a partial solution to the problem of rail-highway planning. The position of these elected officials had broader implications too: faced with a choice between a regional agency (the District) that would combine a large measure of popular regional control with local fiscal accountability and another (the PNYA) which would involve neither, they chose the latter. As Wood characterizes the phenomenon, they preferred to take "regional government out of regional politics in the customary sense of the word" in order to avoid financial responsibility.[17]

By the end of April, the New Jersey sector was essentially divided into two *ad hoc* coalitions: a minority, led by Bergen County interests, favored creation of the Transit District—an approach now approved in New York State—but the dominant sentiment was opposed to that bill and had largely coalesced around A-16.

REGIONAL PROBLEMS IN THE STATE ARENA

If transit policy could have been decided by an assembly of elected officials in the New Jersey sector of the region, the District bill would have been rejected, and perhaps A-16 would have been adopted. In the absence of regional institutions, however, the fate of the competing philosophies underlying the two bills was determined by state officials—some elected from the New York region, others from outstate areas. At Trenton, as at Albany, state action depended on four factors: the kinds of regional interests affected; the representation given these interests at the state capital; alliances formed between regional and outstate legislators; and the tradition of previous state action on the particular policy issue.

In New York State, the range of interests directly affected by the District proposal was relatively narrow—one central area, Manhattan, and two commuting counties oriented toward it. In addition, those groups from the region most favorable toward the plan were also those with the best access to the Republican leadership of both houses; and the opposition forces were mobilized only belatedly.

In New Jersey, however, the interests involved were far more diverse. The District would have embraced Manhattan-oriented suburbs faced with imminent loss of rail services (especially in Bergen), Manhattan-oriented suburbs in central New Jersey, where loss of important services was not likely in the near future, and such major employment centers as Hudson County and Newark, where opposition to the MRTC's perspective of the region was widespread. Moreover, all these diverse interests were effectively represented at Trenton. Legislators from the District area held a majority of Assembly seats and 10 of 21 places in the state Senate. In addition, different political parties controlled the two houses: Senate control was in the hands of an alliance of suburban and rural Republicans, while Democratic urban centers held sway in the lower house.

To bring these diversities of party and geography to bear on a specific bill, another element was needed—alert spokesmen who could point out the advantages or weaknesses of the proposal and thus generate active support or opposition within the legislature. In Trenton as in Albany, those favoring the District bill were active from the beginning of the year. But, in marked contrast to New York, opposition forces in New Jersey were also quickly activated—by the IMGBRS, the Motor Bus Association, Hudson County spokesmen, and others. Traditional hostility toward three symbols—railroads, Manhattan, and the Port Authority—made New Jersey legislators especially receptive to these attacks. As a result, those opposed to the District plan, although largely excluded from the MRTC and New York State deliberations, wielded considerable influence in Trenton.

These competing forces contended for support at Trenton throughout 1958. The first victory went to the District plan. With legislative action still pending, Governor Meyner announced his support for the District bill in mid-April. Several factors motivated his decision. In spite of the continuing deterioration of rail service during the 1950s, Meyner had not yet felt compelled to take direct responsibility for seeking a feasible solution. The District bill now offered a double advantage. It was a route to action, and Meyner had no positive alternative to offer. Moreover, the District plan would largely place the burden of responsibility for the complex transit problem upon a new regional agency, siphoning off the growing pressure for gubernatorial leadership. Here the motivations of the Governor and the Port Authority coincided. Confronted by a regional problem that promised many headaches and few rewards, both favored the creation of a new regional institution—an agency with sufficient powers to meet the burden of rail transportation, yet so limited that it would not infringe upon the traditional prerogatives of the PNYA and the state government in shaping the development of highway transportation in the region.[18]

The Senate proved to be more recalcitrant than the Governor, but in early June it too was won over to the District plan. An alliance of metropolitan and outstate legislators, primarily along party lines, provided most of the favorable votes; and the Governor and the Port Authority contributed their efforts in order to obtain the deciding tally.

The New Jersey Senate had long provided one of the most extreme illustrations of representation by acreage rather than population. Until 1965, under the State constitution, each of the twenty-one counties elected one senator. As a consequence, Essex, the largest county, with a population of more than a million, and Cape May, with less than 50,000, were equally represented. The ten counties in the proposed Transit District had about four-fifths of the state's population but only ten of twenty-one votes in the Senate.[19]

State legislators do not necessarily divide into alliances of metropolitan versus outstate representatives, however. On any policy issue confronting an urban region, metropolitan legislators are likely to be sharply divided among themselves; and

where the issue is of little direct importance to the rest of the
state, the legislative division is likely to reflect the particular
intraregional conflict, extended by the ability of each metropolitan faction to obtain outstate support—especially along
party lines.[20] These were the patterns of behavior that determined
Senate action on the transit issue in 1958.

Soon after the MRTC report was released, Senator Jones of
Bergen County endorsed the District plan and introduced a
bill (S-50) to carry out the Commission recommendation.[21] His
views carried great weight with other Republican members of
the upper house, especially when their own counties were not
directly affected, for Bergen was the state's largest Republican
county and its pluralities were important in statewide electoral
contests. By mid-February Jones had lined up support for his
bill from seven of the eight Republican senators from counties
outside the District region. In addition, the Republican senators
from two District counties, Monmouth and Somerset (both
suburban counties with a substantial number of commuters
and little organized opposition) agreed to support the bill.

Ten Republican senators were now willing to vote for S-50,
but the decisive eleventh vote would not be easily obtained. In
the face of strong constituency opposition to S-50, Republican
senators from two regional counties, Union and Morris, refused
to support the bill; and they were able to persuade the thir-
teenth Republican senator, Wayne Dumont of outstate Warren,
to join them.[22] Nor would the eight-man Democratic contingent
support Senator Jones. All five Democratic senators from the
region—representing Essex, Hudson, Mercer, Middlesex, and
Passaic—either actively opposed the District bill or were unwilling to vote until further discussion clarified the implications
of the measure. Their three Democratic colleagues from outside
the region supported them.

In sum, the situation confronting the District bill in February was that shown in Table 1.

TABLE 1

	For S-50	Unwilling to support S-50
From the District:	3	7
Republicans	3	2
Democrats	0	5
Outside the District:	7	4
Republicans	7	1
Democrats	0	3
Total	10 (all Republicans)	11 (8 Democrats, 3 Republicans)

During the spring, opposition within the region became more vociferous, and as of late April Jones was still unable to obtain the eleventh vote. Governor Meyner then sought the needed tally. With the legislature due to meet on April 22, Meyner urged the Democratic senators from Camden and Salem, both outside the District area, to cast their votes for the Jones bill. They were willing to consider supporting the measure; but after talking with their northern colleagues and finding them still opposed, they told Meyner and Jones they could not vote for the bill. Senators Donal C. Fox (Essex) and William F. Kelly, Sr. (Hudson), were irate at Meyner's maneuver. Fox commented,

The governor has a right to his opinion but he owes to the senators, particularly the Democratic senators from the state's two biggest counties, the decency and courtesy of discussing the matter before he acts. We have never received a word from him on this move, yet he certainly must have known our sentiments.[23]

As Governor Meyner's failure in this case illustrates, the party alliance within the legislature is frequently stronger than the ties that join legislators to their own party's governor.[24] Even stronger than the legislative party in this case was the county party, for in New Jersey the county is the basic unit of political organization. Here, the Port Authority had a strategic advantage, since one PNYA commissioner, Thorn Lord, served also as

Democratic county chairman of Mercer County. During the first months of the legislative campaign, the PNYA had largely avoided an active role, but with the District bill stalled, the Authority's officials decided to lend assistance. The importance of the bill was discussed with Lord, and he agreed to talk with Mercer's Democratic state senator, Sido L. Ridolfi, who had thus far opposed the District.

On June 16, the Senate held its last meeting of the spring session. After an hour's debate, the transit bill was moved for passage and approved 11–7. Ten of the votes were provided by Republicans, with seven of them from counties outside the District. The deciding vote was cast by Ridolfi. Where Governor Meyner had failed, the Port Authority succeeded.

The final distribution of Senate votes is shown in Table 2.

TABLE 2

	For S-50	Against S-50	Abstentions
From the District:	4	6	0
Republicans	3	2	
Democrats	1	4	
Outside the District:	7	1	3
Republicans	7	1	0
Democrats	0	0	3
Total	11	7	3

The Transit District bill now faced only one major hurdle, ratification by the New Jersey Assembly. But here the measure would have its most serious test, for the New Jersey portion of the region and its most populous subdivisions were far better represented in the Assembly than in the Senate. The region commanded only 10 of 21 votes in the upper house, but 46 of 60 in the Assembly; and while the six counties in the region opposed to the District could muster only six votes in the New Jersey Senate, they held 34 of 60 Assembly seats.

The difficulties facing the District measure were amplified by the existence of a concrete legislative alternative, Musto's Assembly bill 16. A-16, which would assign responsibility for meeting the region's rail problem to the PNYA, had won considerable support in central New Jersey and in Hudson County. Members of the Assembly responded to local sentiment by pressing for approval of the bill. As a result, the New Jersey Assembly provided the only real forum for joining the issue between the Transit District and the Musto bills and for exploring the contrasting philosophies of transportation policy which shaped these two measures.

The campaign for Assembly action was cast against a backdrop of increasing urgency, for in the summer of 1958, the railroads succeeded in removing some of the shackles of state regulatory control. The rail carriers had long recognized that state commissions were less responsive than the ICC to railroad pleas to curtail service and increase fares on deficit-producing passenger lines. For several years they had urged Congress to increase ICC responsibility for acting upon railroad requests in these areas. The 1957–58 recession gave added impetus to the rail carriers' pleas, and in July Congress approved the Transportation Act of 1958, which enhanced ICC control at the expense of the states. President Eisenhower signed the bill on August 12.[25] Within two days, the New York Central and the Erie moved to eliminate their trans-Hudson ferry services, and during the fall several railroads threatened to curtail or abandon passenger services if public subsidies were not soon provided.[26]

These developments underscored the need for positive state and local action to meet the transit problem, but they did not overcome the sharp division of opinion in the Assembly over which approach—the District or Musto's PNYA plan—should be adopted. Support for the Musto bill was especially strong in the Assembly's Committee on Federal and Interstate Relations, to which the bill had been assigned. Committee members realized that the measure stood no chance of Assembly approval, however, unless a sound case for turning the transit problem over to the Port Authority were first developed. The Committee therefore employed S. J. Flink, professor of economics at Rutgers University, to evaluate the case for PNYA action.

In three reports, submitted to the Committee in May, September, and November, Flink asserted that "the Port Authority is the logical agency to assume this responsibility and that it is in a financial position to do so." It was essential, Flink argued, to coordinate the planning and development of rail and road facilities in the region; and giving rail responsibilities to the Port Authority would facilitate such coordination. Moreover, PNYA action was viewed by Flink as financially feasible. The annual deficit from the transit program might be reduced to $6 million or less by selecting a less expensive plan than that favored by the MRTC, by increasing the fare structure, and by undertaking other economies. The PNYA would be able to absorb most or all of a $6-million deficit out of excess revenues from other projects, and if necessary it might increase automobile, bus, and truck tolls to meet these losses. Should the deficit exceed available PNYA revenues, Flink argued, state and federal subsidies could be given directly to the Authority.[27]

While the Assembly committee considered Flink's arguments in support of A-16, the alliance favoring the District and opposed to the Musto bill also sought legislative support. Each member of this group—the MRTC, the PNYA, other elements of the rail and highway coalitions, and Governor Meyner—approached the problem with a distinct set of priorities but found itself loosely joined with the others in a temporary marriage of convenience.

The Transit Commission opened its final campaign in September, urging that the Assembly take immediate action on the District bill. The MRTC now sought to convince its critics that the bill involved only a minimal policy commitment. During the fall, the Commission agreed to the suggestion that the

Assembly adopt a resolution, stating that no District plan calling for financing through local tax resources would be acceptable. At a final Assembly hearing in November, co-chairman Tuttle disregarded the interests of the MRTC's financial benefactor and expressed the view that the District might negotiate with the Port Authority for funds to meet any deficits. The Commission also denied that the bill committed the new agency to any specific physical plan. "The District . . . can formulate and recommend any physical plan whatever, or no plan at all," the MRTC asserted in pleading for Assembly approval.[28]

The Port Authority joined the debate on the Transit District and the Musto plans during the summer of 1958. For a year after the release of the Page Report, the PNYA had avoided taking part in the public discussion of transit policy and had hoped that the District scheme would be adopted. But with the MRTC bill now blocked in the Assembly and support for Musto's A-16 growing, the Authority broke its silence. The District measure was a "sound proposal" for meeting the transit crisis and should be enacted, Tobin and his colleagues argued before the legislators in Trenton. The Musto bill, on the other hand, would have "disastrous consequences" and must be rejected.

The Authority's position on A-16 contrasted sharply with that of Assembly consultant Flink and illustrated both the general perspective of those who supported a highway-dominant system in the region and the specific strategies used to defend continued autonomy for the Port Authority. Flink had argued that closer coordination between rail and highway planning was needed in the New York region and that such coordination would be facilitated by assigning rail duties to the PNYA. Tobin challenged the rail-oriented reasoning underlying the argument; there was no need for such coordination, he maintained, for integrated planning would not significantly increase rail patronage or take motor vehicles off the road.[29]

The PNYA also argued that it could not possibly meet rail

deficits out of its own limited income. Here the Port Authority employed a tactic that it hoped would keep it entirely free from rail. It avoided the question of whether it might contribute funds to meet some rail losses and instead discussed the inability of the Authority to meet all rail deficits in the region. MRTC consultants had estimated the New Jersey railroad deficit for 1955–56 at $13 million. By 1958, the PNYA calculated this had reached an annual loss of $20 million. "But that's just the New Jersey segment," Austin Tobin commented. The New York City subways, he noted, run at a yearly deficit of over $100 million, the Staten Island ferry at $6 million, and "then . . . you have the deficits of the Central, the New Haven, the Long Island and the Staten Island Railroads." Even without new construction, the total was close to $150 million, and Tobin argued that it was "awfully clear that the Port Authority couldn't assume one little part of this . . . without assuming it all."

In comparison with the immense, indivisible bulk of the region's rail deficits, the PNYA's available resources were viewed as small indeed. In fact, Tobin and the commissioners argued that almost all of the Authority's future net earnings through 1964 were contractually committed to vehicular, airport, and other improvements; not enough excess funds would be available to meet even the deficits of the New Jersey railroads. As to the suggestion that PNYA bridge and tunnel tolls be increased to provide the needed funds, Tobin pointed out that an increase from 50 to 75 cents would be required merely to meet the New Jersey losses, and he helpfully proposed to the legislators that they "leave that suggestion . . . to the automobile associations and the four million of your people who own motor cars and would be asked to pay that."

Finally, the PNYA turned to the proposal that a subsidy be given to the Authority to help meet rail deficits. The "essence" of the PNYA, Tobin argued, "has been its long tradition of non-political corporate management guided by sound business principles." A subsidy would require that the Authority be subject to the same controls as a regular government department, "and with that, what the Port Authority has or could accomplish in the future is gone." To bolster its arguments against assuming rail responsibilities, the PNYA cited the views of spokesmen for the financial community, who asserted that it was "most essential" that the PNYA be "completely free of any responsibility whatsoever" for rail transit, in order to maintain the confidence of investors in Port Authority bonds.

The efforts of PNYA leaders to extricate the Authority from the rail problem extended through the summer and fall of 1958. At a final hearing in November, Tobin made a last plea for the defeat of the Musto bill and for creation of a Transit District. Asked what the future role of the PNYA in rail transit should be, Tobin yielded to optimism and expressed a view he would soon retract:

I think the Port Authority has done everything that it can to help try to find a solution. . . . Thirty years of hard costly studies on this problem. . . . I think that we have, Mr. Chairman, contributed everything that an agency could contribute and we have nothing more to contribute to this problem.[30]

In their campaign to obtain passage of the Transit District bill and to defeat A-16, the PNYA and the MRTC were able to marshal some support from other members of the rail and highway coalitions. Because of a wide range of perspectives on the bills, however, the resulting alliance was a weak and partially conflicting one. Thus, several railroads and Bergen-area commuter associations favored enactment of the District bill. But the rail carriers divided their energies, advocating also that the Port Authority take over operation of the railroad's trans-Hudson ferries until the District scheme or another long-range solution was accepted.[31] Other groups joined the PNYA in opposing A-16, but they divided sharply on the Transit District proposal. Spokesmen for some automobile associations appeared willing to acquiesce in a District or a similar scheme to tax the benefited area; at least, it was viewed as a lesser evil than asking the motorists to subsidize rail transit. The New Jersey Motor Bus Association agreed with the PNYA in its opposition to A-16 but opposed the District because it might carry out the MRTC plan for rail extensions and thus divert passengers from interstate bus lines. The Metropolitan Regional Council opposed both bills and asked the Assembly to postpone action until 1959 to permit the MRC to prepare a new plan; the MRC bill would call for a tristate agency and might make the agency directly responsible to the Council.[32]

Undaunted by the continued opposition of his fellow Democrats in the legislature, Governor Meyner remained committed to the District bill throughout the summer and fall. Under attack for lack of leadership in dealing with the commuter crisis [33] and doubtful that the PNYA should be asked to assume total responsibility for rail problems, Meyner met with Assembly leaders several times in an effort to obtain passage and remove the one remaining obstacle to creation of the District.

In the three legislative bodies dominated by interests outside the proposed District area and responsive only to selective influences from the New York region, these conflicting perspectives did not preclude action. But in the regionally dominated New Jersey Assembly, the full range of contending forces was felt. Confronted by these divergent views, the Assembly committee members tried to devise proposals that could obtain majority support in their own house and in addition would be acceptable to two governors and three other legislative bodies, each with a different electoral base and a different set of perspectives. They first decided to eliminate A-16 from consideration. The committee members were willing to require that the Port Authority assume some transit responsibilities, but such duties would have to be limited in order to insure that the

Authority's net revenues from other facilities would be adequate to meet its rail deficits. A-16 was viewed as defective because it contained no limitations upon PNYA financial responsibility; in any event it was unlikely that the bill would be acceptable to the two states in its present form.

The committee members also opposed the passage of the Transit District bill. From some vantage points, the District measure was attractive. In comparison with regional bodies like the Port Authority, it would establish an institution under relatively direct control of the general public. Also, the bill represented an approach that both the PNYA and the railroads were willing to support. Yet within these advantages lay the seeds of failure. Support of the PNYA and the railroads had been purchased by a bill which excluded both from financial responsibility and focused on local funding. And the effort to devise a formula for local representation raised questions of whether Hudson and other New Jersey interests were properly protected and of the ability of District officials to reach agreement rapidly enough to cope with the immediate transit crisis.

A third alternative, to delay a decision until the Metropolitan Regional Council could develop a concrete plan for tristate action, perhaps under the auspices of the MRC itself, was also rejected. The legislators had heard MRC representatives speak optimistically of the willingness of local elected officials to subsidize rail service under an MRC plan and of the possibility of developing a scheme to coordinate all rail and rubber planning throughout the tristate region. But there was little evidence to indicate that this approach would result in a politically feasible plan in the near future.

The Assembly committees then worked out a compromise plan based upon the District bill but with the facets of that bill which had caused the greatest concern eliminated. The new measure, which was prepared with the assistance of Meyner's legal aides, made no reference to the use of "fiscal resources of the region" and called for appointment of the District board of directors by the two governors rather than local officials—thus ending the legal basis for regional taxation. (Members of the board would be required to be residents of the District area, thus retaining some linkage to local responsibility.) There was no reference in the bill to state financial aid. In fact, the only sources for meeting costs which were specifically mentioned in the committee report were the Port Authority, the federal government, and the railroads themselves. The revised bill also allayed the fear that a plan opposed by most New Jersey members might be adopted by stipulating that all actions would require the affirmative vote of a majority of the directors from each state, voting as separate units. Finally, responding to the urgent nature of the current rail crisis, the emphasis in the bill was shifted from preparation of a long-range plan to immediate steps to preserve essential services and reduce deficits.[34]

The new bill provided for an agency with less power than the proposed Transit District, yet it would have been an interstate agency, with the ability to negotiate and the potential of later evolving into an important regional organization. But by the time the committee members had reached agreement on the modified District bill, on December 8, the legislature was holding its last session of the year. Action on the new measure had to be postponed until January, 1959, with no certainty that bistate agreement would be forthcoming even then. Governor Meyner's comment as the year closed underlined his feeling of frustration and reflected the general confusion in the New York region as to what should be done. Seeking refuge in a nonpolitical interpretation of a highly political problem, the Governor said he would like to find an expert on the transit problem and say to him, "You are the expert. Will you analyze this mountain of information and advise us as to the best solution?" [35]

CHAPTER IX

State Leadership and Partial Remedies

The efforts to devise new transit policies for the New York area during the years 1945–58 took place primarily in a regional framework. The main participants were based within the region, and the debate was centered upon the development of inter-state regional programs to preserve and extend rail service. Even in 1958, when the focus of attention shifted to the state capitals, the most active interests were those from the New York area, and the policy alternatives under consideration were mainly those developed within the region. The governors and state legislators were relatively passive participants during 1945–58.

When measured by the goals of the rail coalition, the efforts of these years were unsuccessful. At the end of this period, the coalition's various demands—for programs that would expand the rail system, coordinate rail and highway planning and financing, or at the very least insure that existing rail services were retained—were still unmet. The struggles of 1945–58 underscored the great difficulty of devising new policies for a metropolitan region when many interests are actively involved, their perspectives of the region and its problems are diverse, and no institutional framework to provide regional leadership exists. These obstacles to policy innovation were compounded by the lack of widespread public concern during these years. Because of the delaying actions of state regulatory commissions, the deterioration of rail service proceeded gradually and fares were increased slowly. The need for public action was never demonstrated in dramatic fashion, and most of the region's residents remained apathetic.[1]

At this point, in the winter of 1958–59, three developments coincided, producing a shift in the pattern of policy-making in the New York region. First, the federal Transportation Act of 1958 sharply reduced the ability of state regulators to retard changes in service, and the announced plans of several rail lines to curtail service increased the level of public concern during the final months of 1958. Meanwhile, the legislative struggle at Trenton underscored the difficulties of relying on intraregional leadership and bistate agreement when prompt action is needed. Finally, a new governor, Nelson A. Rockefeller, was elected in New York—a governor who assigned a high priority to action to meet the rail crisis, who favored state leadership rather than regional schemes, and who after his landslide election in November, 1958, had the political strength to carry out his intentions with alacrity.

As a result of these several factors, in 1959 a pattern of policy-making on the regional transit issue emerged that differed significantly from that of the previous fifteen years. A tradition of intraregional leadership, involving many participants and extensive public debate, was replaced by state-dominant leadership, focused upon a few key actors who devised solutions through relatively private investigation and negotiation.

Also, state leadership involved the use of state funds, and the expensive plans proposed previously were therefore discarded. In comparison with the MRTC and its predecessors, the governors and their aides sought to define the problem narrowly in order to minimize cost and the use of political resources. They focused their attention mainly upon methods of preserving existing rail services in the short run, not upon extensive improvements or even long-run stabilization of commuter service. They viewed the crisis primarily as a railroad problem, and for the most part avoided such larger issues as the coordination of rail-highway planning or the relationship between transportation and the general development of the urban environment. Being responsive to separate state electorates, they tried to construct programs within a relatively self-contained state framework, not in terms of the regional needs of the interstate New York area. Finally, the states settled for organizational changes that disrupted existing patterns to a minimal extent and were relatively easy to accomplish.

In contrast to the previous decades of debate and inaction, the state-dominant pattern produced several important policy changes. New York State reduced taxes, authorized the use of public funds for railroad-station maintenance, and offered low-cost loans for the purchase of new passenger cars. New Jersey provided direct operating subsidies to the commuter lines and allocated funds for some reroutings and service consolidations. Although helpful, these programs were too limited to guarantee the maintenance of essential rail services. Until 1965, the only step taken which was likely to assure the continued existence and improvement of any important segment of the region's rail network was the Port Authority's reluctant acquisition of the H&M. In mid-1965 New York State made an equally reluctant decision to purchase the Long Island Rail Road. The problem of developing adequate long-range solutions for the New Jersey railroads and the lines serving Westchester and Fairfield Counties was still unsolved.

In this chapter, we examine the state-oriented pattern of policy leadership as it evolved during 1959-61. Then in a final section, we look at the region's political system from the vantage point of 1965 and find the situation generally consistent with the patterns that developed through 1961—fragmentation of perspective and responsibility within the region, the vacuum in policy leadership filled by state officials as it had been since

1959 but still characterized largely by minimal, stopgap actions, and the road coalition still successful in resisting demands for closer integration of transportation planning and financing.

FROM REGIONALISM TO STATE RESPONSIBILITY: ROCKEFELLER TAKES THE INITIATIVE

On November 4, 1958, Nelson A. Rockefeller was elected Governor of New York, defeating Averell Harriman by a plurality of more than 500,000 votes. During the gubernatorial campaign Rockefeller had stressed the need for prompt action to meet the threat of service curtailments stimulated by the federal Transportation Act of 1958.[2] To the Governor-elect, the rail crisis provided an opportunity to build a reputation as an effective political leader. This goal required that corrective action be shaped at Albany rather than within the region. Other factors also militated against a regional or bistate approach: the delays inherent in seeking a satisfactory interstate program and the likelihood that under a bistate plan New York might become involved in meeting the financial problems of the hard-pressed New Jersey railroads.

Rockefeller not only had incentives to take action; his political resources in early 1959 were unusually strong. Having just completed a successful campaign which overturned the Democratic incumbent, he enjoyed widespread party and public support. In addition, the Republicans had retained control of the state Senate and the Assembly, giving Rockefeller an advantage never enjoyed by Harriman or Meyner—control of both houses of the legislature by the Governor's own party.

Thus, Rockefeller was in a position to sever his administration from the complex and inconclusive approaches of the past several years and to devise and carry out an immediate program of state action. This he proceeded to do. Shortly after the election, the Governor-elect called for creation of a state Office of Transportation, to be charged with "looking at the whole transportation picture—railroads, waterways, airlines, highways —to insure a healthier transportation for all the state and to meet the commuter problems of our metropolitan areas." [3] Bills to carry out this proposal were introduced in the legislature soon after its return in January, 1959. Then, on January 15, the Governor appointed Robert W. Purcell as special consultant on transportation problems, and asked him to develop a "realistic program" for immediate legislative action. Purcell, a former Chesapeake and Ohio Railway official and an executive with the Rockefeller business interests, was to concentrate mainly upon the "deteriorating condition of the railroads operating within the State." [4]

The rail crisis also led to a tristate conference on February 10. The meeting was sponsored by the three governors and Mayor Wagner in order to obtain the views of a number of organizations in the region. But the headlines were made by Rockefeller. During the conference, the Governor asserted that commuter rail problems should be met by "each state taking action itself on a coordinated basis," and he opposed the creation of an interstate agency with major responsibilities, such as those proposed by the MRTC and the MRC.[5]

Rockefeller's statement had an immediate impact. Bergen's Senator Jones exclaimed that it was a "black day for rapid transit and regional cooperation," and the Transit Committee of Bergen County criticized Rockefeller for a "disservice" to commuters. At Trenton, the Assembly had passed the compromise District bill prepared in December only a day before the governors' meeting, but this effort appeared abortive. The MRTC, which had planned to remain in existence until the new agency was in being, now saw its hopes for an interstate transit body blocked. On March 1, the Transit Commission publicly noted the lack of interest in such an approach at Albany and announced that it was going out of business. A few days later, the life of the bistate agency, which had devoted nearly five years to the region's transportation problems, came to an end.[6]

NEW YORK STATE: GUBERNATORIAL LEADERSHIP AND A MODEST RESPONSE

Unencumbered by the complexities and delays of an interstate approach, Rockefeller and his aides soon devised a program to cope with New York's rail problems. By April, 1959, the state had enacted a tax relief measure and a scheme to assist the railroads in purchasing new passenger cars. These two plans formed the basis for New York State's response to the rail crisis in 1959–61 and during the subsequent three years as well.

Immediate Action and Long-Range Aspirations. On March 12, 1959, Purcell submitted a series of proposals to the Governor. Noting that taxes on railroad property in New York were the second highest in the country on a per-mile basis (only New Jersey had a higher rate), Purcell urged that these taxes be sharply reduced. The total Purcell program would cut rail taxes by about $15 million, with most of the revenue being lost to local governments. In order to soften the impact of the program, the reductions would take place in stages over several years, and one-half of the losses in local revenue would be reimbursed by state aid.

Purcell also proposed public action to meet the problem of deteriorating passenger equipment. Replacement of aged cars was needed, he believed, but the railroads themselves had little financial incentive to undertake a replacement program. Purcell therefore suggested that the Port Authority buy commuter cars and lease them to the rail lines, at a rental which would reimburse the PNYA for its total costs. This plan would permit the railroads to obtain new cars without any down payment and at low financing rates because of the Authority's tax-free status.

"The view has been expressed," Purcell commented, "that

any extensive program of this character might have an adverse effect on the Port Authority's credit." To avoid this possibility, he proposed that the state immediately advance up to $20 million to the PNYA, to be used to commence the program, and that the state later guarantee a special issue of Port Authority bonds for the commuter-car program.[7]

Purcell's plan conflicted with the Authority's long-sought goal of extricating itself from the rail problem. The proposal did not require that the PNYA use its own funds, as had been urged by Assemblyman Musto, New Jersey's IMGBRS, and others. But it did involve a continuing PNYA responsibility in the rail field as well as state financial support and state review of all PNYA decisions made under the commuter-car program. It was somewhat surprising, therefore, that the Authority greeted the release of the program with the announcement that it was "quite pleased . . . a way had been found" for the Port Authority "to be of assistance." [8]

The PNYA's acceptance of the Purcell plan is explained by the fact that it had achieved a reasonably satisfactory compromise after several weeks of difficult negotiations with the Governor's office. Initially, Purcell had advocated a plan requiring the Port Authority to use its own credit to support the commuter-car program. Rockefeller himself had apparently supported this proposal. Concerned with the threat to its policy position and its credit, the PNYA had marshaled the investment community in opposition to the scheme, had obtained the support of Governor Meyner and his aides, and finally had persuaded Rockefeller and Purcell to modify the original plan. The final program announced in March left the Authority's finances untouched; the new commuter-car division of the PNYA would act essentially as an administrative arm of New York State in carrying out the proposal. The negotiations on this program again illustrated the significant influence that the PNYA wielded. Yet the final outcome showed that once the governors and their aides had become centrally involved in the rail crisis, the Port Authority could no longer be confident of its ability to remain unencumbered by rail problems. This lesson would be underscored even more forcefully in 1960.[9]

The tax relief and commuter-car proposals, together with several other recommendations, were endorsed by Governor Rockefeller and released to the press on March 15.[10] Within a few days, bills to carry out the entire program were introduced in the legislature, and the Rockefeller forces moved for quick approval. Objections arose from the Democratic minority and from some Republicans because of lack of adequate time to study the program, reluctance to give up local railroad taxes, and general antagonism to Rockefeller's legislative program. In the Assembly, all 56 Democrats opposed the entire railroad-aid package, and several Republicans joined them. Yet because of Rockefeller's strong political position, coupled with the state's tradition of railroad tax assistance (established in the Long Island Rail Road Act of 1954) and the indirect political impact of tax relief, most of the Governor's party supported his proposals. On the last day of the legislative session, the Assembly approved the major bills, with the main railroad tax relief measure passing by an 81–66 vote, the others by slightly larger majorities. They were immediately rushed to the Senate and approved in a straight party vote, 34–24. Rockefeller signed them into law in April.[11]

Most of the bills passed by the legislature closely paralleled Purcell's recommendations. One measure, however, did not. Purcell had proposed that the interstate rail problem be met through a bistate agency "along the lines" of New Jersey's modified District bill. The legislation finally shaped by the Rockefeller forces differed significantly from the New Jersey bill, and the differences emphasized the Governor's determination to view the rail problem in a state frame of reference rather than in regional terms. The New York bill called for the creation of a "New York–New Jersey Transportation Agency" rather than a "metropolitan transit district." The new agency would be concerned with the "common aspects" of transportation in the two states, not with transportation needs of the "metropolitan area." Rather than a ten-member board of directors, all required to live in the district, the new agency would be composed of two state officials, one appointed by each governor.[12]

The revised bistate agency bill and the Port Authority's involvement in the commuter-car program both required concurrence by New Jersey. Past experience had shown this to be a difficult hurdle. But the commuter-car program did not obligate New Jersey in any way, and Trenton officials could hope that even in its revised form, the bistate agency might prove helpful in resolving the trans-Hudson rail problem. In addition, as legislative leaders noted publicly, favorable action at Trenton on the New York measures might obligate New York to "similarly concur" in any later New Jersey program involving Port Authority action or otherwise requiring bistate approval. Thus, although there was some criticism of both New York bills, they were passed by large majorities and signed by Governor Meyner in early May.[13]

In addition to the immediate legislative program devised at Albany, there were signs in 1959 of more significant long-range plans that might challenge the independence of the highway coalition and provide a more balanced transport policy for the region and for New York State. The Office of Transportation, established in May, was to assist the Governor in developing a "coordinated, overall" policy toward highways, railroads, and other transport facilities and in finding effective ways to meet specific problems of transportation in metropolitan areas. The need for an integrated transportation policy was also underscored in Purcell's report to the Governor in March. He criticized the massive highway construction programs in the New York region, programs that aided automobile travel "with seeming disregard of the economic consequences to the railroads and the bus lines, to say nothing of the impact of the automobile congestion" on business in the metropolis. He leveled a direct attack on the PNYA for siphoning off rail passengers to its bridges and tunnels. Purcell urged that a single agency be given "broad powers" to coordinate all forms of transportation throughout the state; such coordination was, he concluded, a matter of "paramount importance." [14]

A Marginal Impact. The development of New York's programs and policies during the next two years failed to bear out the initial promise. The tax-relief program did not prevent serious financial difficulties on the state's major commuter railroads—the Long Island, the New Haven, and the New York Central. The Long Island Rail Road, beset by a prolonged strike and a continuing loss of traffic to new expressways, absorbed a deficit of more than $1.7 million in 1960. Despite tax relief and several loans guaranteed by the federal government, the New Haven suffered large losses in 1959–60, and by early 1961 bankruptcy seemed imminent. On the New York Central, as on the other two lines, passenger deficits exceeded the tax relief provided by the 1959 legislation, although the Central's freight profits were large enough to give it a slight overall profit in 1960.[15]

The first two years of the commuter-car program were also disappointing. Some state officials hoped that the program would provide the incentive for replacing more than a thousand obsolete cars on the three rail lines. None of the railroads, however, were eager to add financing costs for new cars to their already large passenger deficits, and in spite of arduous negotiations the Port Authority was unable to execute any leasing agreements in 1959 or 1960. At last, in the spring of 1961, the New York Central agreed to purchase fifty-three new commuter cars. But no agreements with the other two commuter lines were completed during 1961.[16]

By the fall of 1960, it had become clear that New York State would have to take additional action or face the prospect of rapid deterioration of commuter service on all three lines. The response at Albany, however, was a series of stopgap measures in 1960–61 and a call for further study. When measured against the growing need for action, state leadership in meeting the commuter crisis now seemed only slightly more effective than the governmental responses of the 1950s.

The most direct steps taken were a series of legislative proposals developed by the state Office of Transportation in the fall of 1960 and signed into law in March, 1961. Whereas the 1959 laws had applied to all railroads in the state, the 1961 measures were focused entirely on the commuter railroads serving the New York region. The New Haven, the Long Island, and the New York Central were granted additional tax relief, and local communities along the rail lines were authorized to assume the costs of maintaining passenger stations. The prospective benefits to each railroad under this legislation were estimated at $2 to $3 million per year. Unlike the 1959 provisions, however, the 1961 legislation tried to use the attraction of financial aid to compel improvements in service, regardless of the financial condition of the rail lines. To be eligible for the 1961 benefits, each rail carrier would have to participate in the commuter-car program and meet standards of service set forth by the state. It was not certain that the three lines, and especially the hard-pressed New Haven, would be able to comply. Even the Governor commented on the shortcomings of the latest effort. "These bills are designed to alleviate an immediate . . . need," Rockefeller warned in approving the legislation. "They do not offer a final solution to the commuter problem." [17]

The crisis on the New Haven produced a broader pattern of responses during 1960-61, extending beyond New York's tax relief legislation. Attempts were made to devise an interstate program to aid the New Haven, and federal officials also became involved. But these efforts suffered from the same limitations as previous attempts at intergovernmental cooperation. No government institution had responsibility for the entire regional problem, each interest was concerned with avoiding financial responsibility and sought to have others act instead, and studies took the place of substantial, direct action at the state and local level.

During the first months of 1960, the New Haven operated at large deficits, and President George Alpert appealed for state and federal tax relief and subsidies in order to keep the New Haven out of bankruptcy. Meanwhile, short of cash to meet operating expenses, Alpert asked the Interstate Commerce Commission in March to guarantee a $10-million loan under the provisions of the 1958 Transportation Act, and the Commission reluctantly agreed. But a second request, for $6 million, was turned down by the Commission in October, 1960, because of doubts that the New Haven would be able to repay any further loans. The ICC said that it would reconsider the request if there were first action "on the local level," promising "substantial relief" for the rail line.[18]

Soon after the ICC announcement, Governor Rockefeller met with Governor Abraham Ribicoff of Connecticut, Mayor Wagner, and Edwin G. Michaelian, Westchester County Executive, to discuss the emergency. After an extended meeting, the four leaders announced that they would seek additional state and local tax relief for the New Haven, as well as ICC assistance. An Interstate Staff Committee, composed of their main transportation aides and chaired by a key Rockefeller adviser, William J. Ronan, was designated to prepare detailed recommendations for action. A few days later, members of this committee, joined by spokesmen for Rhode Island and Massachusetts, traveled to Washington to urge the ICC to grant the New Haven's $6-million loan-guarantee request. This action, they argued, would give the beleaguered line a reprieve while the four states worked out more enduring solutions. The Commission responded by endorsing a $4.5-million loan guarantee; the remaining $1.5 million would be forthcoming once state and local action had been taken.[19]

The events of these weeks once more provided an opportunity for the region's press to demonstrate its remarkable capacity for false optimism. Noting the cooperative efforts of the four states, Westchester, New York City, and the ICC, the New York *Times* concluded that the responsible officials were "united at last" on a program to save and modernize the New Haven. The *Times* criticized the pro-highway bias of previous public policy and saw the recent events as heralding a new era, in which rail would at last be given "something like equity" in public treatment. It now looked forward to the inclusion of New Jersey and the development of a "comprehensive," areawide program to resolve the region's transportation problems.[20]

This optimistic assessment was short-lived. In late January, 1961, Ronan and the Interstate Staff Committee finally announced a detailed program of action, and the governors of the four states served by the New Haven endorsed it several weeks later. The program included expanded tax relief, fare increases, and other actions that would, it was hoped, provide $13 million a year for the railroad. But it was doubtful that action on the program would be taken in time to prevent bankruptcy. In March, Connecticut acted to give $1.2 million in tax relief. During the same month, New York State enacted its 1961 tax-relief and station-maintenance measures; however, the $2.1 million available to the New Haven under this program was conditioned on service improvements and participation in the commuter-car program. During the rest of the spring, while Massachusetts and Rhode Island debated financial aid and all four states appealed for additional federal loans, the New Haven slid toward bankruptcy. On July 7, 1961, the Railroad was declared insolvent; it was the first major railroad in the United States to enter bankruptcy since the Long Island in 1949. The

New York *Times* reversed its sanguine appraisal of nine months before, attacking all levels of government for believing that a "handout of a loan here and tax rebate there and a trifling help with equipment" would solve the commuter problem.[21] Six months later, facing the threat that the New Haven would be liquidated and appealing for federal action to save the railroad, Rockfeller was to admit that the assistance thus far provided by the states had been only a "palliative, only a Band-Aid." [22]

In 1959–61, Albany officials replaced regional study groups in shaping transit programs for the New York region. But the hope in 1959 that state leadership would mean vigorous action and permanent solutions was not fulfilled. The behavior of other regional actors had been heavily influenced by the desire to avoid extensive responsibility; similarly, the Governor and his aides sought to minimize their involvement. Albany defined the transportation problem and responded to it in narrow terms: assistance to New York carriers was limited to short-run efforts to keep the railroads running, and the New Jersey sector of the region was largely excluded from New York State's plans.

In defining the transportation problem narrowly, the state also failed to act on earlier suggestions that it challenge the hegemony of the highway coalition. The demand in Purcell's 1959 report that highway-dominant policies be replaced by a program of balanced public financial assistance and coordinated planning never obtained real support in the governor's office. For a short time, the first director of the state Office of Transportation, Lewis K. Sillcox, did attempt to press forward along the lines suggested by Purcell. In a memorandum in March, 1960, for example, Sillcox criticized the impact of Port Authority facilities on rail-passenger patronage and on traffic congestion in Manhattan, and in a style reminiscent of MRTC co-chairman Charles Tuttle he denounced the attempt to solve the region's transport problems by "constructing vast [highway and parking] projects at taxpayers' expense." Automobile users, Sillcox concluded, should help in meeting the costs of maintaining rail facilities. Like Tuttle, Sillcox was disregarded. His report was not released to the public, and he was soon replaced as director of the Governor's transportation office.[23]

In essence, the strategy of the Rockefeller administration was to follow the path of least resistance. The rail problem could not be entirely neglected by the state after 1958, but it was dealt with in ways which avoided important but politically difficult efforts—cooperative programs with the New Jersey sector of the region, extensive financial involvement by New York State, and any significant challenge to the highway alliance. In the spring of 1961, the new director of the state Office of Transportation stressed the need for a "comprehensive, constructive program" for New York's transportation industry, in order to restore common carrier services to "vigorous health in the private enterprise sector of the economy." [24] But there was no evidence that New York State's political leaders were prepared to meet this challenge.

NEW JERSEY: THE HIGHWAY COMMISSIONER AND THE PORT AUTHORITY AID THE RAILS

Governor Rockefeller's announcement in February 1959 that he opposed a bistate, regional approach to the rail transit problem caught Governor Meyner unprepared. Meyner had hoped to rely upon a regional agency to take responsibility for meeting the rail crisis and for obtaining any necessary funds. When the District bill had been halted in the Assembly in 1958, Meyner's aides had taken an active part in reshaping it to meet North Jersey objections. With the Governor's full support, the modified District bill had been introduced in January, 1959, and on February 9, the day before Rockefeller's pronouncement, the Assembly had passed the measure by a vote of 46–3.

Now, with Rockefeller interested primarily in plans for his own state, a regional agency seemed unlikely to play a major role, if, indeed, New York State were even willing to join in creating it. A second alternative, continued inaction, was no longer politically acceptable. The New Jersey railroads had responded to the greater freedom permitted under the federal Transportation Act with predicted vigor, applying for severe service reductions or threatening to do so. In early December, 1958, the state's largest passenger carrier, the Lackawanna, announced that it would soon ask for permission to end all passenger service unless New Jersey took prompt action to aid the railroad, and the Pennsylvania said it was considering a plan to eliminate much of its off-hour passenger service to Manhattan. The Lehigh Valley, which carried only a few hundred passengers, declared that it would end service in the near future. During the next three months, service on the West Shore ferry and the Erie ferry were abandoned, and several rail lines announced further plans to reduce train service and increase fares. A similar pattern continued throughout the spring.[25]

With the crisis deepening and no authoritative regional leadership available, the state had to act. Political realities require that a governor respond to a major problem facing a large portion of his constituency; and during the early months of 1959 Rockefeller dramatized the potential for policy innovation directed from the statehouse. Yet the shift to active state leadership was more difficult in New Jersey than in New York because of the greater immediate financial problems of the New Jersey railroads, the restricted fiscal resources of the state, and Governor Meyner's continued hope that a regional agency might fill the leadership vacuum.

New Jersey's response to the regional transport problem during 1959–61 evolved through three phases: a slow shift from a passive role to the acceptance of active state leadership, the development of a dramatic but ill-fated plan in 1959 to use New Jersey Turnpike funds, and a 1960 plan that included state subsidies for the rail lines and Port Authority responsibility for the H&M. The 1960 program, which was put into effect after extended negotiations, has provided the basis for New Jersey's response to the rail problem during the past five years.

These efforts to meet New Jersey's transportation problems were marked by characteristics similar to those seen at Albany. A few administrative officials at Trenton shaped the programs in relatively confidential negotiations with executives of the railroads, the Port Authority, and, to a limited extent, the Rockefeller administration. The programs were developed in state terms, providing assistance for Camden and other downstate areas as well as the New York region. Because New Jersey had a far larger percentage of trans-Hudson commuters than did New York, the programs devised at Trenton were, however, directed toward meeting the interstate transit problem as well as toward insuring continued rail service within the state.

In terms of meeting the long-run transportation problems of the metropolitan region, New Jersey's 1959–61 policies, like New York's, were decidedly limited. The state made available to the rail carriers only about $6 million a year—a sum equal to the average cost of one mile of highway in New Jersey. This amount fell far short of full compensation for passenger deficits, and in succeeding years the officials in charge of the program would appeal for more funds for subsidies, capital improvements, and service consolidations. Also, New Jersey's programs left the autonomy of the highway alliance relatively untouched. The program agreed to by the Port Authority did require that it devote a portion of its own funds to the H&M and other rail projects, but the legislation also built a "statutory fence" around the rail allocation, insuring that the greater part of future Authority investment would be excluded from the rail transit field. Meanwhile, the Governor's chief aide on rail problems,

Dwight R. G. Palmer, who also served as State Highway Commissioner, urged that more state funds be provided for the rail program but objected to taking them out of highway construction funds. Rail service is essential, he argued, but it is "supplemental" to the "greatest transportation resource of all —the Federal and State Highway Systems." [26]

From Observer to "Quarterback." "Individuals and organizations," March and Simon comment, "give preferred treatment to alternatives that represent continuation of present programs." [27] To Governor Meyner, the "present program" in the rail field, although it had never gotten off the drawing board, was an interstate agency. Unlike New York State, where a change in top-level personnel had made it relatively easy to abandon old preferences, New Jersey's leaders had to shed their commitment to a Transit District coupled with a passive state role and to devise a more dynamic state program.

New Jersey's problems in reversing past policy were not only those of inertia, however. The immediate financial problems of her railroads were more serious than those of the New York carriers, and New Jersey's financial resources were more limited. Also, the New York program, which was comparatively painless politically, could not be used in the Garden State. Tax relief would have had its main impact on one county, the Democratic stronghold of Hudson, which obtained more than 60 percent of all railroad taxes collected within the state. Such a plan would perhaps have been inequitable in terms of benefits received by Hudson; in any event, it was strongly opposed in the county and was unacceptable to the Democratic governor. State reimbursement to municipalities for tax losses, as provided in the New York plan, would have been difficult to undertake because of the restricted nature of state revenue sources (i.e., lack of a broad-based state tax). A commuter-car program also lacked support in New Jersey; both the railroads and political leaders saw new equipment as a decidedly secondary need.[28]

Given these constraints, finding workable solutions to its transit problems seemed likely to be a more arduous task in New Jersey than it had been in New York. For several weeks after the February 10 governors' meeting, in fact, Governor Meyner continued his campaign for a bistate District, and otherwise the state seemed to be standing still.[29]

During the early months of 1959, however, several developments coincidently provided the state with the first steps needed in meeting the crisis—a general commitment to state action and an institutional focus to provide continuing leadership. In January, when the imminent demise of the West Shore ferry threatened to strand 3,000 rail commuters in Weehawken, Governor Meyner asked State Highway Commissioner Palmer to supervise plans to transport the ferry passengers into Manhattan by bus. In working on this problem during the next several months and in following the deterioration of rail service throughout North Jersey, Palmer became convinced that vigorous state action was necessary; continued loss of rail service would increase highway congestion beyond "tolerable" limits, and no conceivable highway-building program could meet the resulting need satisfactorily.[30]

Meanwhile, in early January, state Senator Wesley L. Lance (R–Hunterdon) introduced a bill to establish a Division of Railroad Transportation at Trenton. Lance, a legislator from outside the New York region who maintained an active interest in the rail problem and in his party's gubernatorial nomination, advocated giving the Division "wide powers" to keep commuter trains in operation. During the next few weeks, Governor Meyner said he would support the proposal to establish a rail division, and the bill was passed by both houses of the legislature without fanfare. On March 12, the Governor signed the measure, which created the Division as part of Palmer's Highway Department; but Meyner devoted his public statement that day to another plea for a bistate District.[31] No one was appointed director of the Division during the next several weeks, and the state failed to act as the Jersey Central announced plans for a 40 percent fare increase, and regulatory agencies approved petitions which would remove more than a hundred trains from the schedules of the Lackawanna and the Susquehanna.[32]

However, Palmer had already begun to explore ways of meeting the crisis, and in mid-May he was joined by Herbert A. Thomas, Jr., who was named to head the Division of Railroad Transportation. After years of inaction, New Jersey now had a Cabinet official, Dwight Palmer, committed to the need for state action and a working agency charged with responsibility for developing a plan. As Palmer later expressed it, the state government would henceforth be the "leader of the team, the 'quarterback' . . . in solving the transportation problems of our urban areas." [33]

A Plan to Use Turnpike Authority Revenues. Obliged to seek immediate steps to halt the threats of the rail carriers, Palmer, Thomas and their aides considered several alternatives, and in early June Palmer reported to the Governor that he thought a solution to the rail problem had been found. He proposed that the surplus revenue of the New Jersey Turnpike Authority be made available to the state to meet the commuter rail problem and other transportation needs. Such funds could be used to establish connections between rail lines, eliminate grade crossings, provide modern equipment, and finance railroad tax relief. Palmer noted that the excellent financial position of the Turnpike made it likely that these surpluses would exceed $10 million a year; in addition, $30 million or more in Turnpike reserve funds could be made available immediately.

"With the financial resources that this plan will produce," Palmer declared, the state's transportation problems could be "progressively and effectively dealt with." [34]

In order to siphon off these surpluses, the state would first have to win the approval of the Turnpike Authority's bondholders. To gain their consent, Palmer recommended that the state place its credit behind the Turnpike bonds, thus giving the bondholders "even better security than at present" in return for freeing the surplus funds. The following steps would be required before the funds would be available to the state: (1) the legislature would have to authorize the Turnpike plan; (2) at the November election, a majority of the voters would have to agree to place the state's credit behind the Turnpike securities; and (3) the bondholders would then have to accept the change in the status of their bonds.

In his report to the Governor, Palmer also set forth the general philosophy that underlay his proposal. "This plan," the Highway Commissioner explained, "is based on the new conception of our responsibility that . . . all means of transportation . . . [are] part of the single problem to be considered and dealt with by the State Highway Department." Palmer's perspective contrasted sharply with the usual approach of members of the road coalition. It was explicable, however, in terms of his concern for the prospective overburdening of the highways because of rail-service curtailments, and of the fact that his recommendations would draw funds from another highway agency—not his own.

On June 16, 1959, Governor Meyner released the Palmer proposal to the press and gave it his full endorsement. He noted that the funds would provide a basis for aiding the railroads without "one penny of additional taxes from New Jersey citizens," and he urged immediate legislative action. A number of legislators had misgivings about drawing off Turnpike funds, especially without a detailed program for using them. But in view of the immediacy of the crisis, the lack of an alternative plan, and the need for prompt legislative action if the question were to be voted upon in November, both houses agreed in August to support the plan. The vote in the Assembly was 53–2 and in the Senate 17–1.[35]

The second hurdle confronting the Turnpike scheme was the November referendum authorizing the state to assume liability for the bonds. Soon after the plan was announced, campaigns for and against it were begun, and they increased in tempo during the fall. The battle illustrated several general obstacles to innovation in transport policy: Being a direct if limited challenge to the road coalition, the Turnpike scheme generated opposition from highway interests. In addition, the plan was viewed as a threat to the economic well-being of one important segment of the region, Hudson County, sparking attacks from that quarter. Finally, because it was a complex proposal and because the need for public aid to private rail corporations was not widely accepted, it faced apathy or opposition from downstate areas and from many residents of the region who did not rely on rail commutation.

Members of the highway coalition carried on a vigorous statewide campaign. The New Jersey automobile associations, the state's Gasoline Retailers Association, and other automotive interests attacked the plan as a "handout" to the railroads and argued that any Turnpike surpluses should be used to reduce Turnpike tolls or to expand the highway system. Highway interests placed advertisements in local newspapers across the state urging a "No" vote, and the American Automobile Association chapters distributed a folder opposing the plan to their 120,000 members in New Jersey.[36]

A strong attack was mounted in Hudson County. Palmer's plan would permit the state to reduce railroad taxes and reimburse local areas out of Turnpike reserves, but the bill contained no guarantee that all lost revenue would be replaced.

The greatest potential tax loss would occur in Democratic Hudson, and it was not at all clear that the legislature, frequently dominated by Republicans, would be willing to compensate the county fully. "Hudson County can be very badly hurt by this bill," declared the county's state senator in August, in casting the sole vote against the proposal. During the fall, the Board of Freeholders and other officials in the county, both Democratic and Republican, pressed a campaign through their party organizations and in the newspapers to obtain a resounding "No" vote in the referendum.[37]

The coalition favoring the Turnpike plan was generally a familiar one. Suburban municipal and commuter organizations and newspapers in Bergen, Morris, and Union counties campaigned vigorously for a "Yes" vote. The state's railroads endorsed the plan, and the major commuter lines agreed to suspend their efforts to curtail service until after the November referendum. About seventy-five rail executives formed a Community Committee of Northern New Jersey, which arranged for a number of discussions of the plan before civic groups. The proposal was endorsed by the Regional Plan Association, several municipal planning boards in North Jersey, the state Chamber of Commerce, and the New Jersey Real Estate Board.[38] In addition, one member of the road coalition, the Port Authority, found the plan favorable to its own interests, and informally supported it. PNYA officials argued that tapping the Turnpike surpluses was far different from using Port Authority revenues, since the Turnpike had only a single purpose, largely completed; using excess revenues for rail transit would not halt additional projects but only slow the rate at which bonds were paid off. From the viewpoint of the PNYA, the Turnpike plan had one especially attractive feature: it would reduce the pressure for action by the Port Authority itself.

The primary burden of obtaining a favorable vote in November fell to Governor Meyner, Commissioner Palmer, and their aides. Although the Turnpike proposal was directed primarily at meeting the needs of the New York region, it had to win acceptance from a statewide electorate. Consequently, the Governor and his aides traveled up and down the state, stressing the benefits that could accrue to South Jersey as well as the northern region, to the "hundreds of thousands" of intrastate rail travelers as well as interstate commuters. The theme of common goals and needs is frequently stressed by those advocating coordinated action within a region; using a similar tactic, Palmer urged his doubting South Jersey audiences to recognize that "we have a great interdependency, all of us, every part of the state," and to vote for the Turnpike plan. But large portions of the public seemed unconvinced. "Our problem in this section of the state is not the commuter problem," argued a former assemblyman from downstate Salem County, "we have no passenger service at all in Salem." [39]

To counter the road-coalition campaign and broaden the base of public support for the Turnpike plan, Governor Meyner and his aides also pointed out that the funds were not limited to rail transit, but could be used to improve bus service and highway facilities throughout the state. The effectiveness of these efforts to build public support was greatly reduced, however, by the need for the Governor and his staff to divide their energies. Much of their time during the few weeks before the referendum was devoted not to public campaigning but to strenuous and ultimately unsuccessful negotiations to win the support of Hudson County officials. [40]

The voters went to the polls on November 3, 1959. The Turnpike proposal was defeated decisively, by 877,000 to 647,000. Only seven of the twenty-one counties returned majorities in favor of the proposal, and only four of these—Monmouth, Morris, Somerset, and Union—were in the New York region. Hudson County voted four to one against the plan, contributing more than 103,000 of the total margin of defeat.

In many of the counties, the arguments of the auto groups appeared to have been effective. An important factor throughout the state was the lack of public understanding of the need for and benefits of the scheme; this reflected the complexity of the plan and the tight schedule under which it had been rushed toward approval. Thus even the voters of Bergen and Essex Counties returned negative majorities, Bergen voting 52 percent and Essex 54 percent against the plan.[41]

The 1960 Palmer Plan: Rail Service Contracts and a Port Authority Role. During the first months after the defeat of the Turnpike plan, another wave of train discontinuances and fare increases enveloped New Jersey, while Palmer and his aides sought a new plan. By early April, 1960, they had hammered out a new set of proposals, which would form the basis for New Jersey's approach to the rail problem during the next several years. In a report to the Governor on April 4, Palmer recommended (1) that the state begin a program of service contracts with the railroads, allotting $6 million for this purpose during the fiscal year 1960–61, and (2) that the Port Authority purchase about ninety new rail cars and lease them to the H&M, and in addition acquire the remaining trans-Hudson ferries and lease them to the railroads for operation until "satisfactory alternative facilities are available." The report also proposed that the H&M be placed under some form of bistate control, that the railroads carry out various service consolidations and other steps to improve service and reduce deficits, and that $1 million be appropriated for South Jersey rail improvements.[42]

In developing these proposals, Palmer, Thomas, and their aides had worked essentially alone, without the close involvement of the Governor or members of the legislature and without much contact with the railroads, commuter groups, or other regional interests. In fact, after the defeat of the Turnpike proposal, Governor Meyner had suggested that it might be best for the state to abandon its efforts and permit rail passenger service to continue its decline; only the concern of Palmer and the Railroad Division kept the state actively engaged in a search for alternative plans.[43]

Once confronted with a set of completed recommendations, however, the Governor was willing to support Palmer, and he urged prompt action on the service-contract program. Impelled by the crisis, the state legislature responded affirmatively. A bill providing $6 million for contracts and $1 million for rail improvements in South Jersey was introduced with bipartisan sponsorship, approved by both houses within a few weeks, and signed by Governor Meyner on June 22, 1960.[44]

As set forth in the bill, the $6 million was to be distributed among the commuter lines in return for agreements to maintain specified schedules of trains and specified fares. During the fall, service contracts for the 1960–61 fiscal year were negotiated with all the major rail companies in the state and several smaller lines. The contracts covered a part of the passenger losses and guaranteed that 95 percent of the existing service would remain in operation during the contract period, with no increases in fares. In 1961 the program was extended for a second year, and Palmer expressed the view that it might be continued for perhaps another three to five years.[45] "This contract relation is but a palliative," Palmer explained to the legislature in 1961. He looked forward to the possibility of route consolidations and other long-range improvements which in time would end the need for state subsidies and "enable the railroads . . . to be self-sustaining." But it was not clear how these long-range improvements would be financed.[46]

Commissioner Palmer's other major recommendations, Port Authority purchase of the trans-Hudson ferries and purchase of rail cars for the H&M, entailed more complex negotiations. In contrast with New York's commuter-car program, the proposal would have required the PNYA to use its own reserves in meeting rail transit needs, and it contained no firm limitation on the future use of PNYA funds for other rail projects. The challenge to the position that the Authority had successfully defended for many years was direct and immediate.

Under other circumstances, the PNYA might have rejected Palmer's proposal out of hand and fought to limit its involvement to a minimum, as it had successfully done in New York a year earlier. But its position was unusually vulnerable in 1960. With the failure of the Turnpike plan, the Authority faced renewed criticism for its "crass indifference" to the plight of the New Jersey railroads. In addition, since the winter of 1959 it had been under vigorous attack in North Jersey and in the state legislature for its proposal to build a new jet airport in suburban Morris County. These difficulties and others led to a congressional investigation in 1960 "to determine whether Congress should legislate to alter, amend or repeal" its consent to the Port Compact of 1921.[47]

Confronting attacks from several quarters, the PNYA decided that there was more to be gained by negotiating with Palmer than by rigid adherence to its traditional position that none of its funds could be used to meet rail deficits. There were several advantages to this approach. First, flat PNYA opposition might have led Palmer to add his voice to those demanding that the Authority be forced to act. This would further weaken the general position of the Authority. Moreover, Palmer was an influential adviser to Governor Meyner, and, while it was known that the governor himself was not yet convinced that the PNYA should devote its funds to rail, Palmer might in time persuade him to use his veto power over Authority actions to bring the PNYA to heel. There was also a positive incentive for a change in Port Authority strategy: if the Authority and Palmer could agree upon a limited PNYA role in meeting the rail problem, this would forestall greater pressures on the Authority in this area and improve the general public image of the agency.

Therefore, the PNYA did not undertake a public campaign against the Palmer report. Instead, in private conferences with the Commissioner and his aides, the Authority's leaders pressed for a program which would protect the agency from continually expanding rail commitments. Several months of intensive negotiations followed, and at a New Jersey legislative hearing on September 27, 1960, Austin Tobin announced that the Authority was prepared to abandon its historic opposition to applying its own funds to the rail problem—if certain conditions were met. The PNYA would be willing to purchase, modernize, and operate the H&M railroad, Tobin said, if the Authority could purchase the H&M properties at "realistic" market values, about $20 million, and if the PNYA could guarantee to its investors that the Authority "would not thereupon become . . . further involved in the deficits of the commuter railroads." [48]

Some of the Governor's aides and several New Jersey legislators and local commuter organizations objected to the latter restriction, and several months of further negotiations followed. Finally, in the spring of 1961, the Port Authority and New Jersey state officials agreed upon a program of PNYA involvement that went beyond the Authority's 1960 proposal but provided the PNYA with the valuable prize it sought—contractual assurance that its role in the rail problem would be severely limited. The Authority would take responsibility for the H&M, and it might later assume other duties in the rail field, but the total annual deficit from its rail operations could not exceed 10 percent of the Authority's General Reserve Fund. The PNYA estimated that during the next decade this formula would allow it to meet a total rail deficit of $7 to $10 million a year; however, $5 million or more of this amount would be absorbed by the H&M program alone. It was essential, the

Authority argued, to have such a "statutory fence" limiting its total rail deficit; otherwise, the investor could not be certain that the Authority would be able to avoid deeper involvement in deficits, in time ending its ability to meet its general financial obligations. Commissioner Palmer agreed, underscoring the bondholder perspective which shapes Port Authority action. "It gets down to how badly we need the H&M," Palmer declared. "Do we want it on the investors' terms or not at all. It seems to me it is almost as simple as that." [49]

The development of any new Port Authority program requires bistate agreement, and once again in 1961 differing perspectives and priorities separated the two states. As New Jersey and the PNYA completed negotiations on the rail bill in early 1961, the Authority also announced the results of a year-long study of a proposal for a World Trade Center on the lower East Side of Manhattan. The Authority supported the construction of such a Center and said that a public agency should build and operate it.[50] At Albany, the PNYA was seen as the agency to build the Trade Center, and this project was given at least equal priority with Port Authority action on the H&M; but New York State officials thought that Trenton might oppose PNYA sponsorship of a vast complex of buildings of particular benefit to New York. Therefore, in late March, 1961, with Governor Rockefeller's support, the New York legislature passed a single bill incorporating the H&M and World Trade Center proposals, thus requiring that New Jersey agree to PNYA action on the Trade Center before the H&M program could be carried out.

The response in New Jersey was familiar and predictable: officials at Trenton objected to the combined bill, and the legislature refused to take action. After several months of negotiations, however, an acceptable compromise was worked out: the World Trade Center would be shifted from the East to the West Side of Manhattan and combined with the redevelopment of the H&M. A bill incorporating both proposals thus appeared to have rational as well as tactical justification, and New Jersey could obtain satisfaction in the fact that the Trade Center would now face not east toward Brooklyn but west into New Jersey. In early 1962, a combined bill was enacted in both states, and on May 10, 1962, the Port Authority Trans-Hudson Corporation (PATH) was created by the Authority to "acquire, operate and develop the Hudson Tubes." [51]

Finally, after a quarter-century of opposition, the Port Authority was obligated to use its own funds in continuing and substantial support of deficit rail facilities. However, the limitations on the use of PNYA funds outlined in the 1961 New Jersey bill were included in the final bistate legislation.[52] And the Authority, while accepting some direct rail responsibilities, continued to deny that close coordination of rail and highway planning and financing in the region would be beneficial.[53]

The Port Authority's plans to rehabilitate the H&M and construct the Trade Center also gained the agency the broader result it had sought. The PNYA was widely praised, and its public position, which had sunk to a low point in 1960, had rebounded strongly by 1962.[54]

In New Jersey as in New York State, the three-year period following the demise of the MRTC was marked by a shift from intra-regional studies and debate to state-dominant leadership. A few state officials now became responsible for devising and carrying out rail transit policies. When measured by the standards of regional needs and rail-highway interdependence, New Jersey's efforts during these years were perhaps more satisfactory than those guided from Albany. While New York State's attempts to rescue the New Haven Railroad were interstate in focus, its attitude toward the major interstate commutation problem in the region, trans-Hudson travel, was decidedly parochial. New Jersey's program, on the other hand, had a substantial impact on maintaining interstate as well as intrastate commutation. Also, through its key role in the Port Authority's acquisition of the H&M, Trenton helped to bring about the only program for long-range maintenance of a major rail artery in the region that was evolved during these years; and this plan was doubly significant, since it also breached the wall that kept the region's opulent highway interests uncontaminated by their impoverished rail cousins.

Yet, despite these important changes the financial assistance provided by New Jersey compensated the rail carriers for only a portion of their passenger deficits, and it was uncertain how long this stopgap program would successfully retard the decline of rail commuter service. As of 1961, New Jersey, like New York, had not devised a politically acceptable program to allocate adequate amounts of public funds to meet the rail problem on a long-range basis. Moreover, in spite of perennial warnings from the RPA and other groups, neither state had yet faced what these regional spokesmen believed to be the underlying issue: how to coordinate the development of rail and highway policy in order to insure a balanced, efficient system of regional transportation for the entire New York area.

PERSPECTIVE 1965

The patterns of fragmented responsibility and hesitant state leadership continued essentially unchanged during the early 1960s. As the financial condition of most commuter lines deteriorated further, political leaders at all levels tried to minimize their own financial involvement and urged others to take action. The possibility that the regional transit problem would be met by the joint efforts of officials from within the metropolis, a prospect long held forth by the MRC, grew dimmer during this period. Instead, dispersion of local responsibility, combined with the difficulty of relating local benefits to local costs, led county and municipal leaders to assume a largely negative stance where financial liability was concerned. The states, too, sought to limit their burden. With no leadership alternative at hand, however, state officials found themselves assuming increasing responsibility for keeping commuter service patched together. The national government also became an active participant during the 1960s, although federal officials showed little enthusiasm for assuming major policy-making or financial burdens.

Meanwhile, the hopes for coordinated planning and financing of rail and highway facilities were unfulfilled, and the financial strength and political autonomy of the highway coalition continued largely intact. Billions of dollars were spent on road facilities during the late 1950s and early 1960s. Yet the problem of traffic congestion remained as serious as it had in the early postwar period, and the solution offered by the road coalition was the familiar one. "The building of roads must catch up and keep pace with the output of cars," proclaimed Robert Moses in 1964. "We are behind and shall keep losing ground unless we act fast. Congestion is here. Strangulation is not far off." In 1964–65, the highway agencies announced plans for more than $1 billion in new river crossings and other arterial projects.[55]

These patterns of fragmentation and piecemeal action were apparent in the diverse attempts made to meet the commuter problem in the early 1960s. In New Jersey, the financial condition of the state's rail carriers continued to deteriorate during these years, and the threat loomed that all passenger service on several lines would be ended.[56] Pressed by other urgent state commitments, however, and lacking a sales or income tax, state leaders were unwilling to invest the large sums needed to modernize rail facilities or even to insure that essential service would be continued. The 1960 service-contract program was continued, but the annual subsidy to the carriers was considerably less than their passenger-service losses and was more than offset by railroad taxes paid to Trenton and to New Jersey municipalities.[57] Meanwhile, state monies were made available to finance only a small part of a proposed $126 million rehabilitation program.[58]

Unwilling to use state funds in the amounts needed, New Jersey officials turned their attention to outside sources of financing. One possibility was the Port Authority. Under the H&M legislation, the PNYA was authorized to aid other rail carriers as long as the total PNYA rail deficit did not exceed $7–10 million a year. By 1962, however, the PNYA had greatly expanded its original cost estimates for H&M modernization and related projects, absorbing essentially all available Authority funds.[59]

Another possible source of funds was the federal government. Legislation enacted in 1961 and 1964 established a program of federal aid for demonstration projects and capital improvements in the mass transportation field,[60] and as New Jersey's transit crisis deepened in 1964–65, state officials sought to use this program to bolster the state's own hard-pressed resources. In the spring of 1965, Palmer and his aides outlined a plan for $50 million in matching federal-state funds for capital improvements, together with several million dollars for passenger-service experiments which might increase passenger revenues. The prospects for carrying out this program were uncertain, however, because of restrictions on the use of federal grants and because of the difficulties of obtaining necessary state matching funds.[61] In the fall of 1965, New Jersey officials were still seeking a politically feasible program to alleviate the immediate crisis and to meet the long-range mass transportation needs of its residents in the New York region.[62]

In New York State, the efforts of the governor and his aides during the early 1960s were directed at the complex and somewhat disparate problems of the New Haven and the Long Is-

land railroads. Because the New Haven provided rail service
in three New England states as well as New York, Albany and
her sister governments were led to cooperate in the search for
a rescue program. At the same time, this interstate dimension
also offered the states and localities an opportunity to minimize
their own obligations and to press for federal action. Their
primary strategy was to divide the New Haven's deficit into
three components (New York suburban service, long-haul passenger service, and freight) and to argue that the suburban
service contributed "negligibly" to the overall deficit. The other
two components, they contended, were beyond the jurisdiction
of state and local governments but were "intimately tied" to
"federal . . . responsibilities for interstate commerce, the national defense, and the postal service." [63]

This strategy was actively pursued by New York State and
her allies during the early 1960s, but the national government
was unresponsive. Meanwhile, the New Haven remained in
bankruptcy, and its financial condition and quality of passenger
service deteriorated still further.[64]

In 1964, the New Haven's overall loss climbed to more
than $15 million, prompting her trustees to take steps to cur-
tail passenger service in New York State drastically; their ultimate goal was to end all passenger service and to be included
as a freight carrier in the proposed merger of the New York
Central and the Pennsylvania.[65] Anticipating that the ICC
would look sympathetically upon the New Haven's request,
Rockefeller responded in January, 1965, with a new plan:
$20 million in matching federal-state funds would be pro-
vided for new passenger cars on the New Haven and for the
rehabilitation of old cars; the new cars would be available
in eighteen to twenty-four months and would then save the
railroad $300,000 a year in maintenance costs. In addition,
Westchester and Connecticut would each provide $400,000 an-
nually for station maintenance.[66] This latest Rockefeller

scheme was, however, met with scorn by spokesmen within the region and by Judge Robert P. Anderson, whose court has supervised the New Haven during bankruptcy. "What is needed is cash in the till," commented Judge Anderson acidly, "not announcements of intentions to do something sometime somewhere." [67]

A few weeks later, state and federal officials finally agreed upon a program which would extend the life of the New Haven's suburban service for another twelve to eighteen months. The trustees agreed to maintain service during this period in return for a $4.5-million demonstration grant, with two-thirds being supplied by the federal government and the rest by New York State and Connecticut. To federal officials, the grant was viewed as providing time for the "states and localities" to work out a long-term cooperative program to support commuter service. Governor Rockefeller still argued, however, that the national government should, in the long run, accept primary responsibility for meeting the New Haven's problems.[68]

In comparison with the intergovernmental complexities involved in the New Haven situation, the allocation of public responsibility for the Long Island Rail Road was relatively clear. The entire railroad was contained within New York State, and the state government had accepted a special responsibility for the LIRR in the early 1950s. Yet Albany's efforts to meet the LIRR's problems in the early 1960s again illustrated the reluctance of state officials to support a program adequate to insure that a major rail artery in the region would remain in existence. Moreover, the solution finally agreed upon in 1965—state purchase and control of the railroad—again illustrated the narrow substantive focus and limited local participation in policy-making that have characterized New York State's approach to the region's transportation problem.

State officials had hoped that the special concessions granted to the LIRR in 1954 would provide it with enough funds to modernize fully, so that it could emerge from its special status in 1966 as an efficient private rail carrier. The LIRR made a strong start on its rehabilitation program, but because of cost inflation and traffic losses to competing highways the program fell behind schedule in the late 1950s. Even under its special status, the railroad operated in the red in 1960, the program fell further behind, and it was uncertain whether the LIRR could survive as a private carrier without considerable additional public assistance.[69]

Meanwhile, although Rockefeller aides described the LIRR situation as "critical," the state's response was minimal. The railroad-aid programs of 1959 and 1961 provided only marginal assistance to the LIRR, and long-range studies substituted for action. A two-year survey led to a report in 1963 which concluded that the LIRR was indispensable for commutation and urged extensive improvements. The report was silent on the costs of the program and on how these costs or the basic financial needs of the LIRR might be met.[70]

In 1964, with the LIRR experiencing its worst year since emerging from bankruptcy a decade before, Rockefeller finally appointed a committee to devise a concrete plan to revitalize the railroad. The committee was chaired by the governor's main transportation adviser, William J. Ronan; and by early 1965 it had devised a plan which won Rockefeller's support. The Ronan Committee recommended that the state purchase the LIRR and create a Metropolitan Commuter Transportation Authority (MCTA) to supervise LIRR operation and undertake a $200-million modernization program. To spread the financial burden of the program, the LIRR would be purchased with general state funds; local governments served by the railroad would be required to triple their present payments for station maintenance, to a total of $2 million per year; and "much if not all" of the modernization plan, it was hoped, could be financed under the federal mass transportation program, with Washington providing one-half to two-thirds of the total. Although the report pointed out that without a modernized LIRR vast additional highway expenditures would be required, it included no recommendations for the use of Triborough Authority or other highway revenues to aid the rail program.[71]

With the Governor's backing, the MCTA bill was passed by the state legislature during the spring, and the Authority was established in June, 1965. Although the MCTA's initial duty is to take over the LIRR, it is empowered to operate commuter facilities throughout the New York section of the region. By the fall the Authority was engaged not only in negotiations for purchase of the LIRR but in an effort to work out arrangements for preserving suburban service on the New Haven.[72]

While the creation of the MCTA implies an increased public commitment to preserving rail-commuter service in the New York metropolis, the MCTA approach also displays several similarities to previous efforts to meet the region's transportation problems. It minimizes local responsibility for policy-making, maintains the separation of rail and highway financing and planning, and creates another semi-autonomous public authority to cope with a piece of the metropolitan transportation problem. Thus, while MCTA operations are limited to the New York region, local elected officials have no direct role in the selection of MCTA members (all members being appointed by the Governor), nor do they have any other direct voice in policy formulation. Also, MCTA rail responsibilities are not closely linked to highway planning and development on Long Island or elsewhere in the region. Finally, in the "authority" tradition, the MCTA legislation formally separates the agency from close state supervision by providing for five members who serve overlapping eight-year terms and by exempting MCTA decisions on fares and schedules from the control of the state utility commission—or of any other state or regional agency.[73]

The MCTA legislation illustrates a general lack of local involvement in regional transport policy-making during the early 1960s. With government divided among many county and municipal units, it was difficult to relate local benefits to prospective costs, and elected officials were therefore wary of financial involvement. Moreover, the plethora of governments encouraged local officials to view the problem as too extensive for localities to handle. Consequently, political leaders in Bergen and Westchester Counties and other parts of the region devoted their energies to urging that those with broader geographic responsibilities—the states, the PNYA, and the federal government—devise solutions and provide whatever funds were needed. Occasionally, local spokesmen went further, suggesting the creation of regionally controlled organizations to establish and carry out rail policy; these plans, too, were premised largely on outside financing. Since, however, the states and other regional surrogates were not eager to cede control over their own limited funds for meeting the rail crisis, local institutions found themselves without significant influence.[74]

Some attempts were made to develop more broadly based regional organizations which could overcome the limitations of the local-benefit perspective and provide a foundation for a positive regionally led program. But these efforts were also defeated by the reluctance of local spokesmen to accept direct constraints on local autonomy in policy-making or to increase local financial responsibilities.

The primary hope for effective regionally based action lay with the Metropolitan Regional Council. In attacking the 1958 Transit District scheme, spokesmen for this voluntary association of local governments had asserted that the MRC would soon provide leadership in meeting the transit crisis and that the Council might itself become the governing body of a tri-state transportation agency. During the next seven years, how-ever, MRC members were unable to reach agreement on any plan for regional control and financing of mass transportation. They were equally unsuccessful in broadening the capability of the MRC to cope with regional problems. Even a modest proposal, to convert the Council into a statutory commission with advisory powers, was attacked as a step which would "pave the way for elimination of home rule" and was rejected by political leaders in several counties. In 1964, the attempt to obtain statutory powers for the MRC was abandoned.[75]

The lack of an effective local-government role in resolving the transit crisis was also illustrated in the development of the Tri-State Transportation Committee. In 1959–60, regional spokesmen called for the creation of a tristate agency to act as a transportation planning or policy-making board; the agency would include representatives of local governments in the region, as well as state appointees.[76] Dubious of the pros-pects for action from such a composite agency, state officials disregarded the proposal and continued to rely on their own agencies. Then, in the fall of 1961, the three governors an-nounced the formation of a Tri-State Transportation Com-mittee. The new body was not a means for involving local representatives in transportation policy-making, however, but primarily a mechanism through which the state capitals would cooperate on mutual problems in the New York region. Ronan, Palmer, and other state officials held twelve of the thirteen places on the Committee, with one post allocated to New York City. No other local governments were directly represented, and although local "cooperating committees" were later ap-pointed, they have not thus far developed any significant role.[77]

The development of the Tri-State Committee has illustrated not only the state-dominant pattern of leadership but two other recurrent themes in metropolitan policy-making—the tendency to concentrate on narrow segments of the transportation problem rather than focusing upon the broader question of coordinated rail and highway development, and the difficulties of devising cooperative interstate programs. Tri-State's initial report in 1961 called for a study of rail and highway transportation "as parts of an integrated regional . . . network." But during the next four years, the Committee's energies were focused upon short-range transit demonstration projects and long-range projections, and it made no significant contribution to such major policy issues as the financial and planning autonomy of the region's highway coalition.[78] Tri-state officials also hoped to convert the Committee into a permanent interstate commission, with planning powers and the potentiality to undertake direct rail operations in the future. This plan, however, met with vigorous objections from local officials and state legislators, especially in New Jersey. Local criticisms were reminiscent of the attacks leveled at the Transit District scheme in 1958: New Jersey's representation on the Commission would be inadequate, the proposed allocation of costs favored the other states, and the new agency would involve the state in extensive commitments for rail operations far beyond any possible benefits. After a two-year delay, the agency was stripped of all but its planning functions, and a revised measure was accepted by all three states in 1965. In this latest attempt as in earlier efforts, local and state fears provided a major obstacle to the development of closer regional coordination.[79]

Spokesmen from within the New York region thus found themselves in 1965 in the position they had occupied since they had defeated the MRTC plan—lacking any significant role in shaping the region's transportation policy. And while the states, working in part with federal assistance, sought ways of meeting at least the most immediate crises, local spokesmen continued their traditional, if ineffectual, roles. Suburbia criticized railroad officials for trying to end passenger service, objected to local financial aid for the carriers, and urged that the states guarantee commuter service if the railroads could not be forced to do so. The New York *Times*, the RPA, and other spokesmen for the central city and for a regional perspective continued their campaign for an agency which would assume responsibility for operating rail service and for coordinating rail and highway transportation throughout the metropolis. "The only permanent, satisfactory solution," asserted the New York *Times* in the spring of 1965, "will be the unification of all commuter lines . . . with the city's subways system, and their joint operation by a public authority." Such an authority should also "take over management of the toll roads, tunnels and bridges" in the tristate area. Yet in view of the fragmentation of political responsibility and perspective in the region, this solution or others involving effective region-wide coordination were, as the *Times* sadly admitted, "as remote as ever." [80]

CHAPTER X

Patterns of Conflict and Cooperation

The search for transit policy in the New York region amply illustrates the fragmentation of responsibility for policy-making in the metropolis. Many groups and individuals are actively involved, each is responsible to only a narrow slice of the region, and most respond in terms of the immediate interests of their specific geographic or functional constituencies. Political leaders, newspapers, and business groups defend the economic needs and political prerogatives of Newark, Jersey City, Morris County, Westchester County, or the 23rd Street section of Manhattan. Spokesmen for specific functional interests also focus on benefits and costs to their own groups. The railroads, the bus lines, the Port Authority, and the commuter and automobile associations represent broader regional concerns only as they can be accommodated to immediate self-interest.

Occasionally, a wider perspective is urged. The New York *Times* and a few other newspapers in the region, together with planning groups like the RPA, assert that the needs of the region "as a whole" must be considered, and the Citizens Budget Commission and other Manhattan business associations now and then adopt a similar view. For most of these spokesmen, however, the call for a wider perspective is primarily an appeal for greater regional effort to preserve the urban core, an effort essential to their own economic vitality.

FUNCTIONAL INTEGRATION IN THE METROPOLIS

Fragmentation does not entail isolation, however. In order to attain positive goals or avert threats to self-interest, groups in the metropolis are frequently drawn into interaction. Where they agree on goals, they may join in cooperative problem-solving. When disagreement exists, they will engage in conflict and bargaining as each attempts to make his aims prevail.[1]

The patterns of conflict and cooperation that develop in metropolitan political systems may, on the evidence of this study, be linked to the functional specificity or narrowness of the issues under consideration. Simply stated, operating organizations in the same functional area, such as highways or urban renewal, are likely to engage predominantly in cooperative efforts, while interaction involving more than one function, or general-government issues, is likely to be heavily infused with conflict. Functional cooperation is particularly likely to develop along vertical lines—i.e., among local, state, and federal agencies in the same functional area. In some areas, such as highways and water supply, cooperation will also extend horizontally, among local units in the same region; in others, such as urban renewal, interaction will be almost entirely vertical. The explanation for the development of cooperation along these lines seems relatively clear. The primary goals of the operating agencies at local, state, and federal levels are to achieve concrete, measurable results; and highways can be built, redevelopment programs carried out, and effective public health measures instituted only through mutual cooperation among a number of institutions. The significance of the vertical lines of cooperation has expanded greatly during the postwar era with the increased availability of federal and state funds in many functional areas of concern to metropolitan regions.[2]

Conflict among operating agencies is not unknown, of course. In the New York region, for example, the PNYA, Moses, and the New Jersey Turnpike Authority have from time to time disagreed over such issues as construction priorities and apportionment of costs, and generally these divisions have emphasized the general conclusion that institutional self-interest is the fundamental basis for action.[3]

If the focus of attention is extended to nonoperating organizations in the same functional field (to users, other beneficiaries, and government regulators), the potential for conflict within the functional arena increases, but cooperation is still a dominant theme. Beneficiaries will generally support operating organizations in their efforts to improve and expand service, as long as direct benefits are perceived and direct costs increase only marginally. The prospects for such cooperation among regional interests are greatly enhanced when (as in urban renewal and highways) only a small portion of the costs is paid from local taxes. If operating agencies seek a reduction in service or an increase in charges without a clear increase in direct benefits, however, conflict with user groups is likely.

Thus, in the highway field, automobile and bus associations generally favor the expansion plans of the PNYA, the New Jersey Turnpike Authority, and other operating units and vigorously oppose any efforts to reduce the funds available for continued highway expansion and improvement (such as Musto's bill to tap PNYA funds or the plan to siphon off Turnpike revenues to aid rail service). Similarly, in his study of urban renewal in Newark, Kaplan found the Newark Housing Authority and its federal allies supported by realtors, downtown corporations, and other beneficiaries of the slum clearance program.[4]

When the relationships among operating units and beneficiaries in a functional field are predominantly cooperative, two additional traits are likely to characterize these sectors. First, the functional subsystem is likely to be relatively independent of the rest of the region's political system, with respect to both definition of goals and implementation of policy. If the operating agencies and major beneficiaries are in agreement, the opportunities for other interests to shape policy are sharply limited. The opposition of residents in the way of highway and urban renewal programs, for example, will be viewed as negative, and it may be difficult to convince mayors, governors, and others with broader political responsibility to intervene.[5] The tendency toward functional autonomy will be strengthened when the operating organizations are relatively free of direct policy and budgetary control by general-government leaders in the region. Thus, independent authorities which rely on user charges (such as the PNYA) and agencies which obtain substantial federal aid (as in the urban renewal and highway fields) are especially likely to be the center of functionally autonomous subsystems in metropolitan regions.[6]

Also, within these functional subsystems, staff members, whose main formal responsibility is to supply administrative expertise and technical skill, will often have crucial policy-making roles. The importance of staff in making policy arises in part because of the complexity of such substantive areas as transportation, urban renewal, and water supply, and in part from the need for extensive interagency cooperation in the development of policy when local, state, and federal agencies are involved. These tendencies are reinforced when the functional subsystem is relatively autonomous, since the apparent need in this case is for identifying the best solution in engineering, economic, or public-health terms, not for interagency bargaining and compromise. In actuality, of course, as studies of the PNYA and the Newark Housing Authority have shown, expertise is a useful adjunct, but staff members are frequently skilled political strategists as well.[7]

The predominance of cooperation and autonomy in policy-making seen in the highway field does not, on the evidence of this study, extend to the rail-passenger field. There, reduced public patronage, combined with the relative paucity of public funds, has led the operating organizations to seek ways of contracting service or of shifting responsibility to others. The railroads' efforts in these directions have been opposed by user groups; and conflict in goals between railroads and beneficiaries and among different classes of beneficiaries has been a major theme. Cooperative efforts have occurred but have generally involved only part of the rail coalition and have often been in opposition to another alliance of interests concerned with rail policy. Thus, the railroads readily joined forces with the MRTC and others who would shift the financial burden of providing rail service to the general public (by means of a Transit District) or to an element of the road coalition (e.g., the PNYA or the New Jersey Turnpike); meanwhile, with the cooperation of their federal ally, the ICC, they pursued the alternative strategy of curtailing service. Bergen commuters and Manhattan business groups allied themselves with the railroads and the MRTC in favor of a Transit District, while the IMGBRS joined with other interests in central New Jersey, where rail services were not in immediate danger of collapse, in opposition to a District and in support of Port Authority action.

Thus far, we have explored the extent to which metropolitan fragmentation is bridged by patterns of cooperation and conflict within any one functional arena. Multifunctional relationships, as between rail and highway or between urban renewal and highway organizations, are relatively infrequent, and where they do exist, conflict is likely to occur. Interaction of any sort is less common because the primary objectives within each functional arena are usually perceived as being attainable without coordination with other functions. When efforts are made to overcome the tradition of functional autonomy, conflict rather than cooperation is probable, for each interest views the other as a competitor for financial resources and public allegiance. The relationships between the PNYA and the transit study commissions prior to the 1955 Memorandum of Understanding and between the MRTC and Moses illustrate these tendencies.

Cooperative efforts do arise, however, when specific benefits are perceived by each participant. Thus, the railroads and the

Port Authority join in support of a Transit District which will reduce the financial burdens on both. Alternatively, some degree of coordination across functions may be obtained through integrating responsibility under one man (as Moses with Long Island highways and parks) or one agency (as the PNYA and the New Jersey State Highway Department, each with its various interests in the broad realm of transportation).

Interaction involving units of general government at the local level—cities, towns, and counties—warrants separate treatment. Since each such government is itself an integrator of numerous functions, any cooperation involving general government is in a sense multifunctional. Such combined efforts, however, generally develop only when specific problems become acute and when the financial costs to be borne by each government can be clearly related to local benefits. Both of these factors motivate local governments to cooperate along narrow functional lines, e.g., to meet water-supply problems or to curb water pollution.[8]

When local benefits are not clearly perceived as being equal to costs, voluntary cooperation involving local financial support is unlikely to develop. Instead, collaboration will be restricted to the establishment of goals for other institutions and to defensive alliances against outside efforts to assign costs locally. The rail problem in the New York region illustrates this pattern of behavior. Only a small percentage of the region's inhabitants use the rail system, and it is difficult to allocate benefits (other than those to users) among the localities served. Because of these characteristics, together with additional complicating factors (e.g., the tradition of private responsibility), local government leaders are unable to agree upon cooperative programs involving significant local financing of rail services. Joint efforts are directed toward obtaining outside assistance and toward the avoidance of local assessments. Thus, municipal and county leaders in central New Jersey joined to press for PNYA action to meet the rail crisis, Westchester's local representatives urged state and federal action to solve the New Haven problem, and the members of the MRC presented a united front against the Transit District and its regional-subsidy implications.[9]

Moreover, attempts to press for cooperation among local government units on a basis other than that of voluntary collaboration run the risk of stimulating widespread intergovernmental conflict in the metropolis. As the reactions to the Transit District scheme in Newark, Hudson County, and other areas illustrate, spokesmen for each part of the region are sensitive to possible incursions on local autonomy, and efforts to impose new policy-making structures are likely to activate underlying hostilities in the metropolis, such as those of city versus city, city versus suburb, local government versus independent public authority, and state versus state.[10]

POLICY INNOVATION AND INERTIA

The content of regional policies—in transportation, water supply, urban renewal, and other areas—is significantly shaped by the goals and interactions of these metropolitan interests. Other factors, "external" to the regional political system, are also of great importance in deciding policy—economic, social, and technological forces and the nature of national political forces. It is no easy task to determine which of these forces are more likely to initiate policy change in the metropolis, for the interaction among them is continuous. Still, the developments analyzed in this study suggest a conclusion that is consistent with other commentaries. The factors labeled above as "external" will generally be the initiators of significant policy change in the metropolis. In comparison, the region's political system (including state institutions which operate within the metropolis) tends to be biased toward the continuation of present policy—i.e., toward the *status quo*. Regional policies and the structure of the regional political system tend to change primarily in response to external forces. The particular characteristics of the response, however, are shaped by the existing regional system.[11]

These relationships can be illustrated by several examples drawn from this study. The development of automotive technology, combined with changes in public demand and other external factors, was the main cause of the changes in transportation policy and political structure in the metropolis during the first half of the twentieth century. However, the specific content of highway-dominant policy and the particular form of the highway coalition vary from region to region, depending on the existing political system (as well as geographic and other factors). In the New York area, the interstate nature of the region, the prior existence of the PNYA, and other local characteristics were critical. Finally, once the region's political system had adapted to the automotive age, the new policy and political structure became highly resistant to change.

Similarly, it was the decline in the use of public transportation, in the face of changes in public demand and the growth of automobile usage, which sparked renewed interest throughout the United States in a search for changes in regional transportation policy following the end of World War II. In response to these changes, study commissions were created in many metropolitan regions, although the nature and evolution of the study groups varied. The New York counterpart, the MRTC, found its work shaped by such local factors as the bistate nature of the region and the perspective which had developed during previous decades of study-group efforts. Then, with the MRTC study in existence, the region failed to take any other significant steps to meet the rail problem during the next four years.

The decline in freight traffic, coupled with the inability of the region and the states to respond more effectively to the rail problem, led the railroads to press for policy change in the national arena. The effort was successful, and in 1958 the rail lines were partially freed from the shackles of state regulatory controls. Again, it was mainly the pressure of external forces which ended the policy inertia within the region, and new policies toward the railroads were established. Then, with these programs in being, the region and its state institutions once more found it difficult to search further. New York State's commitment to its tax reduction and commuter-car programs, for example, encouraged a five-year hiatus in the development of new policies. In time the continued deterioration of the Eastern railroads, underscored by the bankruptcy of the New Haven, the decline of the Long Island, and the impending insolvency of the Erie-Lackawanna and the Jersey Central, made it imperative that New York and her sister states generate new responses to meet the region's transport crisis.

The reasons which underlie this limited role of the region's political system may be summarized briefly and illustrated by reference to the policy-making efforts analyzed in this study. Established policy at any point in time is accompanied by a structure of organized interests, which have carved out roles and developed stable relationships with each other. These interests respond defensively to efforts to alter policy whenever such efforts threaten to curtail their power. The prospects for intraregional political forces overcoming these defensive alliances are generally small, for the interests which might support change are divided (e.g., railroads and their commuters) and weakened by apathy (e.g., note the small number of commuters who join the commuter groups). In addition, they confront a major weakness of the regional political system, the lack of central policy-making institutions which have the formal power and the incentive to act. And those actors who must serve as surrogates for regional government—central-city mayors, county executives, and state governors—face pressures for alternative uses of limited time and funds as well as conflicting views on the policy issue at hand. Consequently, their responses are largely directed toward shifting responsibility to others and responding minimally to crises.

Finally, the ability of the political system to "tackle the renewal problem, the transportation crisis, the urban sprawl in a thoroughgoing manner" [12] is sharply reduced by the substantive complexities of these problems, especially when viewed in their regionwide dimensions. For most actors concerned with the regional transportation problem, there are no clear answers to the questions of what mix of rail, bus, and automobile facilities and of public control and private responsibility will meet the combined tests of economic and social efficiency and political feasibility. Governor Meyner's plea of 1958 for an "expert" who could find the "best solution" illustrates the feelings of uncertainty and impotence of a large number of those directly involved in the transit problem.

These themes are seen in the two types of effort to shape policy for the metropolis analyzed in previous chapters: the extensive study and the states' "direct action" approach. A long-range study is a probable response when the regional problem is complex and of low political intensity (i.e., there is little political pressure for immediate, direct action). A study is attractive under these conditions because it entails a relatively low expenditure of funds and other political resources, it further reduces the pressure on regional leadership groups for immediate action, and it provides a way to obtain additional knowledge about the problem and perhaps a feasible plan of action. In addition, as Huntington points out in his discussion of defense-strategy innovation, study groups are often valuable in "arousing support from strategically located officials and groups." [13]

The development and results of the study are likely, however, to illustrate the weaknesses of the region's polity in seeking paths toward innovation. When governors and other central regional leaders are actively involved, the study may yield politically feasible proposals; but, given the other demands on their time and their preference for avoiding responsibility for complex and costly problems, such involvement does not often occur. A second and more likely source of influence is the range of interests which may anticipate benefits or losses from the study. Of these, existing institutions and groups which obtain direct benefits from present policy are most likely to have the incentives and resources to influence the study group, and their influence is likely to be in the direction of neutralizing any significant threat to their own powers and sustaining policy. As the efforts of the PNYA illustrate, such influence may infuse the entire study-group structure, from the detailed work of technical consultants to the framework of general policy and the tactics of publicity and political influence.

In so far as these outside forces are not controlling, the study organization is left to define its own perspective and strategy. In the absence of clear guidelines from political leaders, the members of the study group may engage in logrolling, adding together their separate preferences into a combined program rather than shaping their recommendations in the light of political feasibility. The result is likely to be an extensive, costly plan satisfactory only to the limited range of interests which have shaped the goals of the study group and guided its deliberations. The recommendations will be attacked by groups which believe that their interests may be adversely affected, including those who generally favor innovation in the policy area under study but fear the adverse consequences of specific proposals on their own position.[14] Thus, study groups frequently suffer the fate of the MRTC: having begun with enthusiasm and high hopes as to the potential for policy innovation in the metropolis, the study-group members find their proposals under fire from a wide range of narrow geographical and functional perspectives, and efforts to introduce even limited versions of their proposed innovations are defeated or succeed only after long delays.[15]

Occasionally, public concern about one or more regional issues reaches such a high level of intensity that studies will not suffice. Direct action to meet the problem is required. The void in regional leadership institutions is not likely to be filled at this point by cooperative action at the local level unless all governments perceive net benefits to their own constituencies. Instead, the governor (or in some single-county regions, the county executive) will generally act as surrogate, for his responsibility embraces all or a large part of the metropolis, and he has the power to act with a minimum of consultation. The contrast between the MRC's inability to agree upon a plan involving local financial commitments and the actions of Rockefeller and his aides in 1959 illustrates the comparative advantages of the state over its local governments in responding to metropolitan crises.

The state's comparative advantages in mobilizing resources and developing new policies do not, however, emancipate it from the constraints of the existing political system. State institutions are already actively involved in the metropolis—in highways, rail transportation, public health, education, and other areas. These state activities are fragmented functionally and are part of the web of functional relationships that reinforce existing policy. Moreover, the responses of governors and state legislatures are shaped by the statewide framework within which they operate. The governor, conscious of the need to avoid antagonizing his non-metropolitan constituency and aware of the complexity of the issue and the divisions of opinion within the metropolis, finds it difficult to act as a regional leader with a clear mandate. When the legislature is involved, its response is shaped by the interaction of urban, suburban, and rural representatives, often under party control antagonistic to the governor.[16]

Consequently, regional problems are likely to be defined by the states in narrow terms and short-range solutions devised. New York temporizes with commuter-car programs and tax reductions, and New Jersey hopes that partial subsidies will solve the rail problem, at least for the present. Effective action is rendered even more difficult when the state seeks cooperation with other units of government, as illustrated by the bistate negotiations to establish a Transit District and by the efforts of state officials to persuade the PNYA and Westchester County officials to join in efforts to meet the rail crisis. Similar political party affiliation can provide an important basis for intergovernmental cooperation, as the Syracuse studies demonstrate.[17] But when the immediate self-interest of different constituencies diverge substantially, common party labels do not bridge the gap; witness the divisions between Albany and Westchester on the New Haven Railroad crisis.[18]

THE FUTURE OF THE METROPOLITAN POLITICAL SYSTEM

The primary characteristics of metropolitan politics identified in this analysis are fragmentation, functional cooperation, and a strong bias toward policy stasis rather than innovation. What are the prospects for continuation and change in these patterns of political behavior?

It seems probable that the involvement of local units of government in cooperative efforts at the local level will continue to expand, as service demands and the problems of meeting them through individual municipal action both increase. These agreements will, however, generally follow the present pattern, joining a few towns together to meet specific functional problems on a voluntary basis. More promising in terms of its potential for significant coordination is the regional council of elected local officials, which now exists in the New York area and half a dozen other regions. In time, these councils may provide a basis for significant, positive cooperation within the metropolis. In fact, a committee which studied the New York MRC in 1958 concluded that through working together during a two-year period the local officials had already "learned to define the regional dimensions of their local responsibilities," and that the MRC had shown "great potentialities for becoming . . . an official regional leadership institution." [19]

It is true that the councils in New York and other regions have been able to cooperate in a number of areas, e.g., in the preparation of a master map of water pollution sources and the establishment of a regional traffic communication system. The evolution of the MRC, however, underscores the limitations that these organizations face when confronted with complex and politically sensitive issues. In the mass transportation field, the MRC reached agreement on a negative position, opposition to a Transit District, but was unable to agree on the politically difficult questions of the use of local funds and how costs might be apportioned among its members. The MRC's failure to obtain legal status as an advisory council on regional problems further emphasized the localism which motivates many of its members.[20]

Experience with the council device in the New York area is consistent with that in other regions to date. Because of the requirements of voluntary agreement and unanimous consent and because such consent can only be obtained when each unit involved perceives net benefits for its own constituency, the regional council is unable to act effectively on most metropolitan issues. Local sensitivities about political and fiscal autonomy make it unlikely that these organizations will become significant centers for determining regional priorities and policies in the foreseeable future.[21]

If voluntary councils do not provide a firm basis for developing regional cooperation and policy innovation, what are the prospects for the widely publicized alternative—the creation of a formal metropolitan government, responsible to a regionwide constituency? This approach would provide the central leadership institutions which the region now lacks. Efforts to establish such organizations have generally failed, however, and the two successes in this country in recent years (Nashville and Miami) both occurred in single-county regions. The possibilities of such governments being formed in multicounty regions are slight and in interstate areas remote indeed. Morever, the experience of Toronto, the well-publicized Canadian experiment with metropolitan federation, reveals many of the same problems found in the New York region. Toronto's governing council is composed of representatives of the thirteen municipalities in the Metro, and the initial hope was that, by working together, these members would adopt an increasingly regional view. After ten years, however, the federation was judged to have made little progress toward this goal. The problem of mass transportation financing and other regional problems have been the cause of considerable conflict, and, in Smallwood's view, "the relations between Council members appear to be growing worse, rather than better, with the passage of years." [22]

In the larger regions, it seems likely that the nearest approach to regional government in terms of territorial expanse will be the regional district or authority. Some of these agencies are governed by officials of local governments or their appointees, while others, like the PNYA, are controlled by appointees of state officials. In either case, the limitations that characterize the PNYA are found in other districts as well. Each is generally restricted to a narrow functional segment of the metropolis, and this limitation is reinforced by the functional expertise of the agency's staff and by the structure of interests that forms around the district. As observers of experience in the Los Angeles region comment, the single-function district "attracts a clientele, comprising users of its service, interested in the service level it will provide and prepared to defend the organization against attacks." [23] Efforts to expand these agencies into multipurpose units have generally been unsuccessful. While many of the special districts are metropolitan in territorial scope, in responsibility and perspective they will continue to stand as another special pleader, another defender of fragmentation in the metropolis.[24]

The continuing demands for action to meet such regional problems as those in transportation, water supply, and pollution, coupled with limitations in organization, perspective, and financing at the local level, will continue to shift the pressures for action upward to state and federal levels. This trend will be accelerated as the proportion of the metropolitan population living in interstate regions—now one-third of the total—increases. State institutions will respond to these pressures and at times, as this study illustrates, assume major policy-making responsibility. The reapportionment of state legislatures under the guidelines of the 1964 Supreme Court decisions should make these institutions more responsive to metropolitan needs. But as legislative action on the Transit District bill illustrates, metropolitan interests in the legislature are divided between cities and suburbs, and reapportionment will not significantly help to unite these factions.

In addition, the multiple constituency pressures on the governor, the tradition of functional separation at the state level, financial limitations, and the inherent complexity of such issues as mass transportation will restrict the interest and ability of state governments to respond to metropolitan problems. The tendencies to seek short-run palliatives and to respond along narrow functional lines are not likely to be replaced by forward-looking, effective action, involving coordinated planning across functional areas in a comprehensive approach to urban development.[25]

The limited response of state institutions, combined with the already well-developed pattern of city-federal relationships, will probably increase the pressure for additional federal action on regional problems. The national government will frequently be responsive to these pressures, owing to its greater financial resources, often combined with the greater political sensitivity

of the President and Congress to urban interests compared
with that of the states. The growing importance of regional
problems that cross state lines, coupled with the great difficulty
of developing cooperative interstate programs, adds an additional
incentive for federal action. Thus, mass transportation has
already followed the path of highways, urban renewal, and
other issues to the federal doorstep.[26] The familiar pattern of
fragmentation of responsibility is repeated, however, at the
national level. As Danielson has noted, federal responsibility
in regional development is scattered "among a host of executive
agencies, independent bodies, and congressional committees,"
and this lack of central focus, combined with the pressures
of other national and international issues, limits the effectiveness
of the federal government in tackling the problems of the
metropolis.[27]

The increasing role of state and federal agencies in the
metropolis reduces the responsibility of locally elected officials
in meeting regional problems. This tendency serves to reinforce another found within the region: the separation into
semiautonomous authorities of responsibility for transport, urban renewal, and other issues central to urban development.
If, as Long suggests, the major danger in the evolution of the
metropolis is not deficiencies in service levels but "the draining
of vitality from local government," [28] are there any countertrends
which might help local institutions develop a more positive,
progressive role in meeting major regional problems?

The tendency in recent federal legislation for financial aid to
the metropolis to be conditioned on coordinated planning within each region might be such a straw in the wind, for it will
provide a concrete incentive for increased cooperation among
the various agencies concerned with regional development.[29]
Conceivably, such pressure could, step by step, broaden the perspectives of cooperating local, state, and federal officials, both
functionally and territorially, and increase their ability to

cope with regional problems in terms of a broad strategy of urban development. In view, however, of the heavy emphasis on functional problems in the sporadic political pressures for action, combined with the narrow constituency base of local elected officials and the real differences in values within the region as to what goals regional development should maximize, it seems doubtful that significant broad-gauged coordination at the local level will result. Ironically, perhaps, the infusion of federal and state funds often has the opposite effect —reducing the pressure for direct coordination among local officials [30]—and the insertion of a "planning" clause is unlikely to reverse the tide.

If significant forward steps in planning and coordination are taken, it is more likely that they will involve closer linkages among state and federal officials in different functional fields, such as housing and highways, emphasizing cross-fertilization among professional staffs. Where powerful, specialized regional agencies like the PNYA exist, they too may become involved. Planning among these interests will often be increasingly effective as the participation and power of local elected officials is reduced, and if agreement on perspectives and goals among these interests can be achieved, the tendency to exclude local representatives will be reinforced. The early experience of the Tri-State Transportation Committee, emphasizing state and federal control over the development of "long-range comprehensive land-use and transportation recommendations" for the New York region, is a prime example of these trends.[31]

Norton Long and other observers of the metropolitan scene have frequently expressed the hope that responsive and responsible political leadership can be developed within the metropolis, permitting the citizens of the region and their leaders to shape their common destiny. Otherwise, Long warns, "local self-government will give way to the administration of people rather than the self-direction of citizens." [32] The available evidence lends little encouragement to Long's hope and considerable justification for his fears. The elected leaders of the region seem destined to preside over fragmented segments of metropolitan real estate, while control over government policy on major regional issues flows increasingly to the intricate and expanding networks of state, federal, and specialized regional institutions.

Notes

This volume is based upon extensive interviews and private files as well as sources which are available publicly. Because of guarantees of anonymity, the Notes are limited to public sources.

CHAPTER I. INTRODUCTION

1. The quotation is from Gladys M. Kammerer, "The Politics of Metropolis: Still a Frontier," *Public Administration Review*, XXIII (December, 1963), 240. For other analyses of politics in major metropolitan areas, see Edward C. Banfield, *Political Influence* (New York, Free Press, 1960), especially Chap. 4; and several studies of the New York area, including Robert C. Wood (with V. V. Almendinger), *1400 Governments: The Political Economy of the New York Metropolitan Region* (Cambridge, Mass., Harvard University Press, 1961); Wallace S. Sayre and Herbert Kaufman, *Governing New York City: Politics in the Metropolis* (New York, Russell Sage Foundation, 1960; paperback edition, New York, Norton, 1965), especially Chap. 15; Herbert Kaufman, "Gotham in the Air Age," in Harold Stein, ed., *Public Administration and Policy Development: A Case Book* (New York, Harcourt, Brace, 1952), pp. 143-97; and Paul Tillett and Myron Weiner, *The Closing of Newark Airport* (University, University of Alabama Press, 1955). See also York Willbern, *The Withering Away of the City* (University, University of Alabama Press, 1964). Most recent studies of metropolitan politics have been concerned with moderate-sized regions and with the issue of general government reorganization rather than with the politics of resolving specific regional problems. See David A. Booth, *Metropolitics: The Nashville Consolidation* (East Lansing, Institute for Community Development and Services, Michigan State University, 1963); Henry J. Schmandt, Paul G. Steinbicker, and George D. Wendel, *Metropolitan Reform in St. Louis: A Case Study* (New York, Holt, Rinehart and Winston, 1961); Edward Sofen, *The Metropolitan Miami Experiment* (Bloomington, Indiana University Press, 1963); Scott Greer, *Metropolitics:*

A Study of Political Culture (New York, Wiley, 1963). The politics of specific regional issues in a one-county metropolitan area are examined in Roscoe C. Martin et al., *Decisions in Syracuse* (Bloomington, Indiana University Press, 1961).

2. See, for example, Victor Jones, "Local Government Organization in Metropolitan Areas," in Coleman Woodbury, ed., *The Future of Cities and Urban Redevelopment* (Chicago, University of Chicago Press, 1953), pp. 485–507; Norton E. Long, *The Polity*, ed. by Charles Press (Chicago, Rand McNally, 1962), pp. 139–64.

3. See Robert C. Wood, *Suburbia: Its People and Their Politics* (Boston, Houghton Mifflin, 1959); Wood, *1400 Governments*, especially pp. 65–113.

4. Edward C. Banfield and Morton Grodzins, *Government and Housing in Metropolitan Areas* (New York, McGraw-Hill, 1958), p. 159.

5. See Sayre and Kaufman, *Governing New York City*, especially Chaps. 18–19; Banfield, *Political Influence*, especially Chaps. 8–9.

6. See Schmandt et al., *Metropolitan Reform in St. Louis*, pp. 39–42; Banfield, *Political Influence*, especially Chaps. 4 and 10; Wood, *1400 Governments*, p. 195 and *passim*; Morris Janowitz, *The Community Press in an Urban Setting* (New York, Free Press, 1952).

7. See, for example, Scott Greer, *Governing the Metropolis* (New York, Wiley, 1962), Chap. 3; Jones, in Woodbury, ed., *Future of Cities*, pp. 500 ff.

8. John C. Bollens, *The States and the Metropolitan Problem* (Chicago, Council of State Governments, 1956), p. 106.

9. Activities of these councils have included studies of recreation, sewerage, and library problems, for example, and creation of a regional traffic communication system in one area and of a regional parks system in another. See Washington Metropolitan Regional Conference, "A Survey of Urban Regional General Intergovernmental Organizations," Washington, D.C., March, 1961, and periodic reports of the individual councils.

10. See Bollens, *States and the Metropolitan Problem*, especially pp. 86–104; Victor Jones, *Metropolitan Government* (Chicago, University of Chicago Press, 1942); Schmandt et al., *Metropolitan Reform in St. Louis;* Booth, *Metropolitics;* and Greer, *Metropolitics.* In the United States, only two attempts to allocate substantial powers to regional governments have been successful during this century: those in Nashville and Miami, both single-county re-

gions. The successful effort in Nashville is discussed in Booth, *Metropolitics;* on Miami, see Greer, *Metropolitics,* and Sofen, *Metropolitan Miami Experiment.* The 1953 reorganization in Toronto is discussed in John G. Grumm, *Metropolitan Area Government: The Toronto Experience* (Lawrence, University of Kansas Publication, 1959).

11. See Bollens, *States and the Metropolitan Problem,* pp. 117–26; John C. Bollens, *Special District Governments in the United States* (Berkeley, University of California Press, 1957), especially Chap. 1; and Robert G. Smith, *Public Authorities, Special Districts and Local Government* (Washington, D.C., National Association of Counties, 1964).

12. The quotations are found in Frederick L. Bird, *A Study of the Port of New York Authority* (New York, Dun and Bradstreet, 1949), p. 183, and Chamber of Commerce of the State of New York, "Statement of American Economic Principles," 1952. For a generally favorable view of interstate authorities and other compact agencies, see Richard H. Leach and R. S. Sugg, *Administration of Interstate Compacts* (Baton Rouge, Louisiana State University Press, 1959).

13. See Woodrow Wilson, "The Study of Administration," *Political Science Quarterly,* II (June, 1887), 197–222, reprinted in Dwight Waldo, ed., *Ideas and Issues in Public Administration: A Book of Readings* (New York, McGraw-Hill, 1953), pp. 65–75.

14. The best analysis of the public authority as a political institution is Sayre and Kaufman, *Governing New York City,* Chap. 9. See also Smith, *Public Authorities.* For studies of particular authorities in action, see especially Martin Meyerson and Edward C. Banfield, *Politics, Planning, and the Public Interest: The Case of Public Housing in Chicago* (New York, Free Press, 1955); Kaufman, in Stein, ed., *Public Administration;* Tillett and Weiner, *Closing of Newark Airport.*

15. Cf. Bollens, *States and the Metropolitan Problem,* pp. 121–23. The quotation is from Austin J. Tobin, "The Work and Program of the Port of New York Authority," 1953, p. 5.

16. Robert C. Wood, "The Metropolitan Governor," unpublished Ph.D. dissertation, Harvard University, 1949. Cf. Coleman B. Ransone, *The Office of Governor in the United States* (University, University of Alabama Press, 1956), pp. 194–97 and *passim;* Banfield and Grodzins, *Government and Housing in Metropolitan Areas,* pp. 160–61.

17. See V. O. Key, *American State Politics: An Introduction* (New York, Knopf, 1956), pp. 230 ff. On the nature and extent of apathy toward public issues, see Robert A. Dahl, *Who Governs? Democracy and Power in an American City* (New Haven, Yale University Press, 1961), Chaps. 16, 19, and *passim*.

18. See Gordon E. Baker, *Rural versus Urban Political Power* (New York, Doubleday, 1955).

19. For illustrations of legislative behavior on metropolitan problems, see Banfield, *Political Influence*, Chap. 4; Wood, *1400 Governments*, pp. 149–54.

20. See Michael N. Danielson, *Federal-Metropolitan Politics and the Commuter Crisis* (New York, Columbia University Press, 1965).

21. See especially Sayre and Kaufman, *Governing New York City*, pp. 592–93; Harold Kaplan, *Urban Renewal Politics: Slum Clearance in Newark* (New York, Columbia University Press, 1963), pp. 37–38, 180–81, and *passim;* York Willbern, "The States as Components in an Areal Division of Powers," in Arthur Maass, ed., *Area and Power: A Theory of Local Government* (New York, Free Press, 1959), pp. 73–74. Although the problem is aggravated by the political structure of the metropolis, fragmentation is characteristic of all levels of the American political system. See Robert A. Dahl and Charles E. Lindblom, *Politics, Economics and Welfare: Planning and Politico-economic Systems Resolved into Basic Social Processes* (New York, Harper and Row, 1953), especially pp. 335 ff.

22. See, for example, David B. Truman, *The Governmental Process: Political Interests and Public Opinion* (New York, Knopf, 1951).

23. Cf. Wood, *1400 Governments*, pp. 121 ff.; Robert S. Friedman, "State Politics and Highways," in Herbert Jacob and Kenneth N. Vines, eds., *Politics in the American States: A Comparative Analysis* (Boston, Little, Brown, 1965), pp. 434 ff.

24. See Wilfred Owen, *The Metropolitan Transportation Problem* (Washington, D.C., The Brookings Institution, 1956), and Lyle C. Fitch and associates, *Urban Transportation and Public Policy* (San Francisco, Chandler, 1964).

CHAPTER II. TRANSPORTATION IN THE METROPOLIS

1. For the purpose of this study, the New York region includes twenty-two counties in three states: nine in New Jersey—Bergen,

Essex, Hudson, Middlesex, Monmouth, Morris, Passaic, Somerset, and Union; five in New York City—New York (Manhattan), Bronx, Queens, Kings (Brooklyn), and Richmond (Staten Island); seven New York counties outside New York City—Nassau, Suffolk, Dutchess, Orange, Putnam, Rockland, and Westchester; and Fairfield in Connecticut. This is the region as defined by the RPA, the area's major private organization concerned with overall planning. For some purposes, one additional county in New Jersey, Mercer, may also be included.

The U.S. Bureau of the Census includes only seventeen of the twenty-two counties in its comparable unit, now called the New York–Northeastern New Jersey Standard Consolidated Area. Excluded from the Bureau's tabulation are several of the outlying counties—Dutchess, Orange, Putnam, Monmouth, and Fairfield (which was subdivided into three separate metropolitan areas in the 1960 census tabulations).

2. See John T. Cunningham, *Railroading in New Jersey* (Newark, Associated Railroads of New Jersey, 1951), pp. 6–16, 35–55, and *passim*, also references therein, p. 107. See also Jean Gottmann, *Megalopolis: The Urbanized Northeastern Seaboard of the United States* (New York, Twentieth Century Fund, 1961), Chap. 3.

3. The first major effort was begun in the 1870s by an engineer, D. C. Haskins. The project was first halted in 1880, when part of the structure collapsed, killing twenty men; in 1882, after building 1,800 feet of tunnel, Haskins' company went into bankruptcy. The company was reorganized eight years later and carried the tunnel forward another 1,800 feet before again going into bankruptcy. See Cunningham, *Railroading in New Jersey*, pp. 62–63.

4. The Pennsylvania then continued the tunnel under the East River to provide direct access to Manhattan for passengers and freight on the Long Island Rail Road, which the Pennsylvania now controlled.

5. See New York State, Public Service Commission for the First District, *Report . . . for the Year Ending December 31, 1913*, Vol. V: *Documentary History of Railroad Companies* (New York, 1914), pp. 605–20, 768–72, 881–84, 978; Alvin F. Harlow, *The Road of the Century: The Story of the New York Central* (New York, Creative Age Press, 1947), pp. 130, 204–06.

6. The system begun in 1904 was the Interborough Rapid Transit (IRT); it was constructed and owned by the city and leased for

operation to a private firm. In 1913 the Brooklyn Rapid Transit Company, later Brooklyn-Manhattan Transit (BMT), entered the subway field, and in 1925 construction of a city-owned system, the Independent (IND), was begun.

7. The joint board, known as the Suburban Transit Engineering Board, included representatives from the Port of New York Authority, Association of Railroad Executives, New York City Board of Transportation, North Jersey Transit Commission, and the county boards of supervisors of Westchester, Nassau, and Suffolk. See Erwin W. Bard, *The Port of New York Authority* (New York, Columbia University Press, 1942), pp. 128–32.

8. In the plans of the North Jersey Transit Commission and the joint board, passengers would transfer in Hudson County from the New Jersey railroads to a new trans-Hudson rail line. This line would carry them under the Hudson River in one of two tunnels and deliver them to stations between 57th Street and the Battery in Manhattan. The Port Authority's 1937 plan was a limited version of this proposal. Another approach to the trans-Hudson problem, used in L. Alfred Jenny's 1936 plan, involved the construction of larger tunnels in order to transport the railroad trains directly into Manhattan; a terminal to receive the trains would be constructed at about 42nd Street and Sixth Avenue. In addition to the New Jersey–Manhattan plans, the North Jersey Commission included several new rail linkages in New Jersey and a new rapid transit line from Manhattan to Westchester, the joint board would have connected Long Island to Manhattan via a new subway loop, and the Port Authority plan included a linkage from the New Jersey–Manhattan system to Staten Island. See L. Alfred Jenny, "Report on the Acute Transportation Problem Existing between Northeastern New Jersey and the City of New York" (Trenton, Department of Conservation and Economic Development, State of New Jersey, 1951), pp. 7–11, 15–29; RPA, *Regional Plan Bulletin*, No. 25 (New York, June 17, 1935); Bard, *Port of New York Authority*, pp. 128–34; PNYA, *Suburban Transit for Northern New Jersey*, March 1, 1937; statements of Austin J. Tobin and Walter P. Hedden on behalf of the PNYA, before the New York Metropolitan Rapid Transit Commission, Nov. 12, 1953.

9. See especially Bard, *Port of New York Authority*, p. 132; Jenny, "Report on the Acute Transportation Problem," pp. 17–23, 27; statement of Austin J. Tobin., Nov. 12, 1953, pp. 2–6.

10. See RPA, *Regional Plan Bulletin*, No. 77 (New York, July, 1951); Wilfred Owen, *The Metropolitan Transportation Problem* (Washington, D.C., The Brookings Institution, 1956), *passim*. On this section and the rest of this chapter, see Robert C. Wood (with V. V. Almendinger), *1400 Governments: The Political Economy of the New York Metropolitan Region* (Cambridge, Mass., Harvard University Press, 1961), especially pp. 123–44.

11. NYMRTC and NJMRTC, *Joint Report* (March 3, 1954), pp. 10–11, 14, 65; RPA, *Regional Plan Bulletin*, No. 77.

12. Federal-aid highway plans for urban areas approved between 1944 and 1955, for example, involved $3 billion in state and federal funds. Owen, *Metropolitan Transportation Problem*, p. 62. The highway program was greatly expanded by the Federal-Aid Highway Act of 1956.

13. On the Port Authority, see Bard, *Port of New York Authority*, Part II, and Wallace S. Sayre and Herbert Kaufman, *Governing New York City: Politics in the Metropolis* (New York, Russell Sage Foundation, 1960; paperback edition, New York, Norton, 1965), pp. 321–22. On the Triborough Authority, see State of New York, Temporary State Commission on Coordination of State Authorities, *Staff Report on Public Authorities under New York State*, March 21, 1956, pp. 26, 30–31, and *passim*.

14. NYMRTC and NJMRTC, *Joint Report*, pp. 12–13.

15. See Gottmann, *Megalopolis*, Chap. 4; Owen, *Metropolitan Transportation Problem*, Chap. 3. The ferry problem warrants a word of explanation. The trans-Hudson ferries carried passengers from the New Jersey railroad terminals across the river to terminals in downtown Manhattan. Because lower Manhattan was narrow, these terminals were within easy walking distance of employment centers in the area. But when the mid-town area expanded rapidly, the railroad-ferry system was unable to serve the new job centers effectively. A longer, up-river ferry trip would have been required, and the greater width of mid-Manhattan would have left the commuters many blocks from their destinations.

16. See Owen, *Metropolitan Transportation Problem*, especially pp. 99–104; Interstate Commerce Commission, "Railroad Passenger Train Deficit," Docket No. 31954, decided May 18, 1959; Robert W. Purcell, "Special Report to the Governor on Problems of the Railroads and Bus Lines in New York State" (New York, March 12, 1959), pp. 51–52.

17. Passenger service problems were especially important factors in the financial difficulties of the Long Island Rail Road and the H&M, both of which went into bankruptcy during the early postwar years.

18. The 240,000 railroad commuters included 106,000 from New Jersey, 59,000 from Westchester and Fairfield, and 75,000 from Long Island. The count included those entering the city between 7:00 and 10:00 A.M. on a weekday. See RPA, *Regional Plan Bulletin*, No. 77, p. 6. According to an estimate made several years later, if all the rail commuters from New Jersey were to shift to automobiles, twenty new expressway lanes in New Jersey, ten trans-Hudson tubes, and 250 acres of parking space in Manhattan would be required to handle the additional traffic. MRTS, *Report of the Project Director* (New York, May 20, 1957), p. 14.

19. RPA, *Regional Plan Bulletin*, No. 77, p. 2. Cf. Owen, *Metropolitan Transportation Problem*, Chap. 9.

20. Harry Eckstein, *Pressure Group Politics: The Case of the British Medical Association* (London, George Allen and Unwin, 1960), p. 34; see also pp. 33–38. Cf. David B. Truman, *The Governmental Process: Political Interests and Public Opinion* (New York, Knopf, 1951), pp. 506–07, 322 ff., and *passim*.

21. For the views of railroad officials on these problems, see, for example, the statement of Roland Davis, Jr., of the Lackawanna Railroad and the statement of E. C. Nickerson of the New York Central system before the NYMRTC, Nov. 13, 1953. In a broad sense, the city agency responsible for the New York City subway system is a member of the rail coalition; but the direct responsibilities of this agency (the Board of Transportation until 1953, the New York City Transit Authority subsequently) are limited to the city, and it has rarely had an important role in the development of transport policies for the broader region. Also, access to large amounts of public funds and other factors place it in a very different political milieu from that of the private railroads. On the politics of the Transit Authority, see Sayre and Kaufman, *Governing New York City*, pp. 323 ff.

22. The quotations above are found in remarks by William Reid, president of the H&M, at the Sixth Regional Plan Conference, Oct. 9, 1951. See also his statement of Feb. 9, 1953, and his "Report on Proposed New York–New Jersey Rapid Transit System," Nov. 1, 1953; statement of Roland Davis, Jr., of the Lackawanna,

and statement of Henry K. Norton, president of the Susquehanna, before the NYMRTC, Nov. 13, 1953; speech by David I. Mackie, chairman, Eastern Railroad Presidents Conference, before the American Association of Port Authorities, Sept. 24, 1953.

23. IMGBRS, "Report," Dec. 1, 1950, pp. 14, 34. This report includes a history of IMGBRS activities through 1950; see also other reports, briefs, and petitions prepared by IMGBRS during the late 1940s and early 1950s.

24. Some of the attitudes and activities of these organizations are outlined in their 1953 statements before the NYMRTC, which are summarized in NYMRTC and NJMRTC, *Joint Report,* pp. 101–02; see also IMGBRS, "Report," Dec. 1, 1950, pp. 11–12; Newark *Evening News,* Feb. 23, 1954, and Dec. 7, 1958. Compare the comments on commuter organizations in Chicago; Edward C. Banfield, *Political Influence* (New York, Free Press, 1960), especially pp. 111–12.

25. "Petition for Reconsideration" by the IMGBRS, before the Interstate Commerce Commission and Board of Public Utility Commissioners of the State of New Jersey, I&S Docket No. 5585, July 1, 1949, p. 52.

26. See IMGBRS, "Report," Dec. 1, 1950, p. 25; statement of Carleton G. MacLean, chairman of the Transit Committee of Bergen County, before the NYMRTC, Nov. 12, 1953; statement of the Westchester County Planning Commission before the NYMRTC, Nov. 13, 1953. Suggestions that the Port Authority consider taking on transit responsibilities are found, for example, in the Newark *Sunday News,* Sept. 27, 1953, and the Bergen *Evening Record,* Sept. 29, 1953. The possibility of local tax support was suggested by the New Brunswick *Daily Home News,* Nov. 6, 1951, and by the Westchester County Planning Commission, statement, Nov. 13, 1953.

27. For a contrasting view of the commuter, see Robert C. Wood, "A Division of Powers in Metropolitan Areas," in Arthur Maass, ed., *Area and Power: A Theory of Local Government* (New York, Free Press, 1959), pp. 53–69.

28. For background information on these central-city interests, see Sayre and Kaufman, *Governing New York City,* especially pp. 76–86, 481–515; Forbes B. Hays, *Community Leadership: The Regional Plan Association of New York* (New York, Columbia University Press, 1965). An analysis of similar interests in Chicago is

presented in Banfield, *Political Influence*, Chaps. 9, 10, and *passim*.

29. The views of the Avenue of the Americas Association are outlined in its memorandum submitted to the NYMRTC and the NJMRTC, Nov. 10, 1953; the quotation is on p. 12. For positions taken by other groups, see, for example, the Report of the New York Chamber of Commerce, December, 1951; RPA, *Regional Plan Bulletin*, No. 77, July, 1951; statement of the Citizens Budget Commission, Nov. 13, 1953; New York *Herald Tribune*, April 9, 1954.

30. The central-city interests took a more sympathetic view of the railroad companies' problems, partly because of the private enterprise orientation of the city associations and partly because they were less directly affected by rail service deterioration than were the commuter groups. In addition, railroad officials were often important members of the city organizations; in the 1950s, for example, the president of the H&M was chairman of the transportation committee of the Avenue of the Americas Association, and a New York Central vice-president held a similar position with the West Side Association of Commerce.

31. Livingston's views are outlined in his statement before the NYMRTC, Nov. 12, 1953. See also Luther Gulick, "The Next Twenty-five Years in Government in the New York Metropolitan Region," Oct. 6, 1954, reprinted in *Metropolis in the Making: The Next Twenty-five Years in the New York Metropolitan Region* (New York, RPA, 1955), pp. 58–77.

32. See especially the sources cited in Notes 21, 22, 24, 26, and 29 of this chapter.

33. For an excellent analysis of the political behavior of these two agencies and other public authorities operating in New York City, see Sayre and Kaufman, *Governing New York City*, Chap. 9.

34. For a more detailed presentation of the early development of the PNYA, see Bard, *Port of New York Authority*, especially pp. 54 ff., 177 ff., 329 ff.

35. PNYA acquisition of the region's airports is described in Herbert Kaufman, "Gotham in the Air Age," in Harold Stein, ed., *Public Administration and Policy Development: A Case Book* (New York, Harcourt, Brace, 1952), pp. 143–97.

36. The PNYA decided to take part in a study of the rail passenger problem in the face of objections by New York Governor Alfred E. Smith. In defense of its actions, the Port Authority

argued that "no adequate or effective transportation development could take place without taking full account of transportation of passengers as well as freight." (Resolution adopted by the Board of Commissioners, June, 1928; see Bard, *Port of New York Authority*, pp. 128–32.) For a later and different Port Authority view of the relation of passenger to freight facilities, see Chap. IV of this volume.

37. PNYA, *Suburban Transit for Northern New Jersey*, March 1, 1937, p. 10; this report is reprinted in U.S. House of Representatives, Committee on the Judiciary, *Port of New York Authority, Hearings before Subcommittee No. 5*, 86th Cong., 2d Sess. (1960) pp. 1965–99. The 1949 plan is described in Jenny, "Report on the Acute Transportation Problem," pp. 31–33, and in Tobin, statement before the NYMRTC, Nov. 12, 1953, p. 6–7.

38. See RPA, *Regional Plan Bulletin*, No. 77; Newark *Sunday News*, Sept. 27, 1953; and Tobin, statement before the NYMRTC, Nov. 12, 1953, pp. 6–10, where the interest of Governor Driscoll is outlined briefly.

39. See Austin J. Tobin, "The Work and Program of the Port of New York Authority," Feb. 10, 1953; PNYA, *Annual Report, 1952*, p. 1. In contrast with many public agencies, whose end-systems are complex and often reflect "compromise among essentially incompatible interests," the Port Authority had a relatively clear and consistent set of goals. Thus, it could pursue its interests in vigorous and single-minded fashion, while its less fortunate brethren followed a more hesitant path. See Edward C. Banfield, "Ends and Means in Planning," *International Social Science Journal*, XI (1959), 361–68; also, Martin Meyerson and Edward C. Banfield, *Politics, Planning, and the Public Interest: The Case of Public Housing in Chicago* (New York, Free Press, 1955), pp. 320 ff.

40. The quotations are from Newark's Mayor Leo Carlin (Newark *Evening News*, March 25, 1954); Newark *Evening News*, editorial, April 30, 1951; and Chamber of Commerce of the State of New York, "A Statement of American Economic Principles," quoted in Tobin, "The Work and Program of the Port of New York Authority," p. 21. For compilations of favorable comments on the PNYA during the early postwar period, see the booklets issued by the Port Authority on its twenty-fifth and thirtieth anniversaries (April 30, 1946 and 1951).

Some of the praise for the Port Authority and other authorities is combined with a strong measure of dissatisfaction with the normal workings of the democratic process. As the New York *World-Telegram & Sun* editorialized, "The truth is that all too frequently men elected to office are not qualified to tangle with complicated, modern municipal management. They may be overly vote-conscious. They may be hogtied to political bosses. They may be just plain imcompetent. But whatever the reason, time after time when the politicians have gotten in a jam they have had to create an authority and call on successful businessmen to bail them out" (March 12, 1952).

41. Meyerson and Banfield, *Politics, Planning, and the Public Interest*, p. 49.

42. PNYA, *Annual Report, 1952*, pp. 54–55, and "List of Port of New York Authority Commissioners and Principal Staff Members and their Corporate Affiliations," submitted to the Antitrust Subcommittee of the Committee on the Judiciary, House of Representatives, May, 1952.

43. Quoted from profile of Tobin, New York *Times*, July 14, 1959.

44. Samuel P. Huntington, *The Common Defense: Strategic Programs in National Politics* (New York, Columbia University Press, 1961), pp. 310–11. LeMay's organization was the Strategic Air Command, Hoover's the Federal Bureau of Investigation.

45. Salary figures are for 1960. See Newark *Evening News*, Feb. 26, 1960; reprinted in U.S. House of Representatives, *Port of New York Authority, Hearings before Subcommittee No. 5*, p. 181.

46. Sayre and Kaufman, *Governing New York City*, pp. 330–31.

47. Tobin, "The Work and Program of the Port of New York Authority," pp. 5–6. Tobin's business-oriented perspective is also reflected in his views on local government: "It is obvious that one of the primary subjects of citizen interest concerns the manner in which a municipality handles its finances. *Above all else*, the people expect their officials to give them prudent and conservative management of public funds." (Austin J. Tobin, "Public Relations and Financial Reporting in a Municipal Corporation," May 23, 1951, p. 11, emphasis added.) For contrasting views of the priorities in local government policy-making, see Meyerson and Banfield, *Politics, Planning, and the Public Interest*, and Sayre and Kaufman, *Governing New York City*, especially Chap. 19.

48. For example, the need to obtain approval of a municipality

before connecting vehicular projects with city streets, the inability to use surplus revenues except for "such purposes as may be directed by the two states," independent audit, requirement for self-support, and removal of the commissioners for cause. The first assistant to the executive director listed these and other limitations on the Port Authority—including its annual reports and information given to the press—in concluding that the PNYA is subject to adequate democratic controls. (M. E. Lukens, "The Port of New York Authority," address before the American Political Science Association, Sept. 12, 1953.)

49. Tobin, "Public Relations and Financial Reporting," p. 9. In Tobin's view, press releases and newspaper editorials could serve as adequate substitutes for the ballot box: "We look upon the press as the medium of exchange between our agency and the millions of people and thousands of businesses . . . for whom we are working in the Port District. During the past six years, the Port Authority has enjoyed approximately 1400 favorable editorials in the New York and New Jersey press. We feel we can interpret this as a vote of public confidence in our program" (p. 8). The effectiveness of the Port Authority's public relations program is attested to by the several awards received by the agency's director of public relations, Mrs. Lee K. Jaffe. In 1950, for example, she received the Silver Anvil of the American Public Relations Association for "the most notable public relations performance in the field of government."

50. In addition to press relations, the PNYA uses several approaches in order to insure the friendly attention of the region's publics. A community relations department maintains continuing contact with the municipalities from which the Authority had leased facilities and operates a speakers' bureau. Port Authority executives meet frequently with investment banking groups and other business associations to explain the Authority's work. And staff members are active in the affairs of several of the nongovernmental associations in the region; during the mid-1950s, for example, one PNYA official was an officer of the New York Real Estate Board, and another was a trustee of the Citizens Budget Commission.

51. The 1960 House investigation uncovered occasional examples of other relationships between the PNYA and its political environment. For several years prior to 1952, for example, the Port Authority handled part of its insurance so as to add to the income of a firm

owned by an important state legislator in New York. During the period 1945–52, this assemblyman introduced twenty bills favored by the PNYA; and several resolutions calling for investigation of the Port Authority died in the Ways and Means Committee, which he chaired. See U.S. House of Representatives, *Port of New York Authority, Hearings before Subcommittee No. 5*, pp. 1173–97, 1448–57.

52. Prior to the postwar period, the minutes of the Port Authority had been vetoed only once, by Governor Herbert Lehman, and that veto had later been withdrawn. Governor Thomas E. Dewey vetoed the minutes relating to award of a bus terminal construction contract in 1949, and Alfred E. Driscoll vetoed between five and ten PNYA resolutions, most of them of little importance, during his two terms as New Jersey's governor (1947–54). The few occasions on which the veto power has been used contrast with the hundreds of action taken by the Port Authority's Board without gubernatorial objection. In general, the governors appear to agree with the views outlined by Governor Alfred E. Smith in 1927 and quoted favorably by the Authority in subsequent years: "The reserved veto power . . . was to safeguard the states against any abuse of power by a Port Authority Commissioner. It was not intended to give the Governor of each state the power to review the acts of Commissioners and to revise their judgments."

53. Quoted in the Port Authority's *Annual Report, 1952*, frontispiece. See the similar views of Governor Driscoll on the page opposite Dewey's statement.

54. In late 1951 and early 1952, three planes crashed in the vicinity of Newark Airport, bringing the PNYA under attack and causing the airport to be closed temporarily. Hearings on the airport problem and on the Port Authority's activities generally were conducted by the New Jersey Joint Legislative Committee and by two committees of the House of Representatives. One of the House Committees, Judiciary, took testimony on a resolution introduced by Representative Alfred D. Sieminski, Democrat of Hudson County, to rescind congressional consent to the compact creating the PNYA. During this period, the agency was vigorously attacked by a number of groups; it was called a "totalitarian government" by one Newark public official and a "Mafia organization" by Sieminski. In spite of intense criticism in a few areas, the Port Authority was able to muster widespread support for its work and emerged

unscathed. See Paul Tillett and Myron Weiner, *The Closing of Newark Airport* (University, University of Alabama Press, 1955); U.S. House of Representatives, Committee on the Judiciary, *Hearing before the Anti-Trust Subcommittee on a Resolution to Rescind the Consent of Congress Creating the Port of New York Authority*, 82d Cong., 2d sess. (1952), 5 vols.; New York *Herald Tribune*, May 22, 1952.

55. Herbert Kaufman, "Gotham in the Air Age" (Washington, Committee on Public Administration Cases, 1950), p. 65. On Moses, see also Sayre and Kaufman, *Governing New York City*, pp. 320 ff., 381–82; John B. Keeley, *Moses on the Green* (University, University of Alabama Press, 1959); Rexford G. Tugwell, "The Moses Effect," in Edward C. Banfield, *Urban Government: A Reader in Politics and Administration* (New York, Free Press, 1961), pp. 462–72. Later additions to the Moses empire include the Throgs Neck Bridge and the Verrazano-Narrows Bridge.

56. New York *Times*, March 24, 1959.

57. See TBTA, *Annual Report*, 1952; State of New York, Temporary State Commission on Coordination of State Activities, *Staff Report*, pp. 30–31.

58. For a detailed presentation of Livingston's views, see his statement before the NYMRTC, Nov. 12, 1953.

59. Letter to Charles H. Tuttle, chairman of the NYMRTC, Nov. 12, 1953.

60. The bond resolutions under which TBTA bonds were sold authorized it to pledge its revenues only for vehicular projects and the New York Coliseum (under the 1952 resolution). Therefore, any attempt to issue bonds for rapid transit projects would appear to subject existing bondholders to risks they could not have foreseen and thus would violate state and federal constitutional provisions against impairing the obligation of contracts. Complete refinancing, a complex procedure, would probably be required before tolls from TBTA projects could be allocated to rail transit. See the analysis in William Miller, *Metropolitan Rapid Transit Financing* (Princeton, N.J., 1957), pp. 27–29, 103–5.

61. The allusion to "close contact" among the various agencies and examples of cooperation are contained in the statement of the district engineer (New York region), New York State Department of Public Works, before the NYMRTC, Nov. 13, 1953. For the attitudes of user groups, see, for example, the praise directed

toward the Port Authority by the bus companies upon the opening of the PNYA Bus Terminal in 1949 (reprinted in U.S. House of Representatives, *Port of New York Authority, Hearings before Subcommittee No. 5*, pp. 1247–54); and Chaps. VIII–IX of this volume. Conflict between Moses and the Port Authority arose during the latter 1940s and early 1950s over the issues of construction of the PNYA bus terminal, responsibility for the region's airports, and a projected mid-Manhattan expressway. By 1954, however, the two agencies had agreed to cooperate in the expansion of arterial facilities in the region. Some of the conflicts are described by Kaufman, in Stein, ed., *Public Administration*. The fruits of cooperation between the agencies, a $570-million arterial program, are outlined in their report, *Joint Study of Arterial Facilities* (New York, January, 1955); the report is discussed further in Chaps. V and VI of this book.

62. Robert C. Wood, *1400 Governments*, pp. 113, 118, and see generally Chaps. 1–3.

63. See Edward Sofen, *The Metropolitan Miami Experiment* (Bloomington, Indiana University Press, 1963); David A. Booth, *Metropolitics: The Nashville Consolidation* (East Lansing, Institute for Community Development and Services, Michigan State University, 1963); RPA, "The Handling of Metropolitan Problems in Selected Regions," 1958.

64. The twenty-one cities are Bayonne (74,000), Bloomfield (52,000), Clifton (82,000), East Orange (77,000), Elizabeth (108,000), Jersey City (276,000), Newark (405,000), Passaic (53,000), Paterson (144,000), Union (51,000), Union City (52,000), and Woodbridge (79,000) in New Jersey; Hicksville (50,000) and Levittown (65,000) on Long Island; Mount Vernon (76,000), New Rochelle (77,000), White Plains (50,000), and Yonkers (191,000) in Westchester; and Bridgeport (157,000), Norwalk (68,000), and Stamford (93,000) in Connecticut (all populations for 1960).

65. As the RPA has commented, "The region has no centralized 'business community' in the sense that some smaller regions have. . . . Leadership in the region's central cities is becoming increasingly concerned with the problems of a particular area such as Newark or downtown Manhattan, rather than with problems of a regional nature." ("The Handling of Metropolitan Problems in the Tri-State Metropolitan Region," June, 1958, p. 12). For a well-documented

study of intraregional conflict in the early years of this century, see Bard, *The Port of New York Authority*, Chaps. 1 and 2.

In 1960, the U.S. Bureau of the Census renamed its seventeen-county unit the New York–Northeastern New Jersey Standard Consolidated Area. (See note 1 of this chapter.) The Bureau then subdivided the Consolidated Area into several Standard Metropolitan Statistical Areas. This change had been urged upon the Bureau by representatives of Newark and other cities in the region and was received in these cities with satisfaction. It was attacked by New York City and other regional spokesmen, however, as being in conflict with the economic interdependence of the entire region.

66. On the discussion that follows, see Sayre and Kaufman, *Governing New York City*, especially Chaps. 13, 15, 18, 19. See also Chapter VII of this volume, concerning the crucial role of the city's mayor and his aides in the establishment of the Metropolitan Regional Council.

67. See discussion of the rail coalition, pp. 21–27 of this volume.

68. On the city's divided transport responsibilities, see Sayre and Kaufman, *Governing New York City*, especially Chap. 9 and pp. 295–98. On the Transit Authority, see also footnote 21 above; State of New York, Temporary State Commission on Coordination of State Activities, *Staff Report*, pp. 35–37 and *passim*; and a study of the conflict leading to creation of the Transit Authority, William Miller, "Metropolitanism, Transit, and Politics in New York City and State, 1953," unpublished undergraduate thesis, Harvard College, 1954.

69. Sayre and Kaufman, *Governing New York City*, p. 699. See generally Chap. 18.

70. Compiled from the *Legislative Manuals* of New York and New Jersey. The incentive for gubernatorial leadership in Connecticut was considerably less, since only part of one county—comprising less than one-tenth of the statewide electorate—was significantly concerned with transportation in the New York region.

71. "By law . . . and by tradition" the Governor of New York has a commanding role in policy and political leadership in the state; see Lynton Caldwell, *The Government and Administration of New York* (New York, Crowell, 1954), pp. 80 ff. With the increased tenure and powers provided by the 1947 Constitution, New Jersey also has a "strong governor" system. On gubernatorial leadership in New Jersey, see Duane Lockard, *The New Jersey Governor:*

A Study in Political Power (Princeton, N.J., Van Nostrand, 1964), especially Chap. 6.

72. On the general reluctance of political leaders to act quickly and decisively, see Banfield, *Political Influence*, p. 270 ff.

73. In 1951 the state created the Long Island Transit Authority and charged it with responsibility for developing a plan to rehabilitate the railroad, if possible under private ownership. As a result of the Authority's efforts, a plan was devised and was accepted by the state in 1954, calling for tax concessions, special rate-making powers, and financial assistance from the controlling corporation (the Pennsylvania Railroad). The plan included a $60-million rehabilitation program and was to last twelve years.

74. Some of these developments are discussed in Jenny, "Report on the Acute Transportation Problem," pp. 31–37; Port Authority Memorandum to Governor Driscoll, November, 1951; Newark *Evening News*, Nov. 4, 1951; Jenny, statement before the MRTC, New York Public Hearing, (New York, Sept. 17, 1957), p. 111; Tobin, statement before the NYMRTC, Nov. 12, 1953.

CHAPTER III. STRATEGY FOR POLICY INNOVATION

1. Cf. Norton E. Long, *The Polity*, ed. by Charles Press (Chicago, Rand McNally, 1962), Chap. 15; Scott Greer, *Metropolitics: A Study of Political Culture* (New York, Wiley, 1963), pp. 37–41; Samuel P. Huntington, *The Common Defense: Strategic Programs in National Politics* (New York, Columbia University Press, 1961), Chap. V; James G. March and Herbert A. Simon (with the collaboration of Harold Guetzkow), *Organizations* (New York, Wiley, 1958), Chap. 7.

2. On the use of studies as a delaying tactic, see Huntington, *Common Defense*, Chaps. III, V; Marver H. Bernstein, *Regulating Business by Independent Commission* (Princeton, N.J., Princeton University Press, 1955), p. 172; Edward T. Chase, "The Longest Way from Thought to Action," *Reporter*, XXV (June 22, 1961), 28–32.

3. On the attitude of the PNYA, see, for example, its Memorandum to Governor Driscoll, November, 1951, in which it argued that creation of a transit commission would "dispel any misunderstanding as to the complete separation of the transit development from the projects placed in the custody of the Port Authority by

the bi-state treaty." On the ability of different groups to agree on immediate aims, while differing on long-range goals, see Charles E. Lindblom, "The Science of 'Muddling Through,' " *Public Administration Review*, XXIX (Spring, 1959), 79–88.

4. NYMRTC and NJMRTC, *Joint Report* (March 3, 1954), p. 3.

5. Huntington, *Common Defense*, p. 287.

6. L. Alfred Jenny, "Report on the Acute Transportation Problem Existing between Northeastern New Jersey and the City of New York" (Trenton, Department of Conservation and Economic Development, State of New Jersey, 1951); RPA, Regional Plan Bulletin, No. 77 (New York, July, 1951): NJRPC, *Report on Improved Rapid Transportation for the Metropolitan Region of New York and New Jersey* (Trenton, 1952).

7. In general, the three reports took similar positions on the issue of rail-highway relationships. The NJRPC did not, however, recommend a combined study of road and rail, although it did maintain that highway expansion was a major cause of rail-service problems.

8. The road alliance maintained that travelers used the two transportation systems largely at different times and for different routes (rail mainly for commuting from areas served by rail connections into large cities; road for commuting where rail service was not available and for midday, evening, and weekend travel). Therefore, there was little need for coordination. Also, where a secular shift from rail to road facilities did occur, road interests argued that basic changes in living patterns and travel preferences were responsible; highway expansion took place in response to these public demands, rather than causing them. Again (since highway agencies must meet their responsibilities even if deterioration of rail service results) no significant advantage could result from a coordinated study. A third argument, applicable to the PNYA, the TBTA, the New Jersey Turnpike Authority, and other authorities in the region, held that independent policy-making was essential to the businesslike efficiency of these agencies. For statements by the PNYA covering several of these points in detail, see Walter P. Hedden, statement on behalf of the PNYA, before the NYMRTC, Nov. 12, 1953; PNYA, Board of Commissioners, statement with respect to Assembly No. 16, Nov. 24, 1958, pp. 27–33.

9. The need for a study of rail problems in the eastern zone of

the region was also lessened because of separate institutional arrangements affecting two major rail facilities in that area. The Long Island Rail Road functioned under special state policies after 1951; and the New York City transit system, operating entirely within the city, was not normally viewed as requiring regional action. (See discussions of the LIRR and the city system in Chap. II of this volume.)

10. The main purpose of a new trans-Hudson tunnel would be to give passengers on the New Jersey railroads a direct ride into Manhattan. Improvement of rail travel within New Jersey was, however, a secondary goal. The recommendations of Jenny and the NJRPC drew heavily on the trans-Hudson studies made in the 1920s and 1930s. (See Chap. II of this volume.)

11. Chap. 453, Laws of 1952.

12. Chap. 194, Laws of 1952. The reaction in New Jersey to the Albany changes is typified by the editorial in the Bergen *Evening Record:* "New York State has decided to go its own way. . . . New Jersey commuters can walk to work as far as it is concerned. To many New Yorkers, we country boys on this side of the Hudson River are just something to be tolerated" (March 29, 1952).

13. Bayonne *Times,* May 23, 1952.

14. Bergen County's commuter organization criticized the lack of action on the part of the two commissions in a public statement in April and in a letter to Governor Driscoll in June, 1953; and in August, Goodhue Livingston, a member of the New York City Planning Commission, attacked the New York Commission and Governor Dewey publicly, noting that "not a port rat had been disturbed" by the agency and accusing the Governor of a "lack of boldness and vision in the field of metropolitan transportation" (Newark *Evening News,* Aug. 12, 1953). See also the summary of developments in NJMRTC, Minutes, Sept. 22, 1952–Oct. 22, 1953.

The 1953 subway controversy involved extensive conflict between city and state leaders concerning the issue of whether the deficits of the city-owned subway-bus system should be met via new taxes or a fare increase. On March 25, 1953, the state created the Transit Authority over the objections of the city administration; and shortly after assuming responsibility for the transit system, the Authority raised the transit fare from 10 to 15 cents, also over the protests of city officials. See William Miller, "Metropolitanism, Transit, and

Politics in New York City and State, 1953," unpublished undergraduate thesis, Harvard College, 1954.

15. NYMRTC, "A Public Forum" (New York, 1953), p. 4.

16. See statements of Austin J. Tobin and Walter P. Hedden on behalf of the PNYA, before the NYMRTC, Nov. 12, 1953; letter from Robert Moses to Charles H. Tuttle, NYMRTC, Nov. 12, 1953.

17. The report of the two commissions and those of its predecessor study groups were similar largely because several of the same men were involved. Three members of the NJRPC were on the NJMRTC, and Jenny served as consultant to the New Jersey Transit Commission. Also, the ranks of those favorable to increased rail-highway coordination were strengthened by the appointment of Alexander H. Elder to the NJMRTC in December, 1953, replacing Hanau, who had resigned because of ill health. Elder was a former Republican mayor of Glen Ridge, retired general counsel of the Central Railroad of New Jersey, and an RPA director. He had for many years been a vociferous critic of the Port Authority.

18. NYMRTC and NJMRTC, *Joint Report* (March 3, 1954); see especially pp. 2–3, 23–24.

19. The quotation is from an editorial in the New York *Herald Tribune*, March 8, 1954. See also Newark *Evening News*, March 5, and other area newspapers, March 5–8.

20. The event of this period which caused the greatest concern was the Lackawanna Railroad's announcement in November, 1953, that it would soon apply to the ICC for permission to abandon its trans-Hudson ferry to Christopher Street in lower Manhattan. Its plans were widely criticized in North Jersey, and the NJMRTC received more than 250 letters and resolutions from commuters and municipal bodies. The New Jersey Assembly also passed a resolution calling on the Commission to report promptly on action needed to meet this problem. (See NJMRTC, Minutes, February 8, 1954.) Meanwhile, railroad freight earnings had suffered a sharp decline beginning in the fall of 1953. Since freight profits were normally used to absorb passenger losses, this decline threatened the economic stability of some of the roads and foreshadowed intensified railroad efforts to reduce passenger service.

21. Spokesmen for the Jersey Shore Commuters, the Morris County Officials Committee on Transportation, and the H&M supported the entire Forbes resolution. The Lackawanna Railroad

supported only the section requiring the PNYA to finance the MRTC study.

22. Austin J. Tobin, statement at a hearing of the New Jersey Senate Committee on Federal and Interstate Relations on Concurrent Resolution introduced by Senator Forbes (Trenton, April 7, 1954). The Forbes Resolution was also opposed by the Newark Chamber of Commerce, RPA, and the Transit Committee of Bergen County.

23. Chap. 801, Laws of 1954 (New York); Chap. 44, Laws of 1954 (New Jersey). Governor Driscoll retired in January, 1954, after serving for two terms, the maximum permitted by the state constitution. Robert Meyner, a lawyer from the northwestern county of Warren (outside the New York region) and a Democratic state senator from 1948 to 1951, opposed Republican Paul Troast in the 1953 campaign and won. Both houses of the legislature, however, remained under Republican control.

CHAPTER IV. THE STUDY COMMISSION AND THE PORT AUTHORITY

1. David B. Truman, *The Governmental Process: Political Interests and Public Opinion* (New York, Knopf, 1951) p. 398; and see generally Chaps. 13 and 14. Cf. Norton E. Long, *The Polity*, ed. by Charles Press (Chicago, Rand McNally, 1962), Chap. 4.

2. MRTC, Minutes, July 8, 1954. Federal funds for transportation planning were not available at this time.

3. "Informal Comment of the New York–New Jersey Railroads in Cooperation with the Activities of the Metropolitan Rapid Transit Commission," reprinted in MRTC, *Interim Report on the Activities of the Commission* (New York, Feb. 18, 1955), pp. 38–39.

4. The RPA had proposed construction of a single trans-Hudson tunnel (press release, June 14, 1954), and the Avenue of the Americas Association had developed a plan requiring two new tunnels under the Hudson (Memorandum to the NYMRTC and NJMRTC, Nov. 10, 1953).

5. MRTC, Minutes, October 18, 1954. The three New York City groups were the New York Board of Trade, the Commerce and Industry Association, and the New York Real Estate Board.

6. *Jersey Journal*, Dec. 9, 1954.

7. Marver H. Bernstein, *Regulating Business by Independent*

Commission (Princeton, N.J., Princeton University Press, 1955), pp. 79–80.

8. See MRTC, *Interim Report*, 1955, pp. 15–16.

9. See James G. March and Herbert A. Simon (with the collaboration of Harold Guetzkow), *Organizations* (New York, Wiley, 1958), pp. 173–74.

10. Certainly, some of the MRTC members belonged to the category of political actors who "are ideologically motivated, and struggle—sometimes at great material sacrifice—for policies that for them are fundamental articles of faith." Herbert Kaufman, *Politics and Policies in State and Local Government* (Englewood Cliffs, N.J., Prentice-Hall, 1963), p. 75.

11. Edward C. Banfield, *Political Influence* (New York, Free Press, 1961), p. 271.

12. Austin J. Tobin, statement at a hearing of the New Jersey Senate Committee on Federal and Interstate Relations on Concurrent Resolution introduced by Senator Forbes (Trenton, April 7, 1954).

13. Meanwhile, rail service continued to deteriorate. In November, 1954, the Interstate Commerce Commission approved the Lackawanna's petition to end service on its Christopher Street Ferry, and the H&M filed a bankruptcy petition; in November and December, the New York Central announced that it planned to discontinue passenger service on its Putnam Division (in Westchester County) and its West Shore Division and trans-Hudson ferry (serving Rockland County, N.Y., and Bergen County, N.J.). On the developments during November, 1954–January, 1955, see Charles H. Tuttle, address before the RPA, Dec. 7, 1954; letter from Tuttle to John R. Zellweger, Borough Clerk, Dumont, N.J., Dec. 21, 1954; Tuttle, address before the New York Board of Trade, Jan. 4, 1955; Bergen *Evening Record*, Dec. 8, 11, 1954; Newark *Star Ledger*, Jan. 6, 1955; New York *Herald Tribune*, Dec. 9, 1954, Jan. 5, 1955; New York *Times*, Dec. 1, 1954; Newark *Evening News*, Dec. 6, 7, 1954; Newark *Sunday News*, Dec. 9, 1954; MRTC, Minutes, Dec. 13, 1954, Jan. 5, 1955.

14. MRTC, Minutes, Jan. 5, 1955. In 1953 Elder had replaced Hanau. See Chap. III, note 17, of this volume.

15. PNYA, Board of Commissioners, Minutes, Jan. 13, 1955.

16. PNYA and MRTC, "Memorandum of Understanding on

Cooperation between the Two Agencies on Studies Designed to Determine Means of Improving Interstate Rapid Transit Service between New Jersey and New York," January, 1955; reprinted in MRTC, *Interim Report*, 1955, pp. 43–55.

17. New York *Times*, Jan. 14, 1955; Bergen *Evening Record*, Jan. 15, 1955. See also Newark *Sunday News*, Jan. 16, 1955; New York *Herald Tribune*, Jan. 16, 1955.

CHAPTER V. CONFLICT AND ACCOMMODATION

1. James G. March and Herbert A. Simon (with the collaboration of Harold Guetzkow), *Organizations* (New York, Wiley, 1958), pp. 129–30; and see generally Chap. 5. Cf. Martin Meyerson and Edward C. Banfield, *Politics, Planning, and the Public Interest: The Case of Public Housing in Chicago* (New York, Free Press, 1955), pp. 304–12.

2. PNYA and TBTA, *Joint Study of Arterial Facilities, New York–New Jersey Metropolitan Area* (New York, January, 1955).

3. MRTC, *Interim Report on the Activities of the Commission* (New York, 1955), pp. 2–11, 26–30; Charles H. Tuttle, address before the Committee on Traffic and Transportation of the City Club of New York, Feb. 8, 1955; Tuttle, address before the Real Estate Board of New York, Feb. 23, 1955; John F. Kraus, address before the IMGBRS and other organizations, Plainfield, N.J., March 11, 1955; Alexander H. Elder, address before the Joint Council of Municipal Planning Boards of Essex County, East Orange, N.J., March 16, 1955; Newark *Sunday News*, March 27, 1955.

4. New York *Herald Tribune*, Jan. 17, 1955; New York *Times*, Jan. 17, 1955; cf. Newark *Evening News*, Jan. 19, 1955.

5. New York *World-Telegram & Sun*, March 3, 1955; Staten Island *Advance*, March 23, 1955; Bayonne *Times*, Feb. 12, 1955.

6. Elder, address before the Bayonne Chamber of Commerce, April 21, 1955; Tuttle, address before the Transportation Section of the New York Board of Trade, March 31, 1955; Bergen *Evening Record*, April 23, 1955.

7. Newark *Evening News*, April 28, 1955; Newark *Star Ledger*, April 29, 1955; *Jersey Journal*, April 29, 1955; Bergen *Evening Record*, April 30, 1955; New York *Herald Tribune*, April 30, 1955.

8. MRTC, Minutes, June 6, 1955.

9. MRTC, *Interim Report*, 1955, pp. 31–36.

10. See New York *Herald Tribune*, Feb. 20, 1955; letter from Mayor Wagner to Tuttle, Feb. 23, 1955. Among the organizations favoring the intrastate study were New York City's Chamber of Commerce, Real Estate Board, Board of Trade, Citizens Union, and Avenue of the Americas Association.

11. Chap. 780, Laws of 1955.

12. The materials in this and the next several paragraphs are drawn in part from reports in the *Hudson Dispatch* (Union City, N.J.), May 10, 1955; Newark *Evening News*, May 3, 17, 27, 1955; Bergen *Evening Record*, May 3, 10, 1955.

13. Newark *Evening News*, June 14, 1955.

14. Newark *Evening News*, June 20, 1955; Bergen *Evening Record*, June 16, 1955.

15. *Jersey Journal*, July 7, 1955; Elizabeth *Daily Journal*, July 8, 1955; Bergen *Evening Record*, July 7, 1955.

16. Chap. 182, Laws of 1955; statement by the Governor.

17. Bergen *Evening Record*, Aug. 3, 1955; Newark *Evening News*, August 2, 1955.

18. *Jersey Journal*, Sept. 22, 1955.

19. MRTC, Minutes, Sept. 7, 20, 1955; PNYA, Board of Commissioners, Minutes, Sept. 15, 1955.

20. New York *Herald Tribune*, Sept. 27, 1955.

21. Bergen *Evening Record*, Sept. 28, 1955.

22. Edward C. Banfield, "Ends and Means in Planning," in *International Social Science Journal*, XI (1959), 361–68. Cf. Meyerson and Banfield, *Politics, Planning, and the Public Interest*, pp. 320 ff., and Herbert A. Simon, *Administrative Behavior: A Study of Decision-Making Processes in Administrative Organization* (New York, Macmillan, 1957), 2d ed., pp. 67 ff.

23. Robert C. Wood, "Metropolitan Governor," unpublished Ph.D. dissertation, Harvard University, 1949. The other two states studied by Wood were Connecticut and Massachusetts. Cf. V. O. Key, *American State Politics: An Introduction* (New York, Knopf, 1956), pp. 76, 230–37.

24. Edward C. Banfield, *Political Influence* (New York, Free Press, 1961), p. 271.

25. See New Jersey Senate, Joint Resolution No. 1 (Jan., 1955), and Senate Resolution No. 3 (June, 1955).

26. Norton E. Long, *The Polity*, ed. by Charles Press (Chicago, Rand McNally, 1962), p. 50.

CHAPTER VI. THE TRANSIT SURVEYS

1. See James G. March and Herbert A. Simon (with the collaboration of Harold Guetzkow), *Organizations* (New York, Wiley, 1958), pp. 129–30.

2. Harold Kaplan, *Urban Renewal Politics: Slum Clearance in Newark* (New York, Columbia University Press, 1963), p. 166, and see generally Chap. VIII of his study.

3. An outline of the interstate studies contracted for in the fall of 1955 is contained in MRTC, *Interim Report on the Activities of the Commission during 1955* (New York, March 1, 1956), pp. 10–11.

4. Page's staff included Forrest E. Brooks, project chief engineer; Joseph McC. Lieper, project technical coordinator; Carl E. Veazie, transportation economist; Allan K. Sloan, transportation planner.

5. The Philadelphia firm of Day and Zimmerman would (1) evaluate the feasibility of a rapid transit line from Brooklyn, across the proposed Narrows Bridge, into Staten Island and (2) determine the present and future mass-transit demand between Long Island and the rest of the region and consider several specific proposals to improve transit facilities on Long Island. Ford, Bacon and Davis would conduct several studies in the Westchester sector of the region. An outline of these studies is found in MRTC, *Interim Report on the Activities of the Commission during 1956* (New York, Jan. 31, 1957), p. 9. In the spring of 1956, the Commission also contracted with Wm. Wyer and Co. of East Orange, N.J., for a brief review and analysis of the New Jersey intrastate problem, at a cost of $8,000. *Ibid.*, pp. 9, 22.

6. New York *Journal-American*, Dec. 10, 1954.

7. PNYA and TBTA, *Joint Study of Arterial Facilities, New York–New Jersey Metropolitan Area* (New York, January, 1955), p. 30.

8. MRTC, press release, March 13, 1956.

9. New York *Times*, April 10, 13, 19, 1956.

10. MRTC, Minutes, May 7, 1956.

11. Day and Zimmerman, Inc., "Alternate Rapid Transit Plan for Staten Island via the Proposed Narrows Bridge," Report No. 5849-B (Philadelphia, Nov. 29, 1956); MRTC, Minutes, Jan. 7, 1957.

12. Charles H. Tuttle, address before the New York Chamber of

Commerce, Feb. 2, 1956; MRTC, *Interim Report*, March 1, 1956, p. 4; Edward J. O'Mara, address before the Joint Council of Municipal Planning Boards of Essex County, May 9, 1956; John F. Sly, address at Rutgers University, June 19, 1956.

13. Bergen *Evening Record*, June 8, 1956; Newark *Evening News*, June 20, 1956; Ramsey (N.J.) *Journal*, June 20, 1956.

14. Charles E. De Leuw, "Trans-Hudson Rapid Transit" (Chicago, Feb. 11, 1957). In preliminary studies, De Leuw also considered several other possible means of improving trans-Hudson travel, including monorail, aerial transit, and tunnels to carry standard passenger trains under the river. With the concurrence of the sponsors, these alternatives were eliminated from the more intensive studies owing to cost and service disadvantages.

15. William Miller, *Metropolitan Rapid Transit Financing* (Princeton, N.J., 1957).

16. On the fare structure, see *ibid.*, pp. 62–64, and De Leuw, "Trans-Hudson Rapid Transit," pp. 60–61, 124.

17. The PNYA's initial public statement on the conditions under which it might be able to undertake a deficit rail operation is contained in "Public Hearing before Senate Commission Created under Senate Resolution No. 7 (1960) to Study the Financial Structure and Operations of the Port of New York Authority" (Trenton, Sept. 27, 1960), pp. 13 ff. See discussion in Chap. IX of this study.

18. Miller, *Metropolitan Rapid Transit Financing*, p. 102; and see pp. 29–30, 100–02.

19. Austin J. Tobin, "Transportation in the New York Metropolitan Region," Oct. 6, 1954, reprinted in *Metropolis in the Making: The Next Twenty-five Years in the New York Metropolitan Region* (New York, RPA, 1955), p. 39.

20. Miller suggested that population and tax ratables be weighted equally in apportioning the deficit between Manhattan and the suburban counties; Manhattan would then pay about one-third of the deficit and the remaining counties two-thirds. In the allocation of the deficit among the suburban counties, population and extent of trans-Hudson travel would be the controlling factors, with the result that Bergen, Essex, and Hudson counties would each pay 19–23 percent of the suburban share and the remaining nine counties between 2 and 10 percent each. The District would certify its deficits to the suburban counties and to New York City based on these

formulas, and the amounts certified would be made "a mandatory charge on the local budgets." This use of indirect tax support was preferred, since it avoided constitutional and other problems that would arise should the District be given direct taxing power. As Miller noted, there were several precedents for these proposals; the Metropolitan Transit Authority in the Boston area was the closest in its financing arrangements. Miller, *Metropolitan Rapid Transit Financing*, pp. 42–53, 65–69.

21. Miller recommended that the District council be composed of thirty-two members, with half from each state as follows: New York City (14), Orange County, N.Y. (1), Rockland County, N.Y. (1), and the ten New Jersey Counties (16). This equal division between the states would not exactly represent the proportion of deficit assumed, but, Miller noted, "In the present state of development of bi-state cooperation . . . some recognition may well be given to the state line."

The New Jersey representation would be divided among the counties on the basis of their estimated 1975 population, one council member per 500,000 of population, with the following result:

New Jersey County	Representation
Bergen	2
Essex	2
Hudson	2
Mercer	1
Middlesex	2
Monmouth	2
Morris	1
Passaic	1
Somerset	1
Union	2
Total	16

The council would meet annually to consider and approve the District budget. A seven-man board of directors, selected by the council from among its number, would be empowered to provide for the internal organization of the District, to let contracts, and to carry out other duties. *Ibid.*, pp. 76–81.

22. *Ibid.*, pp. 61–62.

23. De Leuw, "Trans-Hudson Rapid Transit," pp. 118–19. This latter argument was not used by Page and the MRTC in their subsequent reports.

24. Coverdale and Colpitts, "Four Proposals for Trans-Hudson Railroad Passenger Service" (New York, Dec. 14, 1956).

25. Ford, Bacon and Davis, "Survey of Common Carrier Bus Transportation between Suburban Communities West of the Hudson River and New York City" (New York, March 20, 1957).

26. Ford, Bacon and Davis, "Measures for Reducing Out-of-Pocket Losses of New Jersey Commuter Railroads under a Public Agency" (New York, Feb. 13, 1957).

27. Miller, *Metropolitan Rapid Transit Financing*, pp. 40, 78–79.

28. The staff report, completed in December, 1957, contained the results of the several intrastate studies by independent consultants, together with the analyses of the MRTC staff. The Commission decided to postpone action on the intrastate questions during 1957–58 in order to devote its energies to its recommendations focused on the interstate problem. The MRTC never did act upon these intrastate questions, but the separate states returned to them in 1959 and subsequent years. (See Chap. IX of this study.)

In brief, the primary results of the intrastate surveys were:

1. *Within New Jersey.* A preliminary survey recommended that further studies be made of the possibility of (*a*) a new transit line from Bayonne north through Jersey City and into Bergen County and (*b*) a rapid transit system extending from Newark to Paterson, Elizabeth, and other cities.

2. *Westchester–Fairfield, Conn., and New York City.* The reports concluded that modernization of passenger cars, new equipment, and other improvements were needed on the New York Central and New Haven Railroads. However, the rail carriers had no financial incentive to carry out these improvements, and the proposed Metropolitan District might be extended to this sector in order to take responsibility for suburban rail operations and needed improvements.

3. *Long Island–New York City.* Additional train capacity was needed on the subway system serving Queens-Manhattan; the City Transit Authority might construct additional East River subway tunnels and the other facilities needed, or the Metropolitan District could construct a branch from the bistate transit loop. As to the LIRR, it would be a "modern, efficient railroad property" at the expiration of the Redevelopment Plan in 1966; but if increased tax burdens and other problems at that time threatened

to reduce the level of service, the proposed District might be expanded to include Nassau and Suffolk Counties and to negotiate with the LIRR to insure adequate passenger service.

4. *Staten Island–Manhattan.* The initial study of transit needs in this sector led to a recommendation that bus service, not rail, be provided across the Narrows Bridge. Later, De Leuw evaluated the possibility of a rail transit line from Staten Island to Manhattan via Hudson County. He concluded that such a line was not presently needed but that it might be considered further as commuter traffic in this sector increased.

The results of the intrastate studies are set forth in MRTC, *Staff Report* (New York, December, 1957), Part II.

29. MRTS, *Report of the Project Director* (New York, May 20, 1957).

30. From editorials in the issues of May 23, 1957.

31. MRTS, *Report of the Project Director*, pp. 40–41, 50.

32. The $9-million figure was based on the following set of calculations (*ibid.*, pp. 33 ff.):

	Millions of dollars/year
Present railroad deficits in N.J.–Manhattan sector	– 13
Savings under District (due to rail consolidations and replacement of ferry service by a rail loop)	+ 5
Operating savings from new cars	+ 3
Deficit due to rail improvement program (new and modernized cars, station improvements, etc.)	– 4
Total	– 9

33. Page also recommended that each state provide capital advances of $25 million to meet interest costs during the construction period and that an effort be made to alter federal laws so that a portion of federal highway funds could be allocated to the support of commuter rail service. *Ibid.*, pp. 39–42.

34. Kaplan, *Urban Renewal Politics*, p. 167.

35. *Ibid.*, pp. 169–70.

36. MRTC, *Interim Report on the Activities of the Commission* (New York, Feb. 18, 1955), p. 55; Charles H. Tuttle, address before the New York Chamber of Commerce, Feb. 2, 1956; PNYA, Board of Commissioners, letter to Martin Kesselhart, Chairman, Committee on Federal and Interstate Relations, New Jersey Assembly (New York, Sept. 11, 1958), p. 23.

37. Lyman Bryson, "Notes on a Theory of Advice," *Political Science Quarterly*, LXVI (September, 1951), 334.

38. Samuel P. Huntington, *The Common Defense: Strategic Programs in National Politics* (New York, Columbia University Press, 1961), p. 164. Cf. March and Simon, *Organizations*, p. 126.

39. March and Simon, *Organizations*, p. 152.

40. See Newark *Evening News*, June 20, 1956; Bergen *Evening Record*, June 8, 1956; Metropolitan Regional Conference, Traffic and Transportation Committee, "Final Report," Jersey City, Dec 11, 1956, p. 10; *Jersey Journal*, May 8, Oct. 10, 1956.

CHAPTER VII. REACTIONS TO THE SURVEYS

1. Robert A. Dahl, *Who Governs? Democracy and Power in an American City* (New Haven, Yale University Press, 1961), p. 191.

2. Citizens Budget Commission, press release, May 24, 1957. Active support for the Page proposals came from the New York *Times* and the New York *Herald Tribune* (see, for example, editorials in both newspapers on May 23, 1957) and the New York *World-Telegram & Sun* (May 24, 1957); also New York Chamber of Commerce, Fourteenth Street Association, Avenue of the Americas Association, and RPA, in addition to the organizations listed in the text. The views of these and other organizations can be found in the transcripts of four hearings held by the MRTC on the Page proposals during June and September, 1957. See MRTC, "New York Public Hearing on the Plan and Recommendations of Arthur W. Page, Project Director of the MRTC," June 12, 1957, and Sept. 17, 1957 (cited hereafter as MRTC, "New York Public Hearing," with date); and MRTC, "New Jersey Public Hearing on the Plan and Recommendations of Arthur W. Page," June 18, 1957 and Sept. 10, 1957 (cited hereafter as MRTC, "New Jersey Public Hearing," with date).

3. See MRTC, "New York Public Hearing," Sept. 17, 1957, pp. 18–19.

4. These figures and similar statistics for other sectors of the region, cited below, are taken from MRTC, *Staff Report* (New York, December, 1957).

5. Bergen *Evening Record*, May 25, 1957; New York *Journal-American*, May 31, 1957; "New York Public Hearing," June 12, 1957, p. 82.

6. See Newark *Evening News*, May 24, 1957; telegram from the county attorney of Rockland County to the MRTC, May 23, 1957; New York *Journal-American*, May 31, 1957; MRTC, "New Jersey Public Hearing," June 18, 1957, pp. 25–28, Sept. 10, 1957, pp. 80–86. The commuter groups supporting the Page plan were the Transit Committee of Bergen County, Citizens United Transit Committee (of Bergen), and Susquehanna Transit Commuters Association.

7. Cf. the attitude in the Chicago suburbs: "The commuters of Kane and DuPage counties [Illinois], although favoring measures to keep [the railroad] running, were very much opposed to paying a tax for that purpose. Politicians from those counties met with Governor Stratton one evening . . . to tell him that their constituents 'just won't sit still for a tax increase of any kind.' The state they said, would be responsible for suspension of passenger service and, therefore, it should provide any subsidy that might be needed." Edward C. Banfield, *Political Influence* (New York, Free Press, 1961), p. 111.

8. Augustus Dreier, in MRTC, "New Jersey Public Hearing," Sept. 10, 1957, pp. 38–61. A similar position was adopted by the Boards of Freeholders of Morris, Passaic, and Union Counties.

9. For Wagner's views, see MRTC, "New York Public Hearing," Sept. 17, 1957, pp. 87–92. The MRC developed out of a June, 1956, conference of local leaders in the region. The purpose of the conference, called by Mayor Wagner, was to permit local officials to discuss such areawide problems as transportation and water pollution and to explore the possibilities for coordinated efforts to meet these problems. This meeting led to the creation of the Metropolitan Regional Conference, which in 1957 was retitled the Metropolitan Regional Council. The Council consists of the top elected officials of the counties and larger cities in the region. Mayor Wagner was the chairman for the first decade of its existence, and his office provided funds and staff for the Council. The MRC has no legal standing, and its conclusions and recommendations are not in any way binding upon the member governments.

10. Newark *Evening News*, June 11, 1957, Newark *Star Ledger*, June 14, 1957; Perth Amboy *Evening News*, Dec. 24, 1957. See also the statements of spokesmen from these areas at the New Jersey public hearing in September.

11. Ross Nichols, representing the Newark Economic Development Committee and the Newark Chamber of Commerce, in MRTC, "New Jersey Public Hearing," June 18, 1957, pp. 17–24.

12. *Hudson Dispatch*, May 30, 1957.

13. Leading opponents, in addition to the Merchants Council, were the County Board of Freeholders, public officials of Jersey City, West New York, and Union City, Jersey City's Real Estate Board and Chamber of Commerce, and the *Hudson Dispatch* and the *Jersey Journal*. See, for example, *Hudson Dispatch*, July 6, 17, 1957; *Jersey Journal*, July 17, 1957; Bayonne *Times*, Aug. 28, 1957; MRTC, "New Jersey Public Hearing," Sept. 10, 1957, pp. 34, 96, 104–13; Jersey City Real Estate Board, resolution adopted Oct. 1, 1957.

14. New York *Journal-American*, May 24, 1957; MRTC, "New York Public Hearing," June 12, 1957, pp. 40–54, 71–76, 150, and "New York Public Hearing," Sept. 17, 1957, pp. 22–25, 39–46, 51–56.

15. Bayonne *Times*, May 25, June 12, 1957. See also Bayonne *Times*, Sept. 10, Nov. 1, 1957.

16. Bergen *Evening Record*, Oct. 1, 1957; New York *Journal-American*, May 24, 1957; letter from the 34th Street–Midtown Association to the MRTC, Sept. 26, 1957; statement submitted by Paul Benton of the 23rd Street Association to the MRTC, Sept. 17, 1957, MRTC, "New Jersey Public Hearing," pp. 25–28.

17. Herman T. Stichman, H&M trustee, remarks delivered at a meeting of the New York Security Analysts, New York, Oct. 11, 1957. Railroad labor tended to divide along similar lines, with the H&M unions critical of the proposals concerning the H&M and other labor spokesmen generally favorable to the Page report. See MRTC, "New Jersey Public Hearing," June 18, 1957, pp. 61–62; Sept. 10, 1957, pp. 124–28.

18. MRTC, "New Jersey Public Hearing," June 18, 1957, pp. 64–68. Symington also recommended that the H&M continue to play an important role in meeting the need for commuter service into downtown Manhattan. On the fears of other North Jersey bus lines, see MRTC, "New Jersey Public Hearing," Sept. 10, 1957, pp. 108–09.

19. Robert Moses, statement released to the press, Sept. 22, 1957.

20. Augustus Dreier, IMGBRS counsel, in MRTC, "New Jersey Public Hearing," Sept. 10, 1957, p. 39.

21. For criticisms by public officials, see, for example, *Jersey Journal*, Aug. 20, 1957; MRTC, "New Jersey Public Hearing," June 18, 1957, p. 34; Newark *Evening News*, June 12, 1957.

22. New York *Times*, May 24, 1957.

23. Banfield, *Political Influence*, pp. 253, 271.

24. Albert Benninger, member, Board of Freeholders, Union County, in MRTC, "New Jersey Public Hearing," June 18, 1957, p. 29.

25. Banfield, *Political Influence*, pp. 297–301, 269.

26. See especially MRTC, "New Jersey Public Hearing," Sept. 10, 1957, pp. 6–16, 94–114; "New York Public Hearing," Sept. 17, 1957, pp. 16–58. These conclusions concerning private groups confirm those of Wallace S. Sayre and Herbert Kaufman, *Governing New York City: Politics in the Metropolis* (New York, Russell Sage Foundation, 1960; paperback edition, New York, Norton, 1965), p. 512, and see Chap. XIII generally.

27. *Jersey Journal*, May 23, July 17, 1957; Elizabeth *Daily Journal*, May 25, Sept. 11, 1957; New Brunswick *Daily Home News*, May 24, 1957; Passaic *Herald-News*, Sept. 11, 1957; Perth Amboy *Evening News*, Dec. 24, 1957; *Hudson Dispatch*, July 6, 1957. See similar findings in other regions: Banfield, *Political Influence*, pp. 106, 112; Henry J. Schmandt, Paul G. Steinbicker, and George D. Wendel, *Metropolitan Reform in St. Louis: A Case Study* (New York, Holt, Rinehart and Winston, 1961), p. 41.

28. See, for example, Bergen *Evening Record*, May 25, 1957; New York *Times*, May 23, 1957; New York *Herald Tribune*, May 23, Sept. 19, 1957.

29. Newark *Evening News*, June 18, 1957; Newark *Star Ledger*, Sept. 19, 1957.

30. MRTC, press release, Sept. 6, 1957; Edward J. O'Mara, articles in *Jersey Journal*, Oct. 9–11, 14–15, 1957.

31. Cf. James G. March and Herbert A. Simon (with the collaboration of Harold Guetzkow), *Organizations* (New York, Wiley, 1958), Chaps. 5, 7.

32. The quotation is from MRTC, *Interim Report on the Activities of the Commission during 1955* (New York, March 1, 1956), p. 4.

33. As Executive Director Frank H. Simon commented at one of the hearings, "We have employed the best engineers and consultants in the country. . . . We must certainly give a lot of credence

to their results." MRTC, "New Jersey Public Hearing," June 18, 1957, p. 91. Cf. Charles H. Tuttle, address before the New York Chamber of Commerce, Feb. 2, 1956.

34. There were only nine members of the MRTC during this period, Thomas J. Harkins of New Jersey having resigned on June 1. Harkins, an executive of the Brotherhood of Locomotive Engineers, opposed Page's recommendations for abandoning passenger service on various rail lines because of the impact which these proposals would have on railroad employment. He found that the other members were unwilling to support his position, and this, combined with ill health, led him to resign. Governor Meyner did not appoint a replacement for Harkins.

35. The title was changed from "Metropolitan District" (the title suggested by Miller and endorsed by Page) to "Metropolitan Transit District" in order to avoid criticism of the proposed agency as a potential multipurpose supergovernment.

36. The statements of the Citizens' Budget Commission and other New York City groups, urging that proposals to meet New York State's intrastate needs be developed rapidly, are contained in MRTC, "New York Public Hearing," June 12 and Sept. 17, 1957.

37. At public meetings on June 5 and 11, Page said that a deficit on the loop (Plan 2) could be eliminated by raising the fare from 30 to 35 cents. Newark *Evening News*, June 5, 1957; *Hudson Dispatch*, June 12, 1957. Cf. similar views expressed by William Miller, in MRTC, "New York Public Hearing," June 12, 1957, pp. 60–61.

38. Samuel P. Huntington, *The Common Defense: Strategic Programs in National Politics* (New York, Columbia University Press, 1961), 146–47, 164–65, and *passim.*

39. MRTC, *Report: Rapid Transit for the New York–New Jersey Metropolitan Area* (New York, January, 1958), pp. x, 39–53. The MRTC's District proposal was essentially the same as that outlined by William Miller. (See previous chapter.) The District would be governed by a thirty-two-member council, composed as follows: in New York State, New York City (14), Rockland (1), Orange (1); in New Jersey, Bergen (2), Essex (2), Hudson (2), Mercer (1), Middlesex (2), Monmouth (2), Morris (1), Passaic (1), Somerset (1), Union (2). The MRTC proposal differed from the Miller plan in three ways: the word "Transit" was added to the District title (see Note 35 in this chapter), the New

York City members would be chosen by the Board of Estimate (rather than the City Council), and the seven-man board of directors could be selected by the council from within or outside its own membership. (The Miller plan provided that the board would be selected from among the council members.)

40. *Ibid.*, pp. xi, 9, 33.

41. *Ibid.*, pp. 9, 36, 30. The report referred to the possibility that the District might be asked to prepare an Emergency Plan "to cope with any special critical developments which threaten the continuance of existing commuter rail services" (p. 41). In the view of some who gave high priority to this problem, the Emergency Plan provision was likely to be the key to the future development of the District. They felt that substantial public funds to aid rail transit were likely to be provided only when suspension of a rail carrier's passenger service was imminent. (It could also be argued that the existence of the District might hasten such emergencies, for the regulatory agencies might be expected to look more favorably upon requests for suspension of service by private carriers if the probable result of granting such requests were public assistance by the District, not cessation of the service.)

42. *Ibid.*, pp. 6, 17, 29.

43. *Ibid.*, pp. 18, 45–46.

44. *Ibid.*, pp. xiii–xiv.

45. Cf. Huntington, *Common Defense*, pp. 146–66.

46. See March and Simon, *Organizations*, p. 152.

CHAPTER VIII. A REGIONAL TRANSIT AGENCY?

1. On state legislative behavior on urban and regional problems, see Malcolm Jewell, *The State Legislature: Politics and Practice* (New York, Random House, 1962), especially pp. 53–61; Gordon Baker, *Rural versus Urban Political Power* (New York, Doubleday, 1955), especially Chaps. 3 and 4; John C. Wahlke et al., *The Legislative System: Explorations in Legislative Behavior* (New York, Wiley, 1962); Victor Jones, *Metropolitan Government* (Chicago, University of Chicago Press, 1942); David R. Derge, "Metropolitan and Outstate Alignments in Illinois and Missouri Legislative Delegations," *American Political Science Review*, LII (December, 1958), 1051–65; Richard T. Frost, "On Derge's Metropolitan and Outstate Legislative Delegations," *American Political Science Review*, LIII

(September, 1959), 792–95; Harold Herman, *New York State and the Metropolitan Problem* (Philadelphia, University of Pennsylvania Press, 1964). The 1964 decisions of the U.S. Supreme Court (*Reynolds v. Sims*, 377 U.S. 533, and other cases) applied the "one man–one vote" principle to state legislatures, and the traditional pattern of rural domination is being substantially altered as a result of this judicial standard. See C. Herman Pritchett, "Equal Protection and the Urban Majority," *American Political Science Review*, LVIII (December, 1964), 869–75.

2. The bills were Assembly Introductory 2028 and Senate Introductory 3015. SI 3015 followed the wording of the MRTC draft closely, but Assemblyman Brook made one change in his bill. The states would not "find and declare" that the District "could not provide such [transit] facilities . . . without an income deficit"; instead, they would only report the opinion of the MRTC that an income deficit must be expected. The MRTC's proposed wording on the use of "the fiscal resources of the region" to meet transit deficits was retained in both New York bills.

3. See especially Real Estate Board of New York, letters to Governor Harriman and Mayor Wagner, Jan. 28, 1958; Committee on Lower Manhattan, press release, Jan. 16, 1958; New York *Journal-American*, Jan. 7, 1958; New York *Herald Tribune*, Jan. 7, 1958; Commerce and Industry Association of New York, press release, Feb. 13, 1958; RPA, press release, Feb. 7, 1958. Public policies toward the LIRR and the New York City transit system are described in earlier chapters. In addition, in 1956 New York City had agreed to provide substantial public aid to the Staten Island Rapid Transit Company, a subsidiary of the Baltimore and Ohio Railroad, in order to maintain its rail service on the Island.

4. On the activities of the H&M unions, see New York *Herald Tribune*, Feb. 6, 1958. An attack on the MRTC plan, based in part on the need for giving attention to Long Island's transit needs, is found in *Long Island Business* (March, 1958), pp. 1–6.

5. In 1958, the Republicans controlled the State Senate by 37–21 and the Assembly by 96–54. Republican hegemony in both houses of the legislature continued unbroken for thirty years until the Democratic victory of 1964.

6. New York *Times*, March 13, 14, 17, 1958; Bergen *Evening Record*, March 13, 1958; New York *Herald Tribune*, March 18, 1958.

7. New York *Times,* April 24, 1958. Mayor Wagner also opposed the bill because the District's governing body would be chosen by county officials and thus might not give adequate representation to the region's larger cities. (This criticism did not apply to New York City's members, who would be chosen by the city's main governing body, the Board of Estimate.)

The Mayor's position on the District was in part a reflection of his chairmanship of the regionwide MRC.

8. Chap. 955, Laws of 1958; approval memorandum 106. The change in the legislative declaration made by Assemblyman Brook was incorporated in the statute. (See Note 2 in this chapter.)

9. See Bergen *Evening Record,* Jan. 7, March 12, 19, April 5, 1958; North Arlington (N.J.) *Leader,* Jan. 9, 1958; Transit Committee of Bergen County, press release, January, 1958, resolution, March 28, 1958; Nutley (N.J.) *Sun,* March 27, 1958; Newark *Evening News,* Jan. 7, April 15, 1958; Bayonne *Times,* Jan. 7, 1958; Passaic *Herald-News,* Jan. 24, 1958.

10. New Jersey Motor Bus Association, "Memorandum re Senate No. 50, Assembly No. 115" (Jersey City, Feb. 17, 1958).

11. New Brunswick *Daily Home News,* Feb. 27, March 3, 1958; Plainfield (N.J.) *Courier-News,* Feb. 27, 1958; Newark *Evening News,* Feb. 28, March 6, 7, 1958.

12. See MRTC, press releases, Feb, 27, April 27, 1958; Bergen *Evening Record,* March 12, April 30, 1958; Newark *Evening News,* April 5, 1958; Essex County, Transcript of the Meeting of the Board of Chosen Freeholders (Newark, May 16, 1958); New Jersey Assembly, Committee on Federal and Interstate Relations and Committee on Highways, Transportation and Public Utilities, "Public Hearing on Assembly Bills No. 16 and 115 and Senate Bill No. 50," Trenton, Nov. 24 and Dec. 3, 1958 (hereafter referred to as N.J. Assembly, "Public Hearing," with the date).

13. Essex County, Transcript of the Meeting of the Board of Chosen Freeholders (Newark, May 16, 1958), pp. 71–72, 53.

14. *Ibid.,* p. 78.

15. *Ibid.,* p. 42.

16. See MRC, Traffic and Transportation Committee, "Report" (New York, June 10, 1958), pp. 6–8; MRC, "Memorandum re: Legislation for Bi-State District" (New York, May, 1958); N.J. Assembly, "Public Hearing," Nov. 24, 1958, pp. 56A ff. On June

10, 1958, the MRC voted unanimously to oppose the Transit District legislation. New York *Times,* June 11, 1958.

17. Robert C. Wood, *Metropolis Against Itself* (New York, Committee for Economic Development, 1959), p. 30. Assemblyman Musto had introduced bills similar to A-16 for several years, but he had never been able to garner much support. On the development of backing for the Musto bill in early 1958, see the New Brunswick *Daily Home News,* March 3, 1958; Newark *Evening News,* March 3, 6, 7, 10, 1958; *Jersey Journal,* Feb. 19, 1958; Elizabeth *Daily Journal,* April 19, 1958; Bergen *Evening Record,* May 5, 1958.

18. Governor Meyner announced his support for the District bill on April 20. See New York *Times,* April 21, 1958; *Hudson Dispatch,* April 21, 1958.

19. Based on the 1960 Census. In 1965, New Jersey adopted a revised formula for selecting state senators in order to conform to the 1964 "one man–one vote" standard of the Supreme Court (*Reynolds v. Sims,* 377 U.S. 533, and other 1964 cases).

20. See references cited in Note 1 of this chapter. These tendencies were not illustrated in legislative action on the District bill at Albany because of the limited area of the New York sector which would be encompassed by the District and because of the delay in the development of opposition in New York City.

21. Senate No. 50. Senator Jones' bill contained a change in the legislative declaration similar to that in the New York Assembly bill (Note 2 in this chapter). The New Jersey Assembly counterpart, No. 115, was sponsored jointly by six Republicans and three Democrats; it followed the wording of the MRTC draft.

22. Although Senator Dumont was from rural Warren County, he was an active contender for the Republican gubernatorial nomination and was sensitive to issues which might win Republican and independent votes in statewide balloting.

23. Newark *Evening News,* April 23, 1958.

24. See Jewell, *State Legislature.*

25. P.L. 85-625. Prior to the Transportation Act of 1958, the reduction or discontinuance of passenger rail service was under the jurisdiction of state regulatory commissions (except that the ICC had jurisdiction if complete abandonment of freight and passenger service on a line were involved). The 1958 Act sharply reduced

state control. A railroad might now discontinue any interstate train or ferry 30 days after posting notice, without regard to state action and unless the ICC intervened. Discontinuance could be suspended by the ICC for four months while it investigated the public necessity for the service and whether continued operation entailed an "undue burden" upon the interstate operations of the carrier. In addition, if a rail carrier's petition to discontinue any intrastate train was not acted upon at the state level within 120 days, the railroad might ask the ICC for permission to eliminate the service. The 1958 Act also increased ICC control over intrastate fares.

Although these changes were to have a significant impact on the rail situation in the New York region, regional interests were primarily focused on the continuing debate on state and local policies and contributed little to the shaping of the new federal policy. See Michael N. Danielson, *Federal-Metropolitan Politics and the Commuter Crisis* (New York, Columbia University Press, 1965), Chap. II.

26. See New York *Herald Tribune*, Aug. 15, 1958; New York *Times*, Sept. 4, 1958; New York *Herald Tribune*, Nov. 18, 1958; Bergen *Evening Record*, Nov. 26, 1958; New York *Times*, Dec. 2, 4, 1958; Newark *Evening News*, Dec. 5, 7, 1958.

27. Each of Flink's three reports was forwarded by the Committee to the PNYA for its comments, and the Port Authority responded to each caustically and at great length. See S. J. Flink, "Memorandum re: A-16; A-115" (Newark, May 19, 1958); "Report on Metropolitan Rapid Transit Development and the Port Authority" (Newark, August, 1958); "Report on the Port of New York Authority and Rapid Transit in the Metropolitan Region" (Nov. 5, 1958). The Authority's comments are found in PNYA, Board of Commissioners, letters to Martin Kesselhart, Chairman, Committee on Federal and Interstate Relations, New Jersey Assembly (New York, May 29, Sept. 11, Nov. 24, 1958).

28. MRTC, press release, Sept. 10, 1958; New Jersey Assembly, "Public Hearing," Nov. 24, 1958, pp. 86A–91A; letter to Governor Meyner and the members of the New Jersey legislature, Oct. 21, 1958. The MRTC favored an Assembly resolution against local tax support (rather than an amendment to the bill) in order to obviate the need for New York State to take formal action on the District bill again the following year.

29. Tobin argued that the regional highway system was used

mainly for weekend and holiday travel, for weekday non-rush hour travel, and for rush hour travel between points not directly served by rail lines. Because of convenience and other advantages, Tobin asserted, almost none of these auto travelers would conceivably shift to rail and therefore rail-highway coordination would have no significant effect in solving the problems of highway congestion and under-utilization of rail service. See statement by Tobin in New Jersey Assembly, "Public Hearing," Nov. 24, 1958, pp. 29–31.

In 1958, the Port Authority doubted that coordinated planning was advantageous. A few years later, however, when the New Jersey Turnpike Authority announced a $300-million expansion plan, the PNYA took a different tack. Concerned about the impact of the expansion plan on congestion at the Holland and Lincoln Tunnels, Tobin also noted that the Turnpike parallels several New Jersey rail lines and that expansion "could quite probably have the effect of forcing the abandonment of commuter service" on one or more of the carriers. Tobin urged that the Turnpike halt its plans until a coordinated study could be made of the ramifications on rail services and on other highway facilities of any such expansion. See Newark *Evening News*, Oct. 25, 1964.

30. Tobin's comments are found in New Jersey Assembly, "Public Hearing," Nov. 24, 1958, pp. 9–69. See also PNYA, Board of Commissioners, letters to Martin Kesselhart, Chairman, Committee on Federal and Interstate Relations, New Jersey Assembly (New York, May 29, Sept. 11, Nov. 24, 1958). The views of investment-banking spokesmen are quoted in the Nov. 24, 1958, letter, pp. 9–10.

31. On the rail carriers' position, see Newark *Evening News*, March 15, April 18, 1958; E. T. Moore, President, Central Railroad of New Jersey, statement of June 11, 1958; New Jersey Assembly, "Public Hearing," Dec. 3, 1958, pp. 52–75, 1A–50A. On the commuter groups which favored the District, see New Jersey Assembly, "Public Hearing," Nov. 24, 1958, pp. 124A–134A, Dec. 3, 1958, p. 109A.

32. On the automobile groups, see *ibid.*, pp. 1–42, 111A–114A. On the Bus Association, see New Jersey Assembly, "Public Hearing," Nov. 24, 1958, pp. 25A–38A. On the MRC, see New York *Times*, June 11, 20, 1958; New York *Herald Tribune*, July 14, 1958; New Jersey Assembly, "Public Hearing," Nov. 24, 1958, pp. 56A–69A.

33. See, for example, Bergen *Evening Record*, April 29, June 20, 1958; New York *Herald Tribune*, April 28, 1958.

34. Assembly Committee Substitute for A–115. The bill also stipulated that no District plan "shall provide for financing by means of any tax on real or personal property within the borders of the district" and that the credit of any governmental unit could not be pledged unless it expressly consented. The compromise bill was devised jointly by the Committee on Highways, Transportation and Public Utilities, which held the District bill, and the Committee on Federal and Interstate Relations, which held the Musto bill. See their "Joint Report in respect to A-16, A-115 and S-50 (1958)," Trenton, Jan. 9, 1958.

35. Newark *Evening News*, Dec. 15, 1958.

CHAPTER IX. STATE LEADERSHIP AND PARTIAL REMEDIES

1. The major exception was the Long Island Rail Road, which obtained public assistance in the early 1950s after it entered bankruptcy and suffered a series of disastrous accidents. (See Chap. II of this study.)

2. See New York *Herald Tribune*, Aug. 15, 1958; New York *Times*, Sept. 4, 1958; and press releases.

3. New York *Herald Tribune*, Nov. 18, 1958.

4. Robert W. Purcell, "Special Report to the Governor on Problems of the Railroads and Bus Lines in New York State" (New York, March 12, 1959), pp. 1–2 (cited hereafter as Purcell, "Special Report").

5. New York *Times*, Feb. 11, 1959; Newark *Evening News*, Feb. 10, 1959.

6. Newark *Evening News*, Feb. 17, 1959; Bergen County Transit Committee newsletter, Feb. 16, 1959; New York *Times*, March 2, 1959.

7. Purcell, "Special Report," pp. 1–50. Before the state could guarantee bonds for the commuter-car program, a constitutional amendment authorizing the guarantee would have to be accepted by two successive legislatures and by the state electorate at a general election.

8. PNYA, press release, March 15, 1959.

9. On the negotiations concerning the 1959 commuter-car pro-

gram, see U.S. House of Representatives, Committee on the Judiciary, *Port of New York Authority, Hearings, before Subcommittee No. 5*, 86th Cong., 2nd Sess. (1960), especially pp. 27–51, 277–320.

10. Purcell also proposed that changes be made in the state's Full Crew Law, that public aid be given to bus lines, that New York State join with New Jersey in developing plans to aid interstate rail service, and that the 10 percent federal tax on passenger transportation be repealed. Purcell, "Special Report," pp. 17–20, 51–74.

11. The legislature refused to enact the proposed changes in the Full Crew Law, however. On legislative discussion of the Purcell program, see New York *Times*, March 20, 25, 26, 1959.

12. Chap. 420, Laws of 1959. The New York modifications were discussed with New Jersey legislative leaders before the revised bill was introduced at Albany, and the New York bill retained several provisions from the New Jersey measure that were important to Trenton legislators, including the prohibitions upon a property tax and upon imposing any obligation on a local government without its consent and the reference to the possibility of future PNYA assistance.

13. Chap. 24, Laws of 1959. The interstate compact establishing the New York–New Jersey Transportation Agency received congressional approval on Sept. 10, and President Eisenhower signed the measure on Sept. 21, 1959 (P.L. 86-302). On legislative views at Trenton, see the statement appended to Assembly Bill No. 22, 1959; New York *Times*, March 27, May 5, 1959; Newark *Evening News*, April 14, May 5, 1959.

14. New York State, Annual Message of the Governor, Jan. 8, 1959; Chapter 16, Laws of 1959. Purcell, "Special Report," pp. 75–76.

15. The status of the three railroads in 1959–61 is summarized in New York State, Office of Transportation, *Annual Report, 1960*, pp. 13–22; *1961*, pp. 16–18. In addition to their passenger-service deficits, the Long Island Rail Road and the New Haven suffered from freight service of limited scope and revenue potential, as well as other problems. See Ford K. Edwards, "A Report to the State of New York, Office of Transportation" (on the New Haven Railroad), March 31, 1962; Frederick B. Whitman et al., "Report of the Railroad Professional Survey Group on Various Aspects of

the New York, New Haven & Hartford Railroad Company's Problems," Washington, D.C., June 28, 1962; New York State, Special Committee on the LIRR, *A New Long Island Rail Road* (February, 1965).

16. See New York State, Office of Transportation, *Annual Report, 1960,* p. 10; *1961,* pp. 15–16; PNYA, *Annual Report, 1960,* p. 31. A constitutional amendment permitting the State to guarantee $100 million of special PNYA bonds was passed by successive legislatures in 1959 and 1961 and approved by a statewide referendum in November, 1961. Of the $20 million originally advanced for the commuter-car program by the State, about $4 million had been expended by the fall of 1961.

17. Chap. 199, Laws of 1961. The provisions of the legislation are outlined in New York State, Office of Transportation, *Annual Report, 1960,* pp. 17–21.

18. New York *Times,* Jan. 6, April 14, Oct. 2, 25, 1960. The 1958 Act provided that the federal government would guarantee loans made by private sources at commercial interest rates, but such guarantees could be given only if prospective earnings of the carrier were such that there was "reasonable assurance" the loan could be repaid.

19. New York State, Office of Transportation, *Annual Report, 1960,* p. 14; New York *Times,* Oct. 26, Nov. 2, 1960. Ronan, the Interstate Staff Committee chairman, was secretary to Governor Rockefeller. During 1960–61, he became the Governor's primary aide on transportation matters. In the fall of 1960, Rhode Island and Massachusetts formally joined the Interstate Staff Commitee.

20. New York *Times,* Oct. 28, 1960.

21. New York *Times,* July 8, 1961. The four-state program to aid the New Haven is summarized in New York State, Office of Transportation, *Annual Report 1960,* pp. 14–15, 17–22.

22. New York *Times,* Jan. 17, 1962.

23. Lewis K. Sillcox, "The Port of New York Authority Trans-Hudson Crossings" (March 23, 1960). Sillcox resigned in April, and Arne C. Wiprud replaced him in August, 1960.

24. New York State, Office of Transportation, *Annual Report, 1960,* p. 31.

25. See New York *Times,* Dec. 2, 4, 1958; Newark *Evening News,*

Dec. 5, 7, 12, 25, 1958, March 3, 4, 24, 31, April 3, 10, 28, May 2, 6, 1959.

26. Dwight R. G. Palmer, address before the Second Annual Meeting, Institute for Rapid Transit, Washington, D.C., May 10, 1963, p. 7.

27. James G. March and Herbert A. Simon (with the collaboration of Harold Guetzkow), *Organizations* (New York, Wiley, 1958), p. 173.

28. In order to keep commuter service in operation, the rail carriers demanded direct financial assistance, not new equipment with its additional financing burdens. For reactions of the New Jersey railroads and other New Jersey interests to the New York program, see New York *Times*, March 16, 1959; Newark *Evening News*, March 16, 1959. New Jersey's state revenue sources are analyzed and compared with New York State's in Robert C. Wood (with V. V. Almendinger), *1400 Governments: The Political Economy of the New York Metropolitan Region* (Cambridge, Mass., Harvard University Press, 1961), pp. 25–26, 80 ff.

29. See New York *Times*, March 13, 1959; Newark *Evening News*, March 16, April 3, 1959.

30. See New Jersey Senate Committee on Highways, Transportation and Public Utilities, "Public Hearing on Assembly Bill No. 692" (Trenton, Aug. 21, 1959), pp. 5 ff.; New Jersey State Highway Department, Division of Railroad Transportation, *New Jersey's Rail Transportation Problem* (Trenton, April, 1960), pp. 10–11 (hereafter cited as New Jersey State Highway Department, April, 1960, Report).

31. See Senate Bill No. 4, introduced Jan. 13, 1959 (by Lance and four Republican co-sponsors); New York *Times*, March 13, 1959; Chap. 14, Laws of 1959.

32. Newark *Star Ledger*, March 4, April 29, 1959; Newark *Evening News*, May 2, 1959.

33. Dwight R. G. Palmer, "State Government and Transportation," *State Government*, XXXV (Summer, 1962), p. 15.

34. New Jersey State Highway Department, Division of Railroad Transportation, *A Proposal toward Solving New Jersey's Transportation Problem* (Trenton, June 15, 1959).

35. New York *Times*, June 18, 1959; Newark *Evening News*, Aug. 11, Sept. 1, 1959.

36. A summary of the highway-coalition campaign is contained in New Jersey State Highway Department, April, 1960, Report, p. A24. The Turnpike Authority chairman accepted the plan, but one of the three commissioners, Cornelius E. Gallagher, attacked it vigorously and argued that the Authority's surplus funds should be used to expand the Turnpike in congested areas. Gallagher also served as a Democratic Congressman from Hudson County.

37. See, for example, New Jersey Senate, "Public Hearing on Assembly Bill No. 692," pp. 49A–63A; Newark *Evening News*, Sept. 10, 1959; and summary in New Jersey State Highway Department, April, 1960, Report, pp. A23–A24.

38. New Jersey Senate, "Public Hearing on Assembly Bill No. 692," pp. 14–16, 1A ff., 19A ff.; Citizens United Transit Committee (Bergen), newsletter, June, 1959; Bergen *Evening Record*, July 25, 1959; Newark *Star Ledger*, July 27, 1959; New Jersey State Highway Department, April, 1960, Report, pp. A20–A29. The state's labor organizations split on the plan, the CIO in favor, the AFL opposed.

39. New Jersey Senate, "Public Hearing on Assembly Bill No. 692," pp. 11, 13A, and see pp. 10A–18A.

40. New York *Times*, Aug. 19, Oct. 15, 1959; Newark *Evening News*, Sept. 10, 1959. The Governor and his aides were caught between the demand by Hudson County leaders that the referendum be amended to guarantee full reimbursement for any lost railroad taxes and the refusal of the legislature to reconvene to amend it.

41. See N.J. State Highway Dept., April 1960 Report, p. A32; New Jersey Senate Commission [created under Senate Res. No. 7, 1960, 1961] to Study the Financial Structure and Operations of the Port of New York Authority, "Second Public Hearing" (Trenton, Jan. 26, 1961), pp. 43–44, 55.

42. New Jersey State Highway Department, April, 1960, Report, pp. 12–27. Railroad efforts to curtail service following the defeat of the Turnpike plan are summarized on p. 12 of the Report.

43. On Governor Meyner's views, see, for example, his statement in the New York *Times*, Feb. 3, 1960. The Governor also expressed this view frequently in private discussions with his aides.

44. Chap. 66, Laws of 1960.

45. The amounts paid to the rail carriers in 1960–61 and 1961–62 were as follows:

| Railroad | Amount paid, millions of dollars | |
	1960–61	1961–62
Erie–Lackawanna	1.99	2.80
Pennsylvania	1.40	2.10
Jersey Central	1.10	1.55
New Jersey & New York	0.08	0.09
Reading	0.01	0.02
Total	4.59 *	6.56

* Figures do not add up to total because of rounding.

SOURCE: New Jersey State Highway Department, Division of Railroad Transportation, *Second Annual Report and Recommendations* (Trenton, January, 1962), p. 41 (hereafter cited as New Jersey Highway Department, January 1962, Report).

The funds for the first two years of the service contract program were diverted by the state legislature from highway construction funds, the first year with Palmer's acquiescence (in view of the emergency situation), the second year over his objections and those of highway user groups. Meanwhile, state officials devised a plan which provided $6–7 million a year for the contract program in 1962 and thereafter and ended the diversion of highway funds. The scheme, enacted in 1961, provided for the levying of a commuter benefit tax on the income of all persons who live in New York or in New Jersey and derive income from the other state. New Jersey had no general income tax, and all these persons had paid an income tax in New York. But because New York State law permits a person working in another state to credit any income tax paid to that state against the New York levy, the net effect of the New Jersey commuter tax was to transfer $6–7 million in tax payments from Albany to Trenton. The plan met constitutional limitations by allocating all funds derived from the tax to the interstate transportation problem. (Originally, New Jersey had hoped to collect $30–40 million through the tax, but New York officials, outraged at the New Jersey plan, changed the tax-credit provisions of New York law so that most tax payments of interstate commuters were retained by Albany.)

46. New Jersey Senate Commission, "Second Public Hearing," pp. 34, 43. In Palmer's April, 1960, Report, several plans for reroutings, service consolidations, and schedule changes were described, and it was suggested that the Division of Railroad Transportation "coordinate the efforts of the carriers, municipalities, commuter and labor organizations" to obtain these improvements. Again in 1962, Palmer urged that all interests "cease carrying on

studies and holding meetings," and join together to improve rail service. He said he hoped that substantial state funds would soon be made available as part of this joint effort. See New Jersey State Highway Department, April, 1960, Report, pp. 16–27, January, 1962, Report, pp. 8–28; cf. New Jersey State Highway Department, Division of Railroad Transportation, *The Railroad Program and Recommendations for Legislative Action* (Trenton, April, 1964), pp. 28 ff. (hereafter cited as New Jersey State Highway Department, April, 1964, Report).

47. See, for example, the statement of Senator Lance in New Jersey Senate Commission [created under Senate Res. No. 7, 1960] to Study the Financial Structure and Operations of the Port of New York Authority, "Public Hearing" (Trenton, Sept. 27, 1960), pp. 2–4; David D. Gladfelter, "Jets for the Great Swamp?" in Richard T. Frost, ed., *Cases in State and Local Government* (Englewood Cliffs, N.J., Prentice-Hall, 1961), pp. 302–18; U.S. House of Representatives, *Port of New York Authority, Hearings before Subcommittee No. 5.* The House investigation was initiated and directed by Congressman Emanuel Celler, New York City Democrat and chairman of the Judiciary Committee. Celler was a long-time critic of the PNYA.

48. New Jersey Senate Commission, "Public Hearing," pp. 13–27. The PNYA set a third condition—that the Pennsylvania Railroad would be willing to transfer its agreements for operation of H&M trains into Newark to the PNYA "on reasonable financial terms."

49. New Jersey Senate Commission, "Second Public Hearing," p. 11.

50. The report on the World Trade Center was submitted on March 10, 1961, and is summarized in PNYA, *Annual Report, 1960,* pp. 35–37.

51. PNYA, *Annual Report, 1962,* p. 32. The twelve commissioners of the PNYA were designated as the board of directors of PATH, the PNYA executive director as the president of PATH, the PNYA deputy executive director as PATH's senior vice-president, and the director of the PNYA rail transportation department as the vice-president and general manager of PATH.

Several hurdles had to be surmounted before the Port Authority could carry out its program for the Hudson Tubes: New Jersey and New York approved the program on Feb. 13 and March 27, 1962, respectively; the New York County Supreme Court granted the

PATH application to acquire the Tubes and the New York terminal buildings on July 26, and the New Jersey Supreme Court approved on Aug. 9, 1962. On Aug. 28 the ICC granted PATH a certificate of public convenience and necessity, and PATH assumed operating responsibility for the Tubes on Sept. 1, 1962. But the power of the Port Authority to carry out the combined Hudson Tubes–World Trade Center project was challenged on constitutional grounds (by tenants who would be forced out of the Hudson Terminal buildings), and on Feb. 19, 1963, the New York Appellate Division held that the bistate authorizing legislation contained constitutional defects (condemnation powers too broad in scope). PATH immediately suspended its rehabilitation plans and served only as a caretaker for the properties during the next ten months. The Port Authority and the states appealed the decision, and on April 4 the New York State Court of Appeals reversed the Appellate Division and upheld the bistate legislation. The U.S. Supreme Court concurred in decisions of Nov. 12 and Dec. 4, 1963, and PATH then resumed work on its modernization program.

52. The 1962 authorizing legislation provides a constitutionally protected statutory covenant with bondholders; under the statute, no new rail transit facility involving a pledge of its revenues from other facilities may be undertaken by the PNYA if the estimated annual deficits of all Port Authority rail facilities (including the facility to be added) would exceed 10 percent of the amount then in the PNYA General Reserve Fund. (The Fund had a balance of $62.6 million at the end of 1961, and it was expected that this amount would increase slowly in subsequent years.) The legislation does permit the Port Authority to undertake additional rail duties, beyond those permitted by this formula, in so far as the states are willing to guarantee any deficits.

53. On the PNYA attitude toward coordination, see Austin J. Tobin, address before the RPA, Oct. 5, 1960; Frank W. Herring, paper presented at the Annual Meeting of the Highway Research Board, Jan. 12, 1961; PNYA, *Metropolitan Transportation—1980* (New York, 1963), pp. 299–304 and *passim*.

54. See, for example, New York *Herald Tribune*, Feb. 15, 1962, New York *Journal-American*, May 16, 1962, and New Jersey Senate, Special Senate Investigating Committee (under Senate Res. No. 7 of 1961), *Report*, June 28, 1963. The bipartisan Senate Committee concluded unanimously that "the basic framework and philosophy

of the Port Authority with respect to its financing policies and its adherence to the principle of administering self-supporting facilities are soundly conceived," and its record of performance in contributing to the development of the Port was rated as "excellent." Special praise was reserved for Austin Tobin for "his thorough and most intimate knowledge of every project. . . . He had at his fingertips all of the data of the Port Authority's activities when he was testifying and in addition thereto, on our personal inspection of the facilities, when he had his experts advise us, . . . Mr. Tobin always had supplemental remarks that even went into greater detail, showing his constant attention to every facet" (*Report*, pp. 12, 26, 37).

The New Jersey legislature did not, however, accept the Port Authority's proposal for a jetport in Morris County, and as of 1965 the PNYA was still engaged in a search for a feasible site for an additional major air terminal in the region. Meanwhile, the investigation by the House Judiciary Committee uncovered some interesting materials on previous PNYA activities (see House of Representatives, *Port of New York Authority, Hearings before Subcommittee No. 5;* and references to the hearings in Chap. II of this volume and in this chapter); but the PNYA's reputation was not significantly damaged nor congressional controls increased. A demand by Congressman Celler for the internal documents of the PNYA was rejected by the Port Authority; the House thereupon voted to cite three PNYA officials for contempt, but these citations were nullified by a 1962 decision of the U.S. Court of Appeals.

55. Robert Moses, Remarks, May 8, 1965; Moses, *Arterial Progress*, November 8, 1965; and 1964–65 reports of the New Jersey Turnpike Authority, New Jersey State Highway Department, and New York State Department of Public Works.

56. On all New Jersey passenger carriers except the Pennsylvania Railroad, passenger deficits were combined with only moderate freight profits (or with freight deficits on some railroads), resulting in systemwide deficits in 1961, 1962, 1963, and 1964. Large losses each year were reported by the major passenger carriers—the Erie-Lackawanna (formed by merger in 1960) and the Jersey Central; and continuing deficits were also absorbed by the smaller carriers—the Susquehanna, the Reading, the New Jersey and New York, and the Pennsylvania-Reading Seashore. See N.J. State Highway

Dept., April, 1964, Report, pp. 8 ff., and annual reports of the rail corporations for 1964.

Noting their continuing financial losses, the Erie-Lackawanna, Jersey Central, and Susquehanna announced in 1964–65 that substantial increases in public assistance would be needed if commuter service was to be continued. The Erie-Lackawanna said it would petition to eliminate all commuter service unless state aid were increased to four times its present total, and its officials foresaw the need for $80 million in public funds to rehabilitate aging cars and purchase new ones. See Newark *Evening News*, June 23, 1964; New York *Times*, Jan. 26, 30, March 26, 1965.

The Pennsylvania Railroad was the only exception to these trends. With its extensive freight network yielding substantial profits, the Pennsylvania saw its financial condition strengthened during 1961–64; and in 1965 it seemed likely that the railroad's commuter service would be continued indefinitely under a program of modest state-federal grants, primarily for the purchase of new passenger cars.

57. During 1960–63, state payments under the contract program totaled $22.7 million, while suburban passenger deficits of the railroads under contract totaled $82.7 million, according to estimates of the state Division of Railroad Transportation. See N.J. State Highway Dept., April 1964, Report, p. 9. (The deficit estimates were based on the ICC method of fully allocated costs; using other accounting methods, the passenger deficits would vary considerably.)

Taxes paid by the railroads in the early 1960s averaged more than $12 million a year, most of which was absorbed by Hudson County municipalities. After years of debate, Trenton lawmakers finally enacted a bill in December, 1964, which will reduce the carriers' tax bill by $2–3 million a year. This generosity was moderated, however, by the legislature's decision to postpone the effective date of the change until January, 1966.

58. The rehabilitation program was announced by the state Division of Railroad Transportation in 1962 and includes plans for rail consolidations, new passenger cars, and other improvements. See N.J. State Highway Dept., January, 1962, Report. Progress in carrying out the program is discussed in N.J. State Highway Dept., April, 1964, Report, pp. 6 ff., and N.J. State Highway Dept.,

Report to Governor Richard J. Hughes: The Erie-Lackawanna Railroad Company and Suburban Passenger Service in New Jersey (Trenton, March, 1965), pp. 18 ff. (hereafter cited as N.J. State Highway Dept., March, 1965, Report).

59. See PNYA, "The Hudson & Manhattan–World Trade Center Project," Jan. 29, 1962; PNYA, *Annual Report, 1962*, pp. 35–36.

60. The 1961 federal program, adopted as part of the Housing Act of 1961, authorized $25 million for demonstration grants, to be allotted to specific projects which would test ways of improving transit service and reducing costs. An additional $50 million was set aside for federal loans for the acquisition, construction, and improvement of mass transportation facilities; and federal planning assistance was authorized to assist in solving urban transportation problems within a framework of regional planning. The program was administered by the Housing and Home Finance Agency. In 1964, Congress expanded the program, authorizing grants as well as loans for capital improvements and providing for the expenditure of $375 million during a three-year period. The developments culminating in the federal mass transportation program are analyzed in Michael N. Danielson, *Federal-Metropolitan Politics and the Commuter Crisis* (New York, Columbia University Press, 1965).

61. Palmer's new plan called for the expenditure of $50 million (half in federal funds) for route consolidations and other capital improvements on several railroads; and for a federal demonstration grant of $3.8 million (combined with $1.9 million in state funds) for the Erie-Lackawanna, to be used to experiment with schedule changes and other service adjustments which might increase passenger revenues on that carrier. As of November, 1965, neither federal nor state funds for the plan had been approved.

62. The prospects for a broad-based state tax and increased state action in the regional transit field were enhanced by the reelection of Democratic Governor Richard J. Hughes in November, 1965, in a landslide which gave his party control of both houses of the reapportioned legislature. (Hughes had been elected Governor in 1961, following Meyner's retirement after serving two terms, the maximum permitted under the state constitution.)

63. The strategy pursued by New York State and her allies (Connecticut, Massachusetts, Rhode Island, Westchester County, and New York City) was based on a New York State-sponsored study by Ford K. Edwards. Edwards concluded that the New

Haven's suburban services (those from New Haven to New York City, including intermediate points) yielded a deficit in 1961 of between $409,000 and $5.5 million; the rest of the railroad's deficit ($17–25 million) was attributed to long-haul passenger services and to freight. Political leaders in the New Haven area emphasized the smaller suburban deficit in urging that the national government take primary responsibility for the railroad. See Interstate Staff Committee on the New Haven Railroad, Report, Feb. 15, 1963 (the quotation in the text is on p. 3); Ford K. Edwards, *A Report to the State of New York Office of Transportation*, March 31, 1962. For a critical analysis of the Edwards report, see Institute of Public Administration, *Suburbs to Grand Central* (New York, August, 1963), Chapter III.

64. On the efforts to enlist more substantial federal assistance for the New Haven, see New York *Times*, Jan. 17, 1962, Jan. 16, 1964, Feb. 24, March 3, 1965; Nelson A. Rockefeller, Text of Testimony Prepared for Presentation to the Senate Commerce Committee (Albany, March 10, 1965). The federal government's stand is outlined by John C. Kohl and C. D. Martin, Jr., in *Statements before the Senate Committee on Commerce* (Washington, D.C., March 10, 1965).

Only in Connecticut, which viewed the New Haven as a major freight and passenger artery, was there evidence of a willingness to take further direct action at the state and local level. In the summer of 1963, with the railroad's deficits climbing, Connecticut created a state Transportation Authority and authorized it to provide several million dollars in grants and loans to the New Haven if a cooperative program with New York State could be developed. But officials at Albany were unresponsive. Meanwhile, the New Haven absorbed deficits of more than $12 million in 1962 and again in 1963.

65. See New York *Times*, Jan. 19, Feb. 19, 1965. In March, it was reported that the New York Central and the Pennsylvania had agreed to include the New Haven on this basis. New York *Times*, March 30, 1965.

66. New York *Times*, Jan. 21, 1965.

67. New York *Times*, Feb. 5, 1965. Criticisms were voiced by Westchester County spokesmen, RPA, and New York City newspapers; see New York *Times*, Jan. 23, Feb. 10, 15, 19, 1965, and New York *Herald Tribune*, Jan. 22, 1965. In addition, legislators

from upstate areas attacked the proposed use of state tax funds to help a railroad operating in only one area of the state. New York *Times*, March 9, 1965.

68. See Kohl, Statement before the Senate Committee on Commerce, March 10, 1965; Rockefeller, Text of Testimony Prepared for Presentation to the Senate Commerce Committee, March 10, 1965; New York *Times*, April 21, 29, 1965.

69. The 1954 plan included tax concessions, an unusual degree of rate-making freedom, and financial assistance from the LIRR owner, the Pennsylvania Railroad. With this aid, the LIRR maintained a net income every year until 1960, when it absorbed a loss of $1.1 million. The financial situation was moderately improved during the next three years, with profits of $0.6, 2.3, and 0.7 million, but in 1964 the LIRR lost $2.1 million. In mid-1964, the railroad's president reported that in spite of rehabilitation efforts, three-quarters of the LIRR fleet were more than sixteen years old, and 10 percent of the passenger cars were more than fifty years of age. State of New York, Office of Transportation, *Annual Report, 1963*, p. 36; *Long Island Press, A*ugust 12, 1964.

70. See New York State, Office of Transportation, *Annual Report, 1960*, pp. 17, 31–32; *Annual Report, 1963*, pp. 31–32; New York State, *Long Island Journey-to-Work Report—1963* (August, 1963).

71. New York State, Special Committee on the LIRR, *A New Long Island Rail Road* (February, 1965); New York *Times*, Feb. 26, 1965.

72. The MCTA was established under Chap. 324, Laws of 1965; Ronan was appointed chairman. During the fall, the MCTA was also negotiating with the New York Central (which was in relatively sound financial condition and maintained its commuter services without substantial losses), looking toward the possibility that Central and New Haven commuter services might be operated under a single management, subject to MCTA control. See New York *Times*, June 3, Oct. 27, 1965; William J. Ronan, Excerpts of Remarks, Oct. 21, 1965.

73. The legislation also provides that all MCTA facilities are exempt from state and local taxation or assessment and that the total cost of operation and maintenance of all passenger stations will be borne by the county within which the station is located (or by New York City, if a city station). On the LIRR, this would increase the total local contribution from $600,000 to $2 mil-

lion a year. In contrast to the PNYA, MCTA actions are not subject to gubernatorial veto; and control within the MCTA is highly centralized, with the chairman serving also as executive officer and receiving a salary of $45,000 per year (while the four other members are paid on a per diem basis, to a maximum of $15,000 a year each). The MCTA's independence is modified by Ronan's dual position as Secretary to the Governor and MCTA Chairman, facilitating close linkage between state and MCTA policy, at least temporarily, and by the probable need for state and federal funds to carry out the MCTA modernization program, thus providing a basis for external influence on the Authority.

74. The reactions of Westchester officials in 1964–65 to proposals that local and state tax support be provided to underwrite the New Haven's suburban service were typical of local views during these years and were similar to reactions in 1957–58 to the MRTC's Transit District plan. "The idea of taxing municipalities for a direct subsidy," asserted Westchester's county executive, "seems neither practical nor realistic. It would be resisted by the local taxpayer." Westchester officials argued that the major responsibility "rests with the states and the federal government." See E. G. Michaelian, Statement, Jan. 13, 1964; New York *Times*, Jan. 14, Sept. 22, 1964.

Illustrating the narrowness with which local officials may perceive the transportation problem, the New Haven subsidy issue not only led Westchester officials to seek outside help but divided the county as well. In early 1964, a program was devised which would provide some assistance to the railroad from New York State and Connecticut if Westchester would contribute $400,000 for station maintenance during the next year. In September, the county supervisors rejected the plan, with supervisors from towns served by the New Haven voting in favor and those from the New York Central service area opposed. (In early 1965, with Rockefeller's $20-million aid program apparently dependent on Westchester participation, the supervisors reversed their position but agreed to make the $400,000 available only if all present New Haven service were continued.) See William J. Ronan, Letter to Alfred F. Sulla, Jr., Westchester County Board of Supervisors, July 24, 1964; New York *Times*, Sept. 22, 1964, Feb. 2, 1965.

During the early 1960s, local interests continued their traditional attempts to persuade state regulatory commissions and other state officials to maintain service on lightly used lines. Aided by similar labor-union efforts, their campaigns did retard the effort to eliminate these high-cost lines.

75. The decision to discontinue efforts to gain legal status for the MRC was made at the April 24, 1964 meeting; at this meeting the MRC also voted to change from a voluntary association of governments to an association of elected officials. See New York *Times*, April 25, 1964; MRC, *Bulletin*, October, 1964. The *Times* found the evolution of the MRC disheartening:

"Sooner or later the desperate need for planning for the common problems of the tri-state metropolitan area, and for giving the local communities a powerful voice vis-a-vis the respective state governments and the Federal Government, will compel the establishment of something like the Metropolitan Regional Council.

"Fantastic fears of planning, local jealousies and political parochialism have joined to kill it for the present—to the shame and injury of the metropolitan area." (May 5, 1964.)

On MRC developments during the early 1960s, see New York *Times*, April 7, 1963, April 25, 1964; Bergen *Evening Record*, April 25, 1964; MRC Executive Board, Minutes, Jan. 3, 1964; Robert F. Wagner, Jr., Remarks at Meeting of MRC, April 24, 1964, and Remarks, May 14, 1965; MRC, *Bulletin, passim.*

76. The RPA and MRC were in the forefront of the campaign for creation of a tristate agency. See New York *Times*, April 20, 1959; MRC, *Bulletin*, March, 1960.

77. The membership of the Tri-State Committee included:

New Jersey: Commissioner of Highways, Director of the Division of Railroad Transportation, State Highway Engineer (all from the State Highway Department), and Commissioner of Conservation and Economic Development.

New York State: Secretary to the Governor, Director of the Office of Transportation, Superintendent of Public Works, Director of the Office of Regional Development.

Connecticut: Executive Aide to the Governor, Commissioner of Highways, Chairman of Public Utilities Commission, Chairman of Development Commission.

New York City: Chairman of City Planning Commission.

Later, four federal representatives were added, two from the Housing and Home Finance Agency, one from the Bureau of Public Roads, and one from the Federal Aviation Agency.

Until 1961, state officials had shown little interest in development of a tristate body. Their decision to create an agency in the fall of 1961 was based on several factors, including the continuing campaign for an agency by regional interests, increased federal interest in coordinated regional planning, and the ability of the states to devise a plan that kept policy control in state hands.

78. The Committee's activities are summarized in its "First Interim Report," October 30, 1961, and subsequent reports. In terms of the Committee's orientation, it is interesting to note that its staff was headed from 1961 until 1964 by Roger H. Gilman, PNYA director of port development, while on leave from his permanent position.

The Tri-State Committee assumed responsibility for coordinating the demonstration projects being carried out in the region under the federal transit programs of 1961 and 1964. These have included experiments with automatic fare collection on the LIRR, expanded parking facilities at New York Central and Pennsylvania Railroad stations, coordinated bus-rail service for commuters from Rockland County to Manhattan, and other projects. See Tri-State Transportation Committee, "Third Interim Report," May 10, 1963, pp. 32–38; New York State, Office of Transportation, *Annual Report, 1964*, pp. 34–36. The New York–New Jersey Transportation Agency was inactive until 1961; subsequently it has conducted studies jointly with Tri-State.

79. The two-year campaign for the permanent Tri-State Transportation Commission is summarized in New York *Times*, Dec. 10, 1963, Feb. 6, March 17, 1964, March 10, April 6, 1965.

80. New York *Times*, Dec. 31, 1964, and March 12, 1965.

CHAPTER X. PATTERNS OF CONFLICT AND COOPERATION

1. See Chap. V above, and James G. March and Herbert A. Simon (with the collaboration of Harold Guetzkow), *Organizations* (New York, Wiley, 1958), pp. 129–30.

2. Patterns of cooperation in various functional fields are analyzed in several other studies. See, for example, Harold Kaplan, *Urban Renewal Politics: Slum Clearance in Newark* (New York, Columbia University Press, 1963); Roscoe C. Martin et al., *Decisions in Syracuse* (Bloomington, Indiana University Press, 1961); Harold Herman, *New York State and the Metropolitan Problem* (Philadelphia, University of Pennsylvania Press, 1963); Vincent Ostrom, Charles M. Tiebout, and Robert Warren, "The Organization of

Government in Metropolitan Areas: A Theoretical Inquiry," *American Political Science Review*, LV (December, 1961), 831–42.

3. For example, see Chap. VIII of this book, Note 29; Herbert Kaufman, "Gotham in the Air Age," in Harold Stein, ed., *Public Administration and Policy Development: A Case Book* (New York, Harcourt, Brace, 1952), pp. 143–97.

4. Kaplan, *Urban Renewal Politics*, Chap. VIII.

5. See, for example, *ibid.*, Chap. VII.

6. See Chap. II of this book; Wallace S. Sayre and Herbert Kaufman, *Governing New York City: Politics in the Metropolis* (New York, Russell Sage Foundation, 1960; paperback ed., New York, Norton, 1965), Chap. IX; Kaplan, *Urban Renewal Politics*, Chap. VIII.

7. Chap. III ff. of this book; Paul Tillett and Myron Weiner, *The Closing of Newark Airport* (University, University of Alabama Press, 1955); Kaplan, *Urban Renewal Politics*. See also Sayre and Kaufman, *Governing New York City*, especially Chap. XI; Martin et al., *Decisions in Syracuse*, pp. 311 ff. and *passim;* York Willbern, *The Withering Away of the City* (University, University of Alabama Press, 1964), pp. 127–28.

8. See Ostrom et al., *American Political Science Review*, LV (1961), 840–41; John C. Bollens and Henry J. Schmandt, *The Metropolis: Its People, Politics, and Economic Life* (New York, Harper and Row, 1965), Chap. 13.

9. The response to the mass transportation problem in other regions illustrates some of these themes. See, for example, Frank Smallwood, *Metro Toronto: A Decade Later* (Toronto, Bureau of Municipal Research, 1963), pp. 30–32; Edward C. Banfield, *Political Influence* (New York, Free Press, 1961), Chap. 4; Winston W. Crouch and Beatrice Dinerman, *Southern California Metropolis* (Berkeley, University of California Press, 1963), p. 28. The San Francisco Bay Area, where a new rapid transit system largely financed by the region's taxpayers is now under construction, is in part a contrasting case. However, the extended conflict on routes, stations, financing, and other questions among the local communities to be served by the system and the withdrawal of two of the original five counties illustrate familiar patterns of behavior. On transit developments in the Bay Area, see San Francisco Bay Area Rapid Transit District, *Rapid Transit, passim; Wall Street Journal*, May 27, 1965.

10. Cf. Henry J. Schmandt, Paul G. Steinbicker, and George D. Wendel, *Metropolitan Reform in St. Louis: A Case Study* (New York, Holt, Rinehart and Winston, 1961); Scott Greer, *Metropolitics: A Study of Political Culture* (New York, Wiley, 1963); Don Becker, "The Fight for Seattle Metro," in Richard T. Frost, ed., *Cases in State and Local Government* (Englewood Cliffs, N.J., Prentice-Hall, 1961), pp. 292–301.

11. Cf. Robert C. Wood (with V. V. Almendinger), *1400 Governments: The Political Economy of the New York Metropolitan Region* (Cambridge, Mass., Harvard University Press, 1961), especially Chap. 5; Willbern, *Withering Away of the City*, pp. 29–33; William L. C. Wheaton, "Integration at the Urban Level," in Philip E. Jacob and James V. Toscano, eds., *The Integration of Political Communities* (Philadelphia, Lippincott, 1964), pp. 134–35; Michael N. Danielson and Jameson W. Doig, *The Politics of Development in the New York Region* (Berkeley, Institute of Governmental Studies, University of California, 1966). See also Sayre and Kaufman, *Governing New York City*, pp. 716–19.

12. These are goals for the regional political system urged by Robert C. Wood in *Metropolis Against Itself* (New York, Committee for Economic Development, 1959), p. 40.

13. Samuel P. Huntington, *The Common Defense: Strategic Programs in National Politics* (New York, Columbia University Press, 1961), p. 290. See also sources cited in Chap. III of this book, notes 1 and 2.

14. For example, the combination of general support for rail-service improvement and criticism of specific elements of the Page plan expressed by the Susquehanna commuters' group (which opposed Page's proposal to end service on its own line) and the 34th Street-Midtown Association (which opposed ending H&M service to 33rd Street).

15. See, for example, Greer, *Metropolitics;* Schmandt et al., *Metropolitan Reform in St. Louis;* Norton E. Long, *The Polity*, ed. by Charles Press (Chicago, Rand McNally, 1962), Chap. 15.

16. On state activities in various functional areas, see for example Herman, *New York State and the Metropolitan Problem*, Chaps. III ff.; Banfield, *Political Influence*, Chap. 4.

17. Martin et al., *Decisions in Syracuse*, pp. 308 ff. and *passim*.

18. The question of a Westchester County contribution to supplement state and federal aid to the New Haven was the subject

of vigorous disagreement between county officials and Rockefeller in the early 1960s. See previous chapter, especially note 74.

19. *The Future of the Metropolitan Regional Council*, Report of the Special Committee on Metropolitan Governmental Affairs to the RPA, January, 1959. Other areas with regional councils are Washington, D.C.; Philadelphia; Detroit; Seattle-Tacoma; Salem, Oregon; and San Francisco.

20. See Chap. IX of this book and Forbes B. Hays, *Community Leadership: The Regional Plan Association of New York* (New York, Columbia University Press, 1965), pp. 152–53.

21. On regional councils in other metropolitan areas, see Roscoe C. Martin, *Metropolis in Transition: Local Government Adaptation to Changing Urban Needs* (Washington, D.C., Housing and Home Finance Agency, 1963), Chaps. III and IV; Bollens and Schmandt, *The Metropolis*, pp. 392–99.

22. Smallwood, *Metro Toronto*, p. 32.

23. Crouch and Dinerman, *Southern California Metropolis*, p. 395.

24. The nature of special districts and prospects for the development of multipurpose districts are discussed in Bollens and Schmandt, *The Metropolis*, pp. 439–52. See also John C. Bollens, *Special District Governments in the United States* (Berkeley, University of California Press, 1957). The experience of Seattle with the multipurpose district concept is instructive; see Martin, *Metropolis in Transition*, Chap. VII.

25. On the characteristics of state and federal action in the metropolis, see, for example, Herman, *New York State and the Metropolitan Problem;* Wood, *1400 Governments;* Crouch and Dinerman, *Southern California Metropolis*, pp. 404 ff.; Michael N. Danielson, *Federal-Metropolitan Politics and the Commuter Crisis* (New York, Columbia University Press, 1965); Bollens and Schmandt, *The Metropolis*, pp. 316 ff., Chaps. 17 and 19; Robert H. Connery and Richard H. Leach, *The Federal Government and Metropolitan Areas* (Cambridge, Mass., Harvard University Press, 1960).

26. See Danielson, *Federal-Metropolitan Politics.*

27. *Ibid.*, p. 189. The federal Department of Housing and Urban Development, created in September, 1965, may provide a focal point for improved coordination of national action in the metropolitan field. However, the limited scope of the responsibilities of the

new agency provides little basis for optimism on this question. The Department is essentially an upgraded Housing and Home Finance Agency and excludes programs in highways, air transportation, pollution, and other areas which are of great importance to regional development.

28. Long, *Polity*, p. 174.

29. For example, the Federal-Aid Highway Act of 1962 stipulates that after July 1, 1965, federal aid can be provided for highway projects only if such projects are based on a comprehensive transportation planning process carried on cooperatively by states and local communities; the federal mass transportation program is also linked to the development of regional planning. See Martin, *Metropolis in Transition*, pp. 140–41; Danielson, *Federal-Metropolitan Politics*, pp. 197–98.

30. See, for example, the illustrations cited in Martin et al., *Decisions in Syracuse*, pp. 331–32; Crouch and Dinerman, *Southern California Metropolis*, p. 383.

31. The Committee is composed of twelve state-appointed officials, four federal officials, and one representative of New York City. (See also Chap. IX of this volume.) The Committee's long-range plans are outlined in detail in its *Prospectus*, April, 1962; the quotation in the text is from a Committee press release of Aug. 12, 1965.

32. Norton E. Long, "Citizenship or Consumership in Metropolitan Areas," *Journal of the American Institute of Planners*, XXXI (February, 1965), 6; and see Long, *Polity*, Chap. 12. Similar concerns are expressed by Robert C. Wood, "A Division of Powers in Metropolitan Areas," in Arthur Maass, *Area and Power: A Theory of Local Government* (New York, Free Press, 1959), pp. 53–69; and Luther H. Gulick, *The Metropolitan Problem and American Ideas* (New York, Knopf, 1962).

Index